Application Development with Qt Creator

Third Edition

Build cross-platform applications and GUIs using
Qt 5 and C++

Lee Zhi Eng
Ray Rischpater

BIRMINGHAM - MUMBAI

Application Development with Qt Creator
Third Edition

Commissioning Editor: Richa Tripathi
Acquisition Editor: Alok Dhuri
Content Development Editor: Tiksha Sarang
Senior Editor: Afshaan Khan
Technical Editor: Gaurav Gala
Copy Editor: Safis Editing
Project Coordinator: Francy Puthiry
Proofreader: Safis Editing
Indexer: Rekha Nair
Production Designer: Joshua Misquitta

First published: November 2013
Second edition: November 2014
Third edition: January 2020

Production reference: 1310120

Published by Packt Publishing Ltd.
Livery Place
35 Livery Street
Birmingham
B3 2PB, UK.

ISBN 978-1-78995-175-2

www.packt.com

Packt.com

Subscribe to our online digital library for full access to over 7,000 books and videos, as well as industry leading tools to help you plan your personal development and advance your career. For more information, please visit our website.

Why subscribe?

- Spend less time learning and more time coding with practical eBooks and Videos from over 4,000 industry professionals

- Improve your learning with Skill Plans built especially for you

- Get a free eBook or video every month

- Fully searchable for easy access to vital information

- Copy and paste, print, and bookmark content

Did you know that Packt offers eBook versions of every book published, with PDF and ePub files available? You can upgrade to the eBook version at www.packt.com and as a print book customer, you are entitled to a discount on the eBook copy. Get in touch with us at customercare@packtpub.com for more details.

At www.packt.com, you can also read a collection of free technical articles, sign up for a range of free newsletters, and receive exclusive discounts and offers on Packt books and eBooks.

About the authors

Lee Zhi Eng is a self-taught programmer who worked as an artist and programmer at several game studios before becoming a part-time lecturer for 2 years at a university, teaching game development subjects related to Unity and Unreal Engine.

He has not only taken part in various projects related to games, interactive apps, and virtual reality but has also participated in multiple projects that are more oriented toward software and system development. When he is not writing code, he enjoys traveling, photography, and exploring new technologies.

Ray Rischpater is an engineer with over 20 years of experience in writing about and developing for mobile computing platforms. He holds a bachelor's degree in mathematics from the University of California and is a member of the IEEE, ACM, and ARRL. He has participated in the development of internet technologies and custom applications.

Currently, he's employed as a technical program manager at Google. In his free time, he enjoys hiking and photography with his family and friends. He provides public service through amateur radio at the licensed station KF6GPE and also irregularly blogs. He has authored this book's previous editions as well as several other books.

About the reviewer

Marthala Vishnu Vardhan Reddy is an enthusiastic software engineer who works predominantly on a machine tool manufacturing platform developed with C++/Qt. His current focus is on the digitization of metal cutting tool data in the direction of Industry 4.1. He completed his masters at the University of Stuttgart, Germany, and has also written an IEEE paper publication on the 5G network. He has been a reviewer for several other Qt books such as *Learn Qt 5*. In addition to this, he is a public speaker and has given many guest lectures at prestigious universities. Vishnu loves to do lots of nature-related activities such as skiing, rock climbing, and hiking. At home, he enjoys streaming games.

Packt is searching for authors like you

If you're interested in becoming an author for Packt, please visit `authors.packtpub.com` and apply today. We have worked with thousands of developers and tech professionals, just like you, to help them share their insight with the global tech community. You can make a general application, apply for a specific hot topic that we are recruiting an author for, or submit your own idea.

Table of Contents

Section 3: Practical Matters

Preface

This latest version of this Qt Creator book provides an in-depth understanding of Qt's massive library and its functionality. Qt is a powerful development framework that serves as a complete toolset for building cross-platform applications, helping you to reduce development time and improve productivity.

This Qt programming book takes you through Qt Creator's latest features, such as Qt Quick Controls 2, enhanced CMake support, a new graphical editor for SCXML, and a model editor. You'll start by designing a user interface, work with multimedia and sensors using Qt Quick, and finally develop applications for mobile, IoT, and embedded devices using Qt Creator. After reading through, you will be able to build a solid foundation in Qt by learning about its core features and create your own cross-platform applications from scratch using Qt Creator and the C++ programming language.

Who this book is for

This book is for beginners and experienced programmers alike who want to dive into GUI programming using the powerful Qt development tools and libraries. This book is suitable for hardcore programmers who are used to object-oriented programming in the C++ language, as well as those who are design-oriented and just trying to learn how to create beautiful and intuitive GUI using Qt Quick.

What this book covers

Chapter 1, *Getting Started with Qt Creator*, covers everything you need in order to get started downloading Qt Creator for Linux, macOS X, and Windows. We will also see how to ensure that your basic configuration is running and take a quick look at a simple QtGui application as well as a Qt Quick application.

Chapter 2, *Building Applications with Qt Creator*, explains how to add files to a project, how to create libraries in a project, and how to use the debugger and the console logger.

Chapter 3, *Designing Your Application with Qt Designer*, covers Qt's notion of signals and slots, explaining how to create user interfaces with Qt Designer. We will also see how to instantiate forms, messages, and dialogs.

Chapter 4, *Qt Foundations*, discusses some of Qt's core classes that you will find especially handy while writing your applications. We will begin with useful data classes and look at Qt's support for multithreading, a key tool in ensuring applications feel responsive. We will look at file and HTTP I/O, an important component in many applications. We will also learn how to use Qt's XML parser to create networked applications and to load XML data from the filesystem.

Chapter 5, *Developing Applications with Qt Widgets*, introduces GUI programming using Qt Widgets. You will learn basic application management, how to create dialogs and error popups, and other major GUI elements. We will also have a look at Qt's flexible layout system, the Model-View-Controller paradigm, and how to use it in Qt for complex controls such as lists and tree views. We will also have a quick look at Qt's support for WebKit.

Chapter 6, *Drawing with Qt*, explains how to do a general drawing in Qt. We will implement concrete examples of offscreen drawings for bitmaps, as well as creating custom widgets that interoperate with Qt Widgets. We will also discuss a newer and lower level of abstraction that Qt provides for graphics management – the graphics view/graphics scene architecture.

Chapter 7, *Doing More with Qt Quick*, looks at Qt Quick in more detail. We will look at fundamental Qt Quick constructs to display shapes, images, and text, as well as how to manage user events. You will also be introduced to the Qt Quick Transition Framework and New Graphical Editor for SCXML. You will also learn how to integrate C++ with Qt Quick.

Chapter 8, *Implementing Multimedia with Qt Quick*, examines Qt Quick's support for multimedia. We will look at various QT Quick components that provide access to audio and video playbacks, and how to access the camera.

Chapter 9, *Sensors and Qt Quick*, looks at Qt's sensor and positioning frameworks as they're supported in QML. You will learn how to determine a device's position on the surface of the earth and how to measure the other characteristics of its environment, as reported by its onboard sensors.

Chapter 10, *Localizing Your Application with Qt Linguist*, explains the task of localization and discusses various tools that QT provides for localization.

Chapter 11, *Optimizing Performance with Qt Creator*, covers how to perform the runtime profiling of QML applications using the QML performance analyzer and explains how to read the reports it generates.

Chapter 12, *Developing Mobile Applications with Qt Creator*, explains how to write a mobile application and how Qt offers better support for iOS and Android applications.

Chapter 13, *Embedded and IoT development with QT Creator*, describes how to create optimized Qt applications specifically designed for embedded devices.

Chapter 14, *Qt Tips and Tricks*, introduces a collection of tips and tricks that you should be familiar with when using Qt Creator and Qt.

To get the most out of this book

Although no prior knowledge of Qt and Qt Creator is required, it would be beneficial to have basic knowledge of C++ programming.

Download the example code files

You can download the example code files for this book from your account at www.packt.com. If you purchased this book elsewhere, you can visit https://www.packtpub.com/support and register to have the files emailed directly to you.

You can download the code files by following these steps:

1. Log in or register at www.packt.com.
2. Select the **Support** tab.
3. Click on **Code Downloads**.
4. Enter the name of the book in the **Search** box and follow the onscreen instructions.

Once the file is downloaded, please make sure that you unzip or extract the folder using the latest version of:

- WinRAR/7-Zip for Windows
- Zipeg/iZip/UnRarX for Mac
- 7-Zip/PeaZip for Linux

The code bundle for the book is also hosted on GitHub at https://github.com/PacktPublishing/Application-Development-with-Qt-Creator-Third-Edition. In case there's an update to the code, it will be updated on the existing GitHub repository.

We also have other code bundles from our rich catalog of books and videos available at https://github.com/PacktPublishing/. Check them out!

Download the color images

We also provide a PDF file that has color images of the screenshots/diagrams used in this book. You can download it here: https://static.packt-cdn.com/downloads/9781789951752_ColorImages.pdf.

Conventions used

There are a number of text conventions used throughout this book.

CodeInText: Indicates code words in text, database table names, folder names, filenames, file extensions, pathnames, dummy URLs, user input, and Twitter handles. Here is an example: "Set the event attribute of the send executable content of red as goGreen and set its delay as 2s."

A block of code is set as follows:

```
Window {
    visible: true
    width: 360
    height: 360
    Rectangle {
```

When we wish to draw your attention to a particular part of a code block, the relevant lines or items are set in bold:

```
#include <QQmlContext>
#include "nativeobject.h"

int main(int argc, char *argv[])
{
    QCoreApplication::setAttribute(Qt::AA_EnableHighDpiScaling);
    QGuiApplication app(argc, argv);
```

Any command-line input or output is written as follows:

```
qmake -project
```

Bold: Indicates a new term, an important word, or words that you see on screen. For example, words in menus or dialog boxes appear in the text like this. Here is an example: "The following screenshot shows you where to set the values on the **Attributes** window."

Warnings or important notes appear like this.

 Tips and tricks appear like this.

Get in touch

Feedback from our readers is always welcome.

General feedback: If you have questions about any aspect of this book, mention the book title in the subject of your message and email us at customercare@packtpub.com.

Errata: Although we have taken every care to ensure the accuracy of our content, mistakes do happen. If you have found a mistake in this book, we would be grateful if you would report this to us. Please visit https://www.packtpub.com/support/errata, selecting your book, clicking on the Errata Submission Form link, and entering the details.

Piracy: If you come across any illegal copies of our works in any form on the internet, we would be grateful if you would provide us with the location address or website name. Please contact us at copyright@packt.com with a link to the material.

If you are interested in becoming an author: If there is a topic that you have expertise in, and you are interested in either writing or contributing to a book, please visit authors.packtpub.com.

Reviews

Please leave a review. Once you have read and used this book, why not leave a review on the site that you purchased it from? Potential readers can then see and use your unbiased opinion to make purchase decisions, we at Packt can understand what you think about our products, and our authors can see your feedback on their book. Thank you!

For more information about Packt, please visit packt.com.

Section 1: The Basics

In the first section of this book, we will look into the basics of Qt Creator and how to build and design applications with it, and also delve into the foundations of Qt. These form the prerequisites for our advanced topics ahead.

This section comprises the following chapters:

- Chapter 1, *Getting Started with Qt Creator*
- Chapter 2, *Building Applications with Qt Creator*
- Chapter 3, *Designing Your Application with Qt Designer*
- Chapter 4, *Qt Foundations*
- Chapter 5, *Developing Applications with Qt Widgets*

Getting Started with Qt Creator

Qt Creator is an integrated software development environment that supports both traditional C++ application development and development using the Qt project's libraries (collectively called **Qt** and pronounced as **cute**).

Qt is available under a commercial license as well as under GPL v3 and LGPL v2. Its development dates all the way back to 1991. For the first 10 years of its life, it was a cross-platform toolkit for Windows and X11; by 2001, support for macOS X had been added.

In this chapter, we will take a look at everything you need to get started, as follows:

- Where to download Qt Creator for Linux, macOS X, and Windows
- New features in the latest version of Qt
- How to ensure that your basic configuration is running
- A quick look at a simple Qt Widgets application as well as a Qt Quick application

Technical requirements

The technical requirements for this chapter include Qt 5.12.3 MinGW 64-bit, Qt Creator 4.9.0, and Windows 10.

The code for this chapter can be found at `https://github.com/PacktPublishing/Application-Development-with-Qt-Creator-Third-Edition/tree/master/Chapter01`.

Downloading Qt and Qt Creator

Qt, the cross-platform toolkit behind Qt Creator, has had a long and illustrious history. Presently a project of The Qt Company, it has its own URL: `http://www.qt.io`. It also has both commercial and non-commercial licenses. To get started with the non-commercial version for free, go to `http://www.qt.io/download-qt-installer`. You should see something similar to the following screenshot:

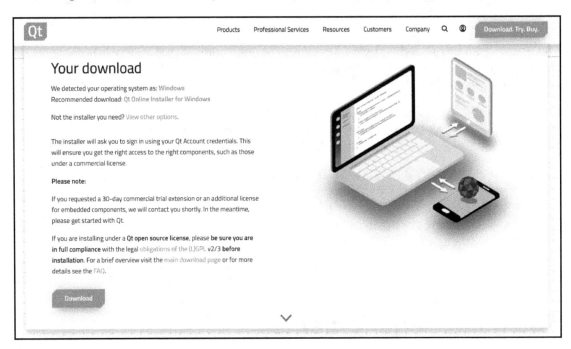

One of the most popular platforms for application development with Qt is Linux. On many Linux variants—notably Ubuntu, my personal favorite – you can get Qt Creator using the package manager. On my Ubuntu box, Qt Creator is just a `sudo apt-get install qtcreator` command away. You'll get a version of Qt that matches your flavor of Linux, although it might not be the latest and greatest build from The Qt Company. If you need to install the latest official version of Qt, it's recommended to download it from the preceding link.

Some downloads include the C++ compiler and the linker that you need. By following the link and downloading Qt, you should now have Qt, Qt Creator, and the MinGW toolkit for developing software on Windows. If you're developing on Linux or Mac, the process will be similar, although it won't include MinGW in your development. On Windows, there's a variant that includes the MinGW toolchain, so you have everything you need to build applications.

However, you can also download Qt Creator for Windows, which uses the Microsoft Visual Studio compiler. So, if you prefer using Visual Studio for your compilation and Qt Creator as your IDE, this is also an option. On macOS X, you'll need to have Xcode and the command-line development tools installed first; you can download Xcode from the macOS X App Store and then use Xcode to download the command-line development tools.

Once the installer downloads, run it in the usual way and it'll launch an installation wizard for your platform. Depending on whether you're running the **online installer** or the **offline installer**, installation for the latter should typically take anywhere from 3 to 4 minutes; however, it may take several hours if you're running the online installer. This is because when you run the installation process, the online installer downloads every single tool and library file from the Qt server uncompressed. On the other hand, the offline installer contains all the tools and libraries in a heavily compressed format packed within the installer itself, which is why the installation process is relatively quicker and simpler, but has a larger-sized installer compared to the online installer.

Other than that, you'll want to have plenty of disk space. Qt Creator doesn't consume that much disk space, but software development does; you'll need at least 500 MB of empty space for the tools and libraries, and you'll need to budget a few free gigabytes on your main drive for your source code, intermediate object files, debugging symbols, and, of course, your compiled application. (It is especially important to plan for this if you're running Qt Creator on a virtual machine; make sure that the virtual hard drive for your virtual machine image has plenty of disk space.)

You should also ensure that your development box has plenty of RAM; the more, the better. Qt Creator runs happily on 2 GB of RAM, but the compiler and linker used by Qt Creator can run a lot faster if they have more RAM available.

New features in Qt

Qt developers are constantly adding new features to Qt while fixing critical bugs that affect its users. This means that we can expect new features in every update of Qt, especially a major release. At the time of writing this chapter, the latest stable version of Qt is 5.12.3, which means it's the third minor update for its major version, 5.12.

Some of the important changes to Qt since the second edition of this book are as follows:

- Qt WebView (WebKit) has been deprecated and replaced by Qt WebEngine (Chromium).
- MinGW 64-bit compiler is now included in Qt's Windows installer.
- Many features have been added to the mobile platforms, including support for in-app purchasing.
- Qt Script, Qt Quick Control 1, and Qt Canvas 3D have been deprecated.
- Added support for new platforms, such as tvOS and watchOS.
- Previously commercial-only features such as Qt Charts, Qt Data Visualization, Qt Virtual Keyboard, Qt Purchasing, and Qt Quick 2D Renderer are now free.
- Added support for embedded platforms.
- Added Qt Automotive Suite.
- Qt binding for Python has been added (using the PySide 2 module).
- New signal and slot connection syntax – you can now directly connect a signal to a C++11 lambda function.
- Added support for JSON format.
- Added Qt 3D Studio.
- Added SCXML and state machine tooling in Qt Creator.

...and there are many more besides!

> To learn more about the new features and changes in the latest Qt release, please check out the official introduction for Qt 5 at `https://doc.qt.io/qt-5/qt5-intro.html`, or head over to the wiki page at `https://wiki.qt.io/Main`.

Finding your way around Qt Creator

The following screenshot shows what you will see when you launch Qt Creator for the first time. Let's take a closer look at each portion of the screen:

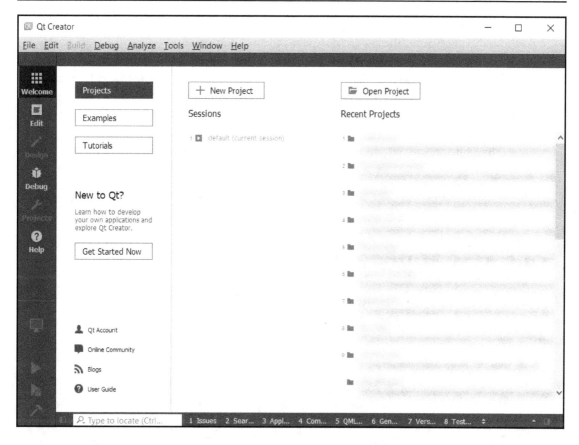

The main window, which currently shows the buttons for **New Project** and **Open Project**, is your workspace. The workspace also includes links to the Qt projects, examples, and tutorials, as well as Qt's developer documentation, such as its online community and blogs. Under normal conditions, this will be located where you'll see the source code for your application. Along the left-hand side of the screen are a series of icons that let you select various views in your application. They are as follows:

- The **Welcome** mode, which shows basic information about Qt Creator
- The **Edit** mode, which lets you edit the files that make up your application
- The **Design** mode, which lets you use Qt Designer to design the user interface for your application

- The **Debug** mode, which lets you debug your application while it's running, including doing things such as viewing the memory and variables, setting breakpoints, and stepping through the application
- The **Projects** mode, which lets you adjust the build and link settings for your project
- The **Analyze** mode, which lets you profile your application's runtime performance
- The **Help** mode, which provides documentation on Qt Creator and the Qt framework

Let's create a new project using C++.

Your first application – Hello World

In Qt Creator, select **New File or Project** from the **File** menu. Qt Creator will present you with the **New File or Project** wizard, which lets you choose the kind of project you want to create, give it a name, and so on. To create your first application, perform the following steps:

1. Select **New File or Project** if you haven't done so already.
2. Qt Creator presents you with a dialog that has a dizzying array of project choices. Choose **Application**, then **Qt Console Application**, and then click on **Choose...**.
3. Qt Creator asks you for a name and a path to the directory where you want to store the files for the project. For the name, enter `HelloWorldConsole` and choose a path that makes sense to you (or accept the default). Then, click on **Next**.
4. Qt Creator asks you for the build system you want to use for your project. Just keep the default option, **qmake**, if you don't have any specific requirements for this. Then, click on **Next**:

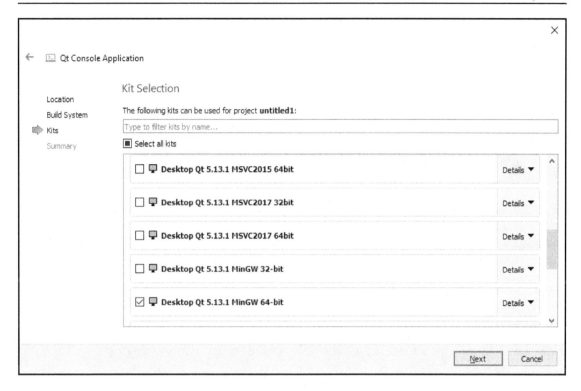

5. Qt Creator can support various kits and libraries against which you can build an application. Select the desktop Qt Kit, which should have been installed by default. If you're running Qt on Windows, please make sure that you select the desktop Qt Kit with **MinGW**, as it is installed by default. Make sure that you have installed Microsoft Visual Studio beforehand if you pick the desktop Qt **MSVC** Kit. Then, click on **Next**.

6. In the next step, Qt Creator prompts you about the version control system for your project. Qt Creator can use your installed version control clients to perform change tracking for your project. For now, skip this and leave **Add to version control** set to **None**. Then, click on **Finish**.

Qt Creator creates your project and switches to the **Edit** view. In the source code editor for the main.cpp file, enter the highlighted code:

```cpp
#include <QCoreApplication>
#include <iostream>

using namespace std;

int main(int argc, char *argv[])
```

```
{
    QCoreApplication a(argc, argv);
    cout << "Hello world!";

    return a.exec();
}
```

You can download the example code files for all Packt books you have purchased from your account at http://www.packtpub.com. If you purchased this book elsewhere, you can visit http://www.packtpub.com/support and register to have the files emailed directly to you.

The QCoreApplication task handles the entire system startup for an application, and every Qt Console app needs to create one and call its exec method as part of your main method. It sets up Qt's event handler and provides a bunch of porting helpers to determine things such as your application directory, library paths, and other details.

For a console application, that's all you need; you can freely mix and match Qt classes with the C++ standard library and **Standard Template Library** (**STL**) although once you master Qt's foundation classes, many STL constructs might feel somewhat limiting.

Next, let's compile and run the application. There are several ways to do this:

1. Click on the green run arrow underneath the **Help** view button on the left to run the application, as follows:

2. Hit *F5* to build and run your application in the debugger.

3. Click on **Start Debugging** from the **Debug** menu, as follows:

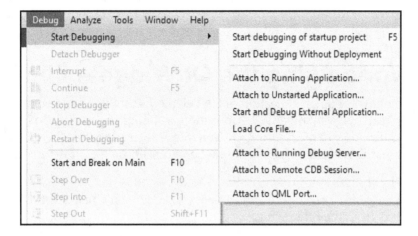

4. Click on the green run arrow with the bug over the arrow in order to debug the application on the left.

5. Choose **Run** from the **Build** menu (or hit *Ctrl + R*).

If you only want to build the application, you can click on the hammer icon under the Run and Debug icons.

Once the application starts, you'll see the **Hello world!** message in a console view, as follows:

When you choose one of these options, Qt Creator invokes the compiler and the linker to build your application. If you choose the **Debug** option, Qt Creator switches to the **Debug** view (which we will discuss in detail in `Chapter 2`, *Building Applications with Qt Creator*) as it starts your application.

Hello World using the Qt Widgets library

One of Qt's strengths is its rich collection of GUI elements that you can use to create windowed applications. Making a GUI application is similar in principle to making a console application; instead of choosing **Qt Console Application**, select **Qt Widgets Application** from the **New** dialog presented when you choose **New File or Project**. Try it now:

1. First, close the current file and project by clicking on **Close All Projects and Editors** from the **File** menu.
2. Next, click on **New File or Project** again and click on **Qt Widgets Application** from the first step of the wizard.
3. Walk through the wizard again, naming your project `HelloWorldGui`.

4. Then, select the default kit. The **New** project wizard will prompt you for the name of the class implementing your main window. Leave the `QMainWindow` subclass as is and the name as `MainWindow`. Skip the build system and version control dialog portions of the wizard.

Qt Creator creates a default subclass of the class that provides the platform's basic window in the `mainwindow.h` and `mainwindow.cpp` files and creates a form that will contain the widgets for your application's window.

The following screenshot shows a default form as you're editing it in Qt Designer. If you run the application at this point, you'll see an empty window. Instead, double-click on the `Forms` folder in the project tree (the second pane) of Qt Creator and then double-click on the `mainwindow.ui` file. Qt Creator switches to the `Design` view, and you'll see something similar to the following screenshot:

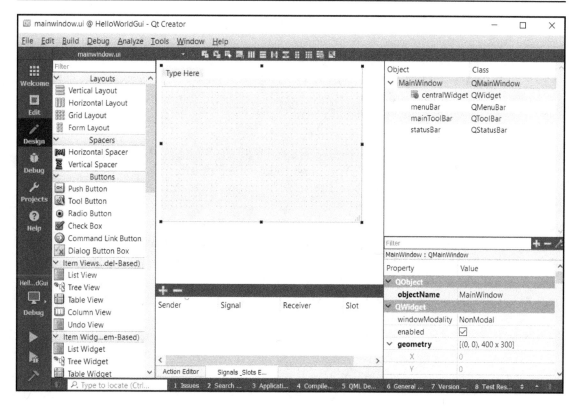

As you can see from the preceding screenshot, on the left-hand side is a list of the layouts that you can choose to organize widgets. These include spacers, views, containers, buttons, and other widgets; other than that, there are a variety of edit and layout options as well. In the middle of the window is the preview of the layout of your application's main window. Further to the right are panes that show the hierarchy of objects in your main window and the properties of any item that you have clicked on in the main window.

Placing widgets in Qt Designer

While we will explore Qt Designer more in `Chapter 3`, *Designing Your Application with Qt Designer*, you can get a feel for using it by building a simple UI. Begin by ensuring that you're in the **Designer** mode, then proceed as follows:

1. Where it says **Type Here**, right-click and choose **Remove menu bar**.
2. Drag a label (under **Display Widgets** in the left-hand side pane) and drop it in the window preview in the center pane.
3. Double-click on the label that appears and type `Hello world!`.

4. Grab a corner of the label and resize it so that the entire text is shown. You can also move it around in the window.

5. Note that when you click on the label, the **Property** field in the lower-right pane is updated to show the properties of your new label.

6. Drag a button (under **Buttons** in the left-hand side pane) and drop it in the window preview in the center pane.

7. Double-click on the button and change its text to Exit.

8. With the new button selected, change the **objectName** field in the **Property** browser to exitButton. You must follow the name described here so that the code generated when adding the slot function will be identical to the one shown in the next sample code snippet.

9. Right-click on the button and select **Go to slot....** A window appears with a list of slots (for now, you can think of a slot as something that is triggered on an action; we will discuss them more in Chapter 2, *Building Applications with Qt Creator*).

10. Choose **clicked()** from the list that appears.

11. Qt Creator returns to the **Edit** view for your mainwindow.cpp file. Change it to read as follows:

```cpp
#include "mainwindow.h"
#include "ui_mainwindow.h"
#include <QApplication>
MainWindow::MainWindow(QWidget *parent) :
    QMainWindow(parent),
    ui(new Ui::MainWindow)
{
    ui->setupUi(this);
}

MainWindow::~MainWindow()
{
    delete ui;
}

voidMainWindow::on_exitButton_clicked()
{
    QApplication::exit();
}
```

Before running your application, let's be sure that you understand the implementation of the `MainWindow` class. The constructor of the `MainWindow` class loads the description of the user interface for the main window and sets it up using the Qt Creator-generated `Ui::MainWindow` class. The destructor deletes the implementation of the code layout, and the `on_exitButton_clicked` method simply terminates the application by calling the `exit` static method implemented by the `QApplication` class.

Finally, we have to add the `on_exitButton_clicked` method declaration to `mainwindow.h` if it's not already added. Double-click on this file in the browser on the left and make sure that it reads as follows:

```cpp
#ifndef MAINWINDOW_H
#define MAINWINDOW_H

#include <QMainWindow>

namespaceUi {
class MainWindow;
}

class MainWindow : public QMainWindow
{
    Q_OBJECT
public:
    explicit MainWindow(QWidget *parent = 0);
    ~MainWindow();
private slots:
    void on_exitButton_clicked();

private:
    Ui::MainWindow *ui;
};

#endif // MAINWINDOW_H
```

The key lines you need to add are highlighted in the previous listing.

We'll learn more about signals and slots in the next chapter; for now, it's enough for you to know that you're declaring a private function to be triggered when you click on the button.

Run the application. It should open a single window with the text **Hello World!**; clicking on the **Exit** button in the window (or on the close-box button in the upper-right corner) should close the application:

At this point, if you think you want to learn more about the Qt Widgets application, go ahead and try dragging other GUI items to the window, or explore the help documentation for the Qt Widgets application by switching to the **Help** view and clicking on **Qt GUI** from the list of help items.

Hello World using Qt Quick

Qt Quick is Qt's newer declarative framework for the user interface. With this, it's incredibly easy to create fluid applications with animated transitions and flowing user interfaces. Using Qt Quick, you can describe your user interface using QML, a JavaScript-like language that lets you declare user interface elements and how they relate; the Qt Quick runtime does most of the heavy lifting in the implementation of your application.

By now, you can guess how to create a Qt Quick project. Choose **New File or Project** from the **File** menu, click on **Qt Quick Application - Empty**, and then follow the wizard.

The wizard will ask you one additional question: the Qt Quick version to use. You should simply choose the latest version. Once you have walked through the wizard, you will end up with a simple application that actually displays **Hello World** in its own window. The code that it supplies is as follows:

```
import QtQuick 2.12
import QtQuick.Window 2.12
```

```
Window {
    visible: true
    width: 640
    height: 480
    title: qsTr("Hello World")
}
```

If you know JavaScript, the syntax of this might look a little familiar, but it's still different. The first two lines are the `import` statements; they indicate which classes should be available to the QML runtime. At a minimum, all of your Qt Quick applications must import `QtQuick`, as this one does.

The QML follows. It declares a Window object of 640 × 480 pixels that determines the size of the application window. Inside the window, we can see two other properties besides the window size: `visible` and `title`. The `visible` property simply means whether you want to display the item by default, which in this case we do. The `title` property is just that: the `Hello World` text placed on your application's window header. Note that the value of the `title` property is actually the result of a function call to the `qsTr` function, which is Qt's built-in localization function. This looks at application resources to return the localized version of `Hello World` if it has been provided.

It's worth making a note of the `qsTr` function here; you can use this if you want your application to support multiple languages. The `qsTr` function is used to display the text in different languages based on the selected locale. You can ignore it if you don't plan on supporting multiple languages.

At this point, you can run the application in the usual way and you'll see a window with the text **Hello World** as the window title.

While the basic concepts and principles are similar, the Qt Quick designer is actually very different from the Qt Widgets designer due to the very nature of it – the Qt Quick designer is specially optimized for creating touch-based applications, while Qt Widgets is designed for creating desktop programs. Before we're able to demonstrate the Qt Quick designer, let's first create a **QtQuick UI File** by going to **File**, **New File or Project**, then select the **QtQuick UI File** under the **Qt** category. After that, use the `MyGui` component name and keep the `MyGuiForm` component form name. Then, press **Next**, followed by the **Finish** button.

Once you're done, Qt Creator will add `MyGui.ui.qml` and `MyGui.qml` to your project, and Qt Quick Designer will be launched automatically. Take a look at the following screenshot:

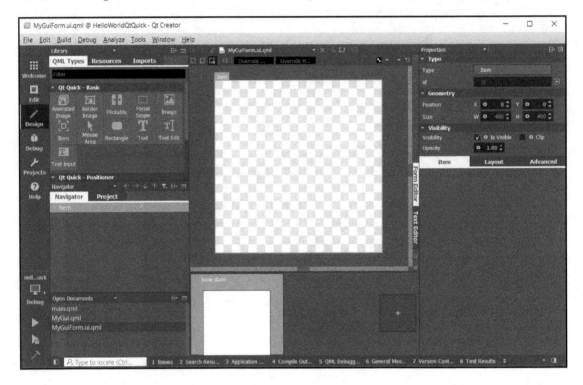

It shows a list of things you can add to the canvas, as well as the hierarchy of objects on the canvas, along with the properties of individual objects.

However, there are far fewer Qt Quick widgets that you can use compared to Qt Widgets. Other than that, the widgets in Qt Quick don't match the look and feel of the native platform to nearly the same extent. That's by design; Qt Widgets is for building conventional applications that match the native platform by using native controls with a native look and feel, while Qt Quick is used for creating device-independent applications with their own look and feel. For example, you'd probably write an enterprise data collection application using Qt Widgets, while you'd create a media center application using Qt Quick.

However, the manner of using the designer is the same in both cases. Let's add `mouseArea` to the main view and give it something to do:

1. Select `MyGuiForm.ui.qml` from the list of files in Qt Creator and click on **Design** to see the **Design** view.

2. In the **Library** pane, select **QML Types** and scroll down until you see **Rectangle**. Drag the rectangle to the center pane and drop it somewhere underneath the parent object called **Item**.

3. With the rectangle selected in the window pane, select the red color for your rectangle under **Colors**.

4. With the rectangle object selected, click on **Layout** in the **Properties** tab and mouse over the layouts until you see **Fill to Parent**. (This is the fifth icon under the **Anchors** and looks like a box with a border.) Click on it.

5. Now, drag a **MouseArea** object out of the **Library** pane and drop it on your new rectangle.

6. With the **MouseArea** object selected, repeat *step 4* to make it fill the parent **Rectangle** object.

7. Click on the small circle icon with an arrow located just beside the `id` property of the **MouseArea**. The icon will turn a red color once it's clicked. This will allow other QML scripts to access this object.

8. Repeat *step 7* for the rectangle object as well.

9. Go back to the **Edit** view and modify `main.qml` to look similar to the following code snippet:

```
import QtQuick 2.12
import QtQuick.Window 2.12

Window {
    visible: true
    width: 640
    height: 480
    title: qsTr("Hello World")

    MyGuiForm {
        anchors.fill: parent
        mouseArea.onClicked: {
            rectangle.color = "blue";
        }
    }
}
```

In newer versions of Qt, the QML script has been separated into two formats: .qml and .ui.qml. The first format (.qml) is for writing the logic and operations you want to perform when a GUI event has been triggered by the user. The second format (.ui.qml) is only for the cosmetic definition of your GUI – where to position the objects, the size and color of the objects, and so on.

You can see that all of the changes made for the MyGui.ui.qml file were done in the **Design** view; as for main.qml, we have to use the text editor to write the logic code demonstrated previously. You can make use of the MyGuiForm class directly in main.qml and tell it what to do when the **MouseArea** is being pressed by the user. You will need to set an ID of the **MouseArea** so that the onClicked handler knows which object will be triggering the event (in this case, it's using the default name, mouseArea). The id property also lets other QMLs access the **Rectangle** by name (in this case, its name is simply the default name, rectangle), and the onClicked handler changes the rectangle item's color property to blue when the user presses on the **MouseArea** item.

Run the application. You'll see your red-colored rectangle fills the entire window, and clicking on the rectangle changes its color to blue.

Summary

Getting Qt Creator is easy; it's either just a web download away or, on most Linux platforms, an optional installation through the native package manager (although the versions delivered by a package manager might be slightly older than those you get from the Qt project's website).

Qt Creator organizes its source code for you in projects; when you first launch it, you can either create a default project or create a new project to contain the source code and resources for your application. Inside Qt Creator are all the options you need to compile and debug your application. In addition, it supports designer tools for developing both Qt Widgets and Qt Quick applications.

In the next chapter, we'll dig into the details of how to configure Qt Creator for compiling and editing your code, including how to add source files to your project, configure compiler and linker options, add dependencies to third-party libraries, and so on.

Building Applications with Qt Creator

2

The first thing you want to do with Qt Creator is figure out how to add source files and build (or debug) your project. This chapter is all about that – we'll go over how to add files to a project, how to create libraries in a project, and how to use the debugger and the console logger. These are the essential skills you need to create a good-quality application using Qt. At the end of this chapter, you'll be driving Qt Creator to develop console applications like a pro.

In this chapter, we will do the following:

- Learn about our sample library
- Look into the Build menu and the `.pro` file
- Link against our sample library
- Debug
- Build our project
- Run and debug our application

Technical requirements

The technical requirements for this chapter include Qt 5.12.3 MinGW 64-bit, Qt Creator 4.9.0, and Windows 10.

Getting started – our sample library

This chapter's example code has two pieces: a library that defines a public function, and a console application that calls this function. Libraries are a great way to break up your applications, and while this example is simple, it also lets me show you how to create a library and include it in your application.

I'm going to stretch your imagination a bit; let's pretend that you're responsible for setting up a library of math functions. In this example, we'll only write one function, factorial. You should be able to recollect the factorial function from introductory programming; it's represented by a ! and is defined as follows:

- 0! is 1
- 1! is 1
- n! is n × (n - 1)!

This is a recursive definition and we can code it in the following way:

```
unsigned long factorial(unsigned int n)
{
    switch(n)
    {
        case 0: return 1;
        case 1: return 1;
        default: return n * factorial(n-1);
    }
}
```

An alternate definition that avoids the cost of function calls is given as follows:

```
unsigned long factorial(unsigned int n)
{
    unsigned long result = 1;
    for(unsigned int i = n; i > 1; i--)
    {
        result *= i;
    }
    return result;
}
```

Let's begin by creating a library that implements our `factorial` function. To do this, follow these steps:

1. In Qt Creator, from the **File** menu, choose **New File or Project**.
2. Select **Library** in the left-hand side pane of the dialog and select **C++ Library** from the center pane:

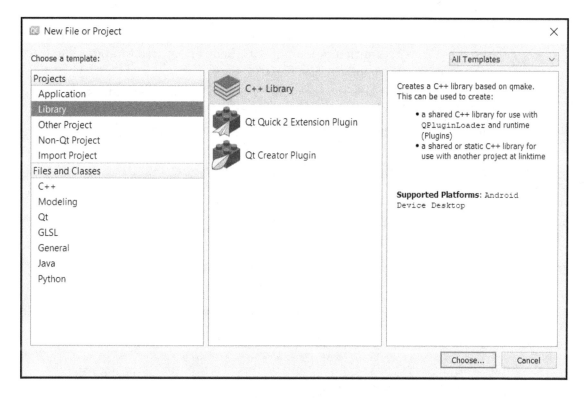

3. Qt Creator can create **dynamic-link libraries** (**DLLs** in Windows parlance), static libraries, or plugins that can be shared between applications. We're going to create a static library, so in the next window that appears, select **Statically Linked Library** and name it `MathFunctions`. Choose a reasonable path for the project.

A statically linked library is included in your program binary and is part of your application. If multiple applications use a static library, each will have its own copy. A dynamically linked library is stored as a separate file and can be shared by multiple applications at runtime because each application loads the dynamically linked library. Qt also supports plugins, which are dynamic libraries loaded at runtime that can extend an application's functionality.

4. Libraries built by Qt Creator can rely on the Qt libraries. Let this library rely on QtCore, the core data structure for Qt. In the **Select Required Modules** window, leave QtCore checked and click on **Next**.

5. In the next window, name the skeleton files that Qt Creator will add to your project. Click on **Next**.

6. In the **Project Management** window, choose **<None>** for the version control choice (we won't use version control for this project) and click on **Finish**.

7. Edit mathfunctions.h to include a static method declaration for our factorial function:

```
#ifndef MATHFUNCTIONS_H
#define MATHFUNCTIONS_H

class MathFunctions
{
public:
    MathFunctions();
    static unsigned long int factorial(unsigned int n);
};
#endif // MATHFUNCTIONS_H
```

8. Open mathfunctions.cpp. You can do this in one of the following ways: by double-clicking on it in the **Project** pane, by right-clicking on the factorial function and selecting **Switch Header/Source**, or by simply hitting the *F4* key. Write your factorial function; mathfunctions.cpp should now comprise something similar to this:

```
#include "mathfunctions.h"

MathFunctions::MathFunctions()
{
}

unsigned long int MathFunctions::factorial(unsigned int n)
{
    switch(n)
```

```
        {
            case 0: return 0;
            case 1: return 1;
            default: return n * factorial(n-1);
        }
    }
```

9. Click on the **Projects** button on the left-hand side and change the output paths for the **Release** and **Debug** builds to point to the same directory by editing the **Build directory** line under **General**. Do this first for the **Build** and then for the **Debug** build configurations. To do this, remove the release and debug portions of the directory path from the **Build directory** path. This way, when you build your library, Qt Creator will place the release and debug builds of your library in folders named `release` and `debug`, respectively:

As you write the code, note that Qt Creator prompts you at various stages about things it can deduce from your header with automatic suggestions (called **autosuggest**). For example, once you type the `MathFunc` class name, it offers to autocomplete the class name or the C preprocessor guard; you can select the class name either using the mouse or just hit *return*.

Similarly, typing the double colons tells Qt Creator that you're trying to enter something in the `MathFunctions` class, and it prompts you with the `MathFunctions` class members; you can use the arrows to select `factorial` and hit *Return*, and it will type that.

Finally, typing an opening parenthesis cues Qt Creator that you're defining a function and it prompts you with the arguments to the function you defined in the header file. You'll see this autocompletion a lot when you type code; it's a great way to learn Qt too, because you can type a class name or part of a function name and Qt Creator prompts you with helpful hints along the way. Qt Creator can also autocomplete variable and method names; start typing a function name and press *Ctrl* + spacebar to see a menu of possible completions.

Before you continue, be sure to build your library in both the release and debug configurations. The easiest way to do this is to click on the Build selector at the bottom-left of the software and select either **Release** or **Debug**, and then click on the hammer icon to perform a build, as shown in the following screenshot:

A combination of *Ctrl + B* offers a mouse-free shortcut to the **Build** menu.

Learning the landscape – the Build menu and the .pro file

In the previous chapter, you learned how to build applications by hitting the hammer button in the corner of Qt Creator's main window or by starting the debugger. To just build your library – or any application – you can either use the hammer icon or the various choices in the **Build** menu. The obvious choice is either **Build All** or **Rebuild All**. Choosing **Build All** recompiles only those files that need to be rebuilt as recognized by Qt Creator; **Rebuild All** cleans the project of all the object files and rebuilds the entire project from scratch.

In most cases, it's sufficient to choose **Build All**, and that's what you want to do because it's faster. Sometimes, you really do want to rebuild the whole project, especially when things are broken and Qt's make system can't reconcile all the dependencies (or you've incorrectly specified them). Select **Build All** now and wait for it to build while we discuss the other options. Learning the landscape - the **Build** menu and the .pro file. You can also clean your project (remove all object files and other autogenerated products) by selecting **Clean All**.

The **Publish** option is available for some add-on kits that let you publish compiled applications and libraries to application stores and repositories; you can find more details about this in the documentation for any Qt Creator add-in.

Behind every Qt Creator project is a .pro file; this serves the same function as a Makefile and, in fact, it is processed by the Qt toolkit qmake command.

A Makefile is a file that describes how your application can be built using the make utility. For more information, go to https://www.techopedia.com/definition/16406/make. Qt provides qmake, a utility that converts the .pro files to Makefiles; you'll work with the Qt Creator GUI most of the time to create the .pro files and ignore the resulting Makefile.

These files are declarative, in that you declare the relationships between the files that make up your application and qmake figures out how to build your application from there. In most cases, you'll need to make few or no changes to a `.pro` file, but it doesn't hurt to understand how they work. Double-click on `MathFunctions.pro` and you'll find this:

```
QT -= gui
TARGET = MathFunctions
TEMPLATE = lib
CONFIG += staticlib
DEFINES += QT_DEPRECATED_WARNINGS
SOURCES += mathfunctions.cpp
HEADERS += mathfunctions.h
unix {
    target.path = /usr/lib
    INSTALLS += target
}
```

The basic syntax of a `.pro` file is variable assignments; the file generated by Qt Creator assigns the following variables:

- `QT`: This variable indicates the Qt modules that your project will link against. By default, all projects include `QtCore` and `QtGui`; there's a plethora of other modules available, which include key features such as the `WebEngine` web browsing engine (`QtWebEngine`) and multimedia libraries (`QtMultimedia`). Our assignment here indicates that we use the default Qt modules, but don't link them against `QtGui`.
- `TARGET`: This variable is the name of the compiled library or executable.
- `TEMPLATE`: This variable indicates the kind of template that qmake should use to generate the binary. In our case, we're saying that it should use the template to create a `lib` file – a static library.
- `CONFIG`: This variable passes an additional configuration to qmake's template. Here, we say that we want a statically linked library.
- `DEFINES`: This variable specifies preprocessors that should be set throughout the build process (the `-D` option). In this case, qmake displays warning messages when detecting deprecated features being used in our project.
- `SOURCES` and `HEADERS`: These variables contain lists of the source and header files that make up our project.

- `INSTALLS`: This variable indicates where the resulting build product should be installed. Here, it's set in a `scope`. Scopes let you specify conditional options in qmake; the condition for the scope is a variable or an expression, which might be true or false, and the code that follows is executed if the variable is true. The scope at the end of this file says, *if we're building for a Unix variant, set the* `target.path` *variable to* `/usr/lib` *and the* `INSTALLS` *variable to* `target`.

These are the basic variables you'll find in almost any `.pro` file.

 For more information on qmake scopes that you can use to control conditional compilation, see `https://doc.qt.io/qt-5/qmake-advanced-usage.html`.

Another additional variable that you're likely to want to know about is `LIBS`. Now, `LIBS` indicates additional libraries against which Qt Creator should link your project.

Note how variables are managed: you use = for assignment, += to add an item to a list, and -= to remove an item from a list.

Now that we have learned about the Build menu and the `.pro` file, let's move on to learning how we can incorporate the library we just built into another project.

Linking against our sample library

Now, let's make an application that depends on our library. Our application will call the factorial function in the library, statically linking to the library in order to access the factorial function. To accomplish this, you need to perform the following steps:

1. Select **Close All Projects and Editors** from the **File** menu.
2. Choose **New File or Project** from the **File** menu and create a new Qt console application called `MathFunctionsTest` using the wizard.
3. Right-click on `MathFunctionsTest` in the **Project** pane and click on **Add Library**. You can now choose a library in your build tree, a library outside your build tree, an external library on your system such as the Unix math library, `fftmpeg`, or another library that you've created. Select **External Library** and click on **Next**.

4. Browse the library file that was built in the previous section by clicking on **Browse...**, next to the line labeled **Library file**. It'll be in a folder named something like `build-MathFunctions-Desktop_Qt_5_12_2_MinGW_64bit-Debug` in your project's folder. Select the `MathFunctions` library in either the `release` or `debug` folders; it doesn't matter which. The dialog box should look something similar to the following screenshot:

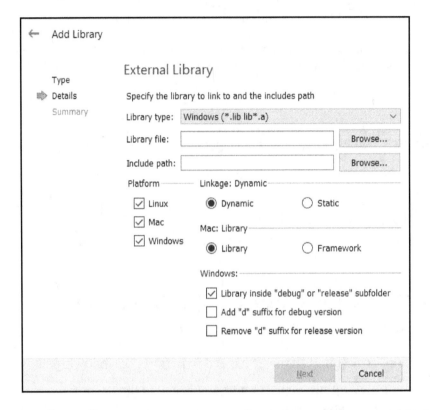

5. Browse the include files for your library by clicking on **Browse...**, which is next to **Include path**. This is the directory where you put the headers for your library.
6. Choose static linking.
7. Leave the other values set to their default values, click on **Next**, and then click on **Finish**.

Qt Creator will work its magic with your .pro file, adding a LIBS variable that includes the output of your library's build and an include path to your library's header files.

We can now call our factorial function. Edit main.cpp to read the following code:

```
#include <QCoreApplication>
#include "mathfunctions.h"

int main(int argc, char *argv[])
{
    QCoreApplication a(argc, argv);
    qDebug("6! is %lu", MathFunctions::factorial(6));
    return a.exec();
}
```

This code first includes our library header file. Note that if you compile the application after adding just the #include declaration, you'll get autosuggest help for every element of the MathFunctions library. This code uses qDebug instead of the C standard library to process its console output.

qDebug() actually has a stream-savvy implementation too. I could have written the qDebug line as follows:

qDebug() << "6! is" << MathFunctions::factorial(6);. The code would have generated the same output. To do this, you'll need to be sure to include the #include <QDebug> line.

Build and run the application now in the **Debug** mode; you should see a console window with the text **6! is 720**. Now, try to build and run the library in the **Release** mode... Wait; why is the debugging output from qDebug still there?

qDebug isn't really a debugging log; it's an output stream for debugging information, regardless of build levels. If you want to turn off its output in release builds, you'll need to edit the .pro file. Double-click on your .pro file and add the following line:

```
CONFIG(release, debug|release): DEFINES += QT_NO_DEBUG_OUTPUT
```

This is another scope; it says that if your build configuration is release, add the QT_NO_DEBUG_OUTPUT preprocessor definition to the list of preprocessor definitions for the project.

Now, if you **Rebuild** (don't choose **Build**, but actually choose **Rebuild** because you want a clean build through the entire system) and run in the **Release** mode, you won't see any output.

Qt actually defines four output streams. One is for debugging messages, another is for bonafide warnings; use `qDebug` for regular logging and `qWarning` to output messages of a higher priority. There's also `qCritical` and `qFatal` for high-priority log messages that will indicate critical failures or failures that cause the application to terminate. You can also turn off warnings in release builds in the same way; simply add the following to your `.pro` file:
`CONFIG(release, debug|release): DEFINES += QT_NO_WARNING_OUTPUT`.

What will you do if you want to add files to your project? You can either do this by manually editing the `.pro` file, which can be faster if you're a good typist, but it is also error-prone and can result in weird build problems if you mess up, or you can do it by right-clicking on your project and selecting either **Add New...** or **Add Existing Files....** The **Add New...** option opens up a short wizard with choices such as these:

- Qt Designer forms, which we'll talk about in the next chapter
- Qt resource files, which we'll talk about in the next chapter
- **Qt Quick Markup** files
- JavaScript files (which can contain the code implementing the logic of a Qt Quick application)
- OpenGL shaders for fragments or vertices in either full OpenGL or OpenGL/ES
- Text files (such as a `Readme` file for your project) or a scratch file to use as a place to stash temporary clipboard items until you're done with an editing session

Before we move on to the important topic of debugging, let's take a look at one more `.pro` file, the `.pro` file for our application, as follows:

```
QT -= gui

# No debug output
CONFIG(release, debug|release): DEFINES += QT_NO_DEBUG_OUTPUT

CONFIG += c++11 console
CONFIG -= app_bundle

DEFINES += QT_DEPRECATED_WARNINGS

SOURCES += main.cpp

# Default rules for deployment.
qnx: target.path = /tmp/$${TARGET}/bin
else: unix:!android: target.path = /opt/$${TARGET}/bin
```

```
!isEmpty(target.path): INSTALLS += target

# Include library
win32:CONFIG(release, debug|release): LIBS += -L$$PWD/../build-
MathFunctions-Desktop_Qt_5_12_3_MinGW_64_bit-Release/release/ -
lMathFunctions
else:win32:CONFIG(debug, debug|release): LIBS += -L$$PWD/../build-
MathFunctions-Desktop_Qt_5_12_3_MinGW_64_bit-Debug/debug/ -lMathFunctions
else:unix: LIBS += -L$$PWD/../build-MathFunctions-
Desktop_Qt_5_12_3_MinGW_64_bit-Debug/ -lMathFunctions

INCLUDEPATH += $$PWD/../MathFunctions
DEPENDPATH += $$PWD/../MathFunctions

win32-g++:CONFIG(release, debug|release): PRE_TARGETDEPS += $$PWD/../build-
MathFunctions-Desktop_Qt_5_12_3_MinGW_64_bit-
Release/release/libMathFunctions.a
else:win32-g++:CONFIG(debug, debug|release): PRE_TARGETDEPS +=
$$PWD/../build-MathFunctions-Desktop_Qt_5_12_3_MinGW_64_bit-
Debug/debug/libMathFunctions.a
else:win32:!win32-g++:CONFIG(release, debug|release): PRE_TARGETDEPS +=
$$PWD/../build-MathFunctions-Desktop_Qt_5_12_3_MinGW_64_bit-
Release/release/MathFunctions.lib
else:win32:!win32-g++:CONFIG(debug, debug|release): PRE_TARGETDEPS +=
$$PWD/../build-MathFunctions-Desktop_Qt_5_12_3_MinGW_64_bit-
Debug/debug/MathFunctions.lib
else:unix: PRE_TARGETDEPS += $$PWD/../build-MathFunctions-
Desktop_Qt_5_12_3_MinGW_64_bit-Debug/libMathFunctions.a
```

Phew! That's pretty dense. Let's see if we can unravel it. It begins by telling the build system that we do not use QtGui.

Next up is the instruction to disable the qDebug messages in release builds, which won't happen by default. The other CONFIG options together say that we're building a console application that supports C++11 standard. The next line with the SOURCES option indicates that we have one source file, a main.cpp file.

The next set of scopes indicate the path to our library and handle the fact that our libraries are in different directories on Windows for release and debug. This is different from Unix systems where there is only one build variant of the library. After this come the INCLUDEPATH and DEPENDPATH variables, which indicate that there are library headers in the MathFunctions directory and that the application depends on those headers. So, if the timestamps on the headers change, the binary should be rebuilt.

The final scope specifies the same dependency on the output library itself; if the library changes, the application executables have to be rebuilt. This is especially important because, that way, we can run multiple copies of Qt Creator, edit our library and application files separately, and rebuild the bits we need after they change, as well as figuring out all the dependencies, with the right bits getting built automatically.

We have learned how to link a C++ library to our Qt project, but we are not really done yet. Next, we will look at how we can debug our application by empowering the tools provided by Qt.

Getting lost and found again – debugging

Qt Creator has a state-of-the-art GUI that hooks into either the **GNU Debugger** (**GDB**), or Microsoft's command-line debugger, CDB, if you use Microsoft tools.

If you've installed Qt Creator on macOS, Linux, or the MinGW version of Qt Creator for Windows, you have everything you need to begin debugging your application. If you already have Microsoft Visual Studio installed and then installed a version of Qt Creator that uses Microsoft's compiler, you also need to install the Microsoft command-line debugger to use Qt Creator's debugging features. Here's how you can install the command-line debugger:

1. Download the debugging tools for Windows, either from
   `http://msdn.microsoft.com/en-us/windows/hardware/hh852365` if you are using the 32-bit version of the compiler and Qt Creator, or from
   `http://msdn.microsoft.com/en-us/windows/hardware/hh852365` for the 64-bit version of the compiler and Qt Creator.

2. Configure the debugging symbol server by going to **Options** under the **Tools** menu, selecting the **Debugger** item on the left-hand side, clicking on the **CDB Paths** pane, and edit the textbox next to the **Symbol Paths** line.

 Usually, the debugger works out of the box with Qt Creator, unless you're using the Microsoft toolchain. However, if you encounter problems, consult the Qt documentation about setting up the debugger at `http://qt-project.org/doc/qt-5/debug.html`.

The following screenshot shows the debugger in action with our test project, stopped at a breakpoint. Let's take a look at the following screenshot in detail to get oriented:

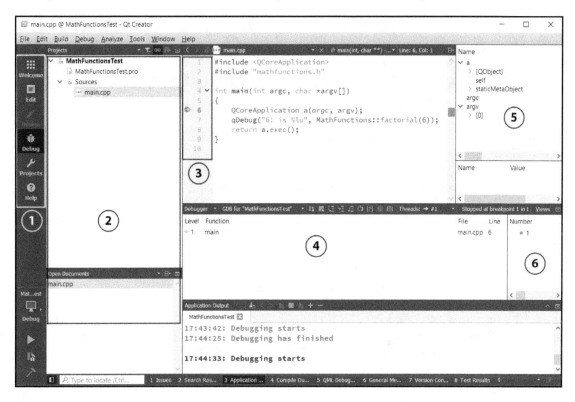

In the screenshot, you'll see the following components (numbered for easy reference):

1. On the left-hand side is the usual row of buttons to pick a view in Qt Creator.
2. Next to the buttons is the view of the project files and the list of open documents.
3. In the main editor pane, every source line has a clickable indicator to let you set and clear breakpoints.
4. The call stack, indicating how the program got to the line the execution is stopped at, is shown in the pane under the editor pane.
5. In the upper-right corner is the variable inspector where you can see the values of the variables in the current stack frame, along with any global variables.
6. Underneath the variable inspector is a list of pending breakpoints, so you can turn on and off breakpoints without needing to hunt through the code.

To generate the screen that you can see in the preceding screenshot, I clicked to the left of line **6**, placing a breakpoint, and then I clicked the **Debug** button on the left after ensuring I'd specified a **Debug** build in the Build selector. Qt Creator built the application in the **Debug** mode, started the application, and let it run to the breakpoint on line **6**.

Setting breakpoints and stepping through your program

A breakpoint, if you haven't encountered one before, is just that – a point at which execution breaks and you can examine the program's state. Once the execution is stopped at a breakpoint, you can step into a function or step over a line, executing your program one line at a time to see how it's behaving. Clicking to the left-hand side of a line number in the **Debug** view lets you set or clear breakpoints. While stopped at a breakpoint, a yellow-colored arrow in the margin of the editor pane indicates the line of code that the processor is about to execute.

While at a breakpoint, several buttons appear above the call stack pane that let you control the program flow, which you can see in the following screenshot:

The buttons are defined as follows (again, numbered for easy reference):

1. The green-colored Continue button, which continues execution at the line indicated by the arrow. You can also continue by pressing the *F5* function key.
2. The red-colored Stop button, which stops debugging altogether.
3. The Step Over button, which executes the current line and advances to the next line before stopping again. You can step over one line by pressing *F10*.
4. The Step Into button, which enters the next function to be called and stops again. You can step into a function by pressing *F11*.
5. The Step Out button, which runs the remainder of the function in the current calling context before stopping again. You can step out of the current function by pressing *Shift + F11*.
6. The instruction-wise button (looks like a little screen), which toggles the debugger between working a source line at a time and an assembly line at a time.
7. There's also a menu of threads, so you can see which thread is running or has stopped.

For example, (in the previous screenshot) from line **7**, if we step over line **8** (pressing *F10*) and then press *F11*, we'll end up inside our factorial function. At this point, if we step into the function again, we'll see the value for *n* change in the right-hand side column, and the arrow advance to point toward line **9** (again, as numbered in the screenshot). From here, we can debug the factorial function in several ways:

- We can examine the contents of a variable by looking at it in the right-hand side pane. If it's in a stack frame above the current calling frame, we can change call frames and see variables in a different call frame too.
- We can modify a variable by clicking on its value and entering a new value.
- With some debuggers, we can move the arrow to different lines in the calling function to skip one or more lines of code, or rewind the execution to rerun a segment of code again.

This last feature, which unfortunately doesn't work with the Microsoft command-line debugger, is especially powerful because we can step through a program, observe an error, modify variables to work around the cause of the error, and continue testing the code without needing to recompile it and rerun the executable. Or, I can skip a bit of the code that I know takes a while to run by substituting the new state in the variables in question and continuing from a new location in the current call frame.

Also, there are a number of other things that we can do, from how we debug the application to various ways in which we can view the state of the application when it's running. From the main **Debug** menu, we can do the following:

- Detach the debugger from a running process by selecting **Detach** from the **Debug** menu (this is handy if the debugger is slowing things down and we know that part of our code doesn't need to be debugged).
- Interrupt the program execution by stopping the execution and examining the current state by choosing **Interrupt** from the **Debug** menu (useful if our application seems caught in a long loop we weren't expecting and appears hung).
- While it is stopped, run to the line that the cursor is on by choosing **Run to Line** or pressing *Ctrl + F10*.
- While it is stopped, skip to the line that the cursor is on by choosing **Jump to Line**. Choosing **Jump to Line** lets you skip the lines of code between the current point and the target line.

Examining variables and memory

The variables pane shows you the values of all the variables in the current stack frame. **Structures** show the values of their members, so you can walk through complex data structures as well. From the variables pane, you can also copy a variable name and value to the clipboard or just a variable value.

In the variables pane, there's a really useful feature called the **Expression Evaluator**, which lets you construct algebraic expressions for the variables in your code and see the results. For example, if I'm stopped at the beginning of the factorial function with n set to 6, I can right-click on the **variables** pane, choose **Insert New Expression Evaluator**, and type in a formula such as n*(n-1) in the dialog that appears. Thus, a new line appears in the pane showing the expression and the value 30. While this is a pretty contrived example, I can view pointer values and pointer dereferences as well.

I can also conditionally break the execution when a variable changes; this is called a **conditional breakpoint** or a **data breakpoint**. For example, let's put a loop in our main function and break as we execute the loop. To do this, first change the main function to read like the following block of code:

```
#include <QCoreApplication>
#include <QDebug>
#include "mathfunctions.h"

int main(int argc, char *argv[])
{
    QCoreApplication a(argc, argv);

    int values[] = { 6, 7, 8 };
    for(unsigned int i = 0; i < sizeof(values)/sizeof(int); i++)
    {
        qDebug() << values[i] << "! = " <<
          MathFunctions::factorial(values[i]);
    }

    return a.exec();
}
```

This will iterate the values stored in the integer array values and print the computed factorial of each value. Start debugging again and let's add a data breakpoint on i. To do this, perform the following steps:

1. Put a breakpoint on the first line of main, the line initializing QCoreApplication.
2. Step over until the for loop, then right-click on i in the right pane and choose **Add Data Breakpoint at Object's Address** from the **Add Data Breakpoint** submenu.
3. Continue by pressing *F5* or the **Continue** button.

The execution will stop at line **11**, the beginning of the for loop, when i is set to 0. Each time I hit *F5* to continue, the application runs until the value of i changes as a result of the i++ statement at the end of the for loop.

You can also inspect and change the individual values of arrays in the variable inspector by clicking on the expansion arrow next to the array name in the variable inspector pane.

In addition to viewing and changing variable values, you can view and change individual memory locations. You might want to do this if you're debugging a decoder or encoder for a binary format, for example, where you need to see a specific location in the memory. From the variables pane, you have several choices by which you can check a memory location; a few of them are given as follows:

- You can right-click on a given variable and open a memory window at this variable's address.
- You can right-click on a given variable and open a memory window at the value that the variable points to (in other words, dereference a pointer to a memory location).
- You can right-click on the variable pane and open up a memory browser at the beginning of the current stack frame.
- You can right-click on the variable pane and open up a memory browser at an arbitrary location in the memory.

The following screenshot shows the memory viewer that contains the array values:

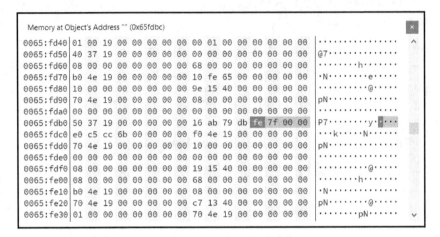

The window shows the memory addresses on the left-hand side, the values of the memory in 16 bytes to a line (first in hexadecimal and then in ASCII), and colors the actual variable you've selected to open the window. You can select a range of values and then right-click on them to do the following:

- Copy the values in ASCII or hexadecimal
- Set a data breakpoint on the memory location you've selected
- Transfer the execution to the address you've clicked (probably not what you want to do if you're viewing data!)

Examining the call stack

The call stack is the hierarchy of function calls in your application's execution at a point in time. While the actual flow varies, typically in your code it begins in `main`, although what calls `main` differs from platform to platform. An obvious use for the call stack is to provide context when you click on the **Interrupt** button; if your program is just off contemplating its navel in a loop somewhere, clicking on **Interrupt** and taking a look at the call stack can give you a clue as to what's going on.

Remember how I defined the factorial function in terms of itself? You can see this very clearly if you put a breakpoint in the factorial and call it, and then continue through the breakpoint a few times before looking at the call stack. You'll see something akin to the following screenshot:

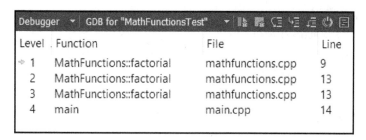

Working from left to right, the fields in the call stack window are the stack levels (numbering starts from the top of the stack and moves down), the functions being invoked, the files that the function is defined in, and the line numbers of the function currently being executed. So, this stack frame says that we're on line **9** of `MathFunctions::factorial` in `mathfunctions.cpp`, called by line **13** of `MathFunctions::factorial`, which is called by line **13** of `MathFunctions::factorial`... and so on, until it bottoms out in our main function and the system startup code that the operating system uses to set up the application process before that.

If you right-click on a line of the call stack pane, you can perform the following actions:

- Reload the stack, in case the display appears corrupted.
- Copy the contents of the call stack to the clipboard – great for bug reports. If your application throws an exception or crashes in the debugger, you can copy the call stack and send it off to the developer responsible for that part of the code (or keep it for yourself as a souvenir).
- Open the memory editor at the address of the instruction, at the line of code indicated by the function call in the call stack.
- Open the disassembler at the address of the instruction, at the line of code indicated by the function call in the call stack.
- Disassemble a region of the memory or the current function.
- Show the program's counter address in the call stack window while debugging.

That's it; we have learned how to use the debugging tools to examine our application. Next, let's learn how to build our project!

The Projects pane and building your project

You've seen how the `.pro` file affects your project's compilation, but there's even more to it than this. If you click on the **Projects** button on the left of Qt Creator, you'll see the project's options, which consist of the following:

- The **Build & Run** options
- The **Editor** options
- The **Code Style** options
- **Dependencies**

Each of these is in its own panel.

 In most cases, you won't need to monkey around with any of these settings, but you might have to tinker with the **Build & Run** settings, especially if you're targeting multiple platforms such as Windows and Linux with cross-compilers or Android. (I will write more about this exciting development in Qt later in this book.)

The final thing that you should know is the build and run kit selector. Qt is one of the best cross-platform toolkits available today, and you can easily find yourself working on a system supporting multiple platforms, such as Linux and Android, or multiple versions of Qt. To support this, Qt has the notion of a build kit, which is just the headers, libraries, and associated things to support a specific platform. You can install multiple build kits and choose which build kit you're compiling against by choosing **Open Build and Run Kit Selector....** By default, if you followed the steps in the previous chapter to install Qt Creator, you'll have one build kit installed; from the Qt website, you can choose others.

The different types of settings in the **Project** mode are as follows:

- For the Build settings, there are configuration options for your release and debug builds. In the **Build** settings editor, you can control whether the build products are placed in their own directory (the default, a so-called shadow build where your build outputs are not mixed with the source code, but placed in their own directory), the qmake configuration for the build (and actually see how Qt Creator will invoke qmake), how Qt Creator cleans your project, and any environment variables you need to set for the build.
- The **Run** settings editor lets you control whether your application runs locally or is deployed on a remote host (not always supported, but usually the case for platforms such as Android), any command-line arguments that you want to pass to your applications, and the settings for the performance analyzer tool, which I will talk about in Chapter 4, *Qt Foundations*.

- In the **Editor** panel, you can set specific editor options for this project. These override the global Qt Creator defaults, which you can set by choosing **Options** from the **Tools** menu and selecting the **Text Editor** option. These options include details such as whether to use tabs or spaces when formatting your code (I strongly suggest you use spaces; they are compatible with editors everywhere!), the number of spaces per tab stop, whether or not automatic indentation should occur, how source files should be encoded, and so on.
- The **Code Style** panel is another override to the global settings for Qt Creator (this time, it's the C++ and Qt Quick panels of the **Options** dialog available from the **Options** menu). Here, you can pick the default styles or edit the styles.

 I strongly recommend that you pick a style that matches the existing source code you're editing; if you're starting from a blank page, the Qt default style is quite readable and is my favorite.

- The **Dependencies** panel lets you set the build order if your project file contains multiple subprojects so that things build in the right order. For example, we could choose to open both our library project and our test project; if we do, we'll see the `MathFunctions` library listed in the dependencies, and we can choose to build the project before the test application is built.

We have gone through how we can build our project. Let's take a step back and review the entire process once again.

A review – running and debugging your application

You'll spend a lot of time editing, compiling, and debugging your code in Qt Creator, so it's wise to remember the following basics:

- The arrow key runs your application without the debugger; to debug your application, choose the arrow key with the bug icon on it.
- You can switch between the **Editor** view and the **Debug** view of your application by clicking on the **Edit** or **Debug** view choice on the left-hand side; if you debug your application, Qt Creator will enter the **Debug** view automatically.

- There's more to breakpoints than just stopping at a line of code! Use data breakpoints to pin down weird bugs that occur only sometimes, or to quickly skip over the first bazillion items of a large loop.
- The variable pane lets you see more than just the contents of variables; you can also add expressions composed of several variables and arithmetic, or view arbitrary memory locations.
- Want to hack around a bug during a debugging session? You can change the values of variables in the variable pane and continue running, changing the program's state as you go.

Hopefully, you have learned how to build and debug your Qt application through all the sections we have covered here. Finally, let's summarize what we have learned from this chapter.

Summary

Qt Creator's **Integrated Development Environment** (**IDE**) contains an editor and tools to start the compiler, linker, and debugger in order to build and debug your applications. Using this, you can start and stop your application, place breakpoints while your application is stopped, or examine the variables or the logical flow of your application.

While Qt Creator manages most of the project for you, sometimes you just have to get down and dirty with a `.pro` file. You can use scopes to handle conditional compilation (things such as when building for a specific platform or whether a file should be included in the **Release** or **Debug** mode). The `.pro` file consists of scopes, variables, and their values; by setting the variables that the `.pro` file feeds qmake, qmake understands the dependencies in your project and magically creates a Makefile to build your application.

In this chapter, we have learned how to build our own C++ library and link it to our Qt application. After that, we also learned how to build and debug our application using the tools provided by Qt.

In the next chapter, we'll move on from the mechanics of making a project build and take a look at Qt Creator's UI designer, as well as give you a brief introduction to the world of Qt Widgets and Qt Quick.

3
Designing Your Application with Qt Designer

Qt is perhaps best known as a cross-platform user interface toolkit, and only in the last few years has Qt Creator really evolved to be a full software development environment. Even in its early releases, however, Qt had an excellent facility for building user interfaces with Qt Designer, now part of Qt Creator. More recently, the developers building Qt have added Qt Quick, as a second option for user interface development. Qt Quick extends the Qt libraries and Qt Designer capabilities of Qt Creator, to build fluid interfaces for touchscreens and **set-top boxes** (**STBs**). This is facilitated by the declarative nature of Qt Quick and the **Qt Meta-Object Language** (**QML**).

In this chapter, we will cover the following topics:

- Introducing signals and slots
- Creating user interfaces with Qt Designer
- Instantiating forms, message boxes, and dialogs in your application
- Wiring the Qt Widgets application logic
- Introducing Qt Quick's support for declarative user interface development
- Understanding the building of a Qt application
- Creating the Qt application

These topics will allow you to dive into the basics of creating an application using Qt, whether in C++ or through QML methods. You will learn how to design your first user interface, using both the Qt form designer and Qt Quick Designer. Then, you will also learn how to make use of the basic functionalities provided by Qt, such as instantiating a message box and connecting user interface interaction with an event function, through the signals and slots mechanism.

At the end of this chapter, you'll be well equipped to decide whether your application should be written using Qt Widgets or Qt Quick and to build your application, with the help of the documentation that accompanies Qt Creator.

Technical requirements

The technical requirements for this chapter include Qt 5.12.3 MinGW 64-bit, Qt Creator 4.9.0, and Windows 10.

Introducing signals and slots

In software systems, there is often the need to couple different objects. Ideally, this coupling should be loose—that is, not dependent on the system's compile-time configuration. This is especially obvious when you consider user interfaces—for example, a button press might adjust the contents of a text widget, or cause something to appear or disappear. Many systems use events for this purpose; components offering data encapsulate that data in an event, and an event loop (or, more recently, an event listener) catches the event and performs some action. This is known as **event-driven** programming or the event model.

Qt offers the *signals and slots* mechanism as interfaces to manage events, such as the click event, selection change event, text input event, and so on. When a user does something and an event is triggered, the object (that is, a push button) generates a signal that gets sent to the Qt's event system. Then, the event system will notify the other object that is linked to the signal that such an event has occurred. Eventually, it will trigger the `slot` function (which is somewhat similar to a callback function) of the receiving object, as a reaction to the signal. In other words, when object A is being instigated (that is, button clicked), it will send a signal to object B and notify it to execute its `slot` function (that is, close the window). Qt objects might emit more than one signal, and signals might carry arguments; in addition, multiple Qt objects can have slots connected to the same signal, making it easy to arrange one-to-many notifications.

Qt provides a macro, `connect`, that lets you connect signals to slots. Equally important is the fact that if no object is interested in a signal, it can be safely ignored, and no slots will be connected to the signal. Equally important, if no slots are connected to a signal, it will simply be ignored. Any object that inherits from `QObject`, Qt's base class for objects, can emit signals or provide slots for connection to signals. Under the hood, Qt provides extensions to C++ syntax, to declare signals and slots.

A simple example will help make this clear. The classic example you find in the Qt documentation is an excellent one, and we'll use it again here, with some extension. Imagine that you have the need for a counter—that is, a container that holds an integer. In C++, you might write something like the following block of code:

```cpp
class Counter
{
public:
    Counter() {}

    int getValue() { return myValue; }
    void setValue(int value);

  private:
    int myValue = 0;
};
```

The `Counter` class has a single private member, `myValue`, bearing its value. Clients can invoke `getValue` to obtain the counter's value, or set its value by invoking `setValue` with a new value. Do note that in C++11, you can directly initialize the default value of a class data member—in this case, we set the default value of `myValue` as `0`.

In Qt, we can write the class this way, using signals and slots:

```cpp
#include <QObject>

class Counter : public QObject
{
Q_OBJECT

public:
    Counter(QObject *parent = 0) {}
    int getValue() { return myValue; }

public slots:
    void setValue(int value);
    void increment();
    void decrement();

signals:
    void valueChanged(int newValue);

private:
    int m_value = 0;
};
```

This `Counter` class inherits from `QObject` the base class for all Qt objects. To make all the functionality of `QObject` (such as the signal-slot mechanism) available, subclasses of `QObject` must include the declaration `Q_OBJECT` as the first element of their definition; this macro expands to the Qt code, implementing the subclass-specific glue necessary for the Qt object and signal-slot mechanism. The constructor remains the same, initializing our private member to 0. Similarly, the accessor method value remains the same, returning the current value for the counter. If you don't include the `Q_OBJECT` macro at the beginning, then the compilation will fail.

An object's slots must be public and are declared using the Qt extension to C++ public slots. This code defines three slots: a `setValue` slot, which accepts a new value for the counter, and the `increment` and `decrement` slots, which increment and decrement the value of the counter. Slots might take arguments, but must not return them; the communication between a signal and its slots is one way: initiating with the signal and terminating with the slot(s) connected to the signal. This mechanism is intentionally designed this way by the Qt developers.

The counter offers a single signal. Signals are also declared using a Qt extension to C++ signals. A `Counter` object emits the `valueChanged` signal a single argument, which is the new value of the counter. A signal is a function signature, not a method; Qt's extensions to C++ use the type signature of signals and slots, to ensure type safety between signal-slot connections, a key advantage signals and slots have over other decoupled messaging schemes.

As developers, it's our responsibility to implement each slot in our class with whatever application logic makes sense. The `Counter` class's slots look like this:

```
void Counter::setValue(int newValue)
{
    myValue = newValue;
    emit valueChanged(newValue);
}

void Counter::increment()
{
    setValue(getValue() + 1);
}

void Counter::decrement()
{
    setValue(getValue() - 1);
}
```

We use the implementation of the `setValue` slot as a method, which is what all slots are at their heart. The `setValue` slot takes a new value and assigns the new value to the private member variable of `Counter` if they aren't the same. Then, the signal emits the `valueChanged` signal, using the Qt extension `emit`, which triggers an invocation to the slots connected to the signal.

This is a common pattern for signals that handle object properties: testing the property to be set for equality with the new value, and only assigning and emitting a signal if the values are unequal.

If we had a button—say, `QPushButton`—we could connect its clicked signal to the `increment` or `decrement` slot so that a click on the button increments or decrements the counter. I'd do this using the `QObject::connect` method, like this:

```
QPushButton* button = new QPushButton(tr("Increment"), this);
Counter* counter = new Counter(this);
QObject::connect(button, &QPushButton::clicked, counter,
&Counter::increment);
```

We first create the `QPushButton` and `Counter` objects. The `QPushButton` constructor takes a string, the label for the button, which we denote to be the `Increment` string or its localized counterpart.

Why do we pass this to each constructor? Qt provides a parent-child memory management between the `QObject` objects and their descendants, easing cleanup when you're done using an object. When you free an object, Qt also frees any children of the parent object so that you don't have to. The parent-child relationship is set at construction time: a signal to tell the constructors that when the object invoking this code is freed, `PushButton` and `counter` can be freed as well. (Of course, the invoking method must also be a subclass of `QObject` for this to work.)

Next, call `QObject::connect`, passing first the source object and the signal to be connected, and then, the receiver object and the slot to which the signal should be sent.

Ever since Qt version 5, you are not recommended to use the old `SIGNAL` and `SLOT` macros when calling `QObject::connect`.

Signals can be connected to signals too, and when this happens, the signals are chained and trigger any slots connected to the downstream signals. For example, I can write the following code:

```
Counter a, b;
QObject::QObject::connect(&a, &Counter::valueChanged, &b,
&Counter::setValue);
```

This connects the b counter with the a counter so that any changes in value to the a counter also change the value of the b counter.

Other than that, you can also connect a signal directly to a function, like this:

```
connect(a, &Counter::valueChanged, someFunction);
```

If you're writing C++11 code, you can even connect your signal to a lambda function, which looks something like this:

```
connect(a, &Counter::valueChanged, [=](const QString &newValue)
{
    b->updateValue("senderValue", newValue);
});
```

The lambda function is what we call an anonymous function, which does not need a name or identifier. A lambda function is always getting triggered instantly by a higher-order function, which—in layman's terms—is a function declared within a function. Once its task has been completed, it will cease to exist; hence, there is no need for an identifier.

In this case, when the valueChanged signal is being triggered, we directly declare a lambda function within the connect function, which subsequently calls updateValue and passes the newValue variable to it. This is helpful when you don't intend to reuse the same slot function elsewhere and, thus, if you have written JavaScript before, you should be pretty familiar with this.

There's also disconnect, which breaks the connection between a signal and a particular slot. Invoking disconnect is similar to invoking connect, as follows:

```
disconnect(&a, &Counter::valueChanged(int), &b, &Counter::setValue(int));
```

This disconnects the connection we made in the previous example.

Signals and slots are used throughout Qt, both for user interface elements and to handle asynchronous operations, such as the presence of data on network sockets, HTTP transaction results, and so forth. Under the hood, signals and slots are very efficient, boiling down to function dispatch operations, so you shouldn't hesitate to use the abstraction in your own designs.

Qt provides a special build tool, the meta-object compiler, which compiles the extensions to C++ and is required for signals and slots. It generates the additional code necessary to implement the mechanism.

Using these, we will create a sample form, with the help of Qt Designer.

Creating user interfaces with Qt Designer

Let's create a simple calculator application, using Qt Designer and two forms: one form that takes the arguments for an arithmetic operation, and a second dialog form to present the results.

Bear in mind that we will be using these forms in the following sections of this chapter as well. We'll do this twice in this chapter, first to show how to do this using Qt Widgets, and second, by using Qt Quick. The example is contrived but will show you how to create multiple user interface forms in both environments, and will give you practice in working with signals and slots.

F1 is the keystroke you can use in Qt Creator to get help. As you write code in this and subsequent chapters, for any class or method you're curious about, select it and hit *F1*. You'll be taken to Qt's `Help` mode, with documentation about that class or method.

Creating the main form

In Chapter 1, *Getting Started with Qt Creator*, you learned the basic elements of the Qt Widgets designer, including the palette of widgets you can use, the central **Edit** pane, the tree of objects, and the **Property** view. The following screenshot shows the Qt Designer again:

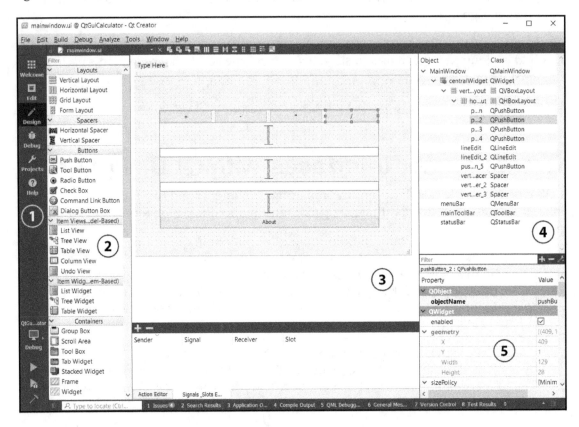

Working from left to right, the parts of the screen you see are as follows:

1. The **Views** selector, presently indicating that the Qt Designer view is active.
2. The palette of possible widgets you can lay out on your form.
3. The form editor, above the connection editor that lets you wire signals and slots between widgets.
4. The object tree, indicating all of the objects that have been laid out on the form and showing their parent-child relationships, through the use of nested lists.

---

5. Under the object tree is the **Property** editor, where you can edit the compile-time properties of any item you select on the form editor.

Let's begin by creating a new Qt Widgets project (click on **Qt Widgets Application** from the **New File or Projects** dialog) and naming the project QtGuiCalculator, and then, follow these steps:

1. In the Forms folder of the project, double-click on the mainwindow.ui file. The designer will open.
2. Drag out a vertical layout from the palette.
3. Right-click on the layout and choose **Lay out**, then choose **Adjust Size....** The layout will shrink to a point.
4. Drag two line editors and drop them on the vertical layout in the object viewer (the far right pane). You'll see the vertical layout grow, to accept each of the line editors. You should now have something that looks like the following screenshot, where the layout now has two text fields:

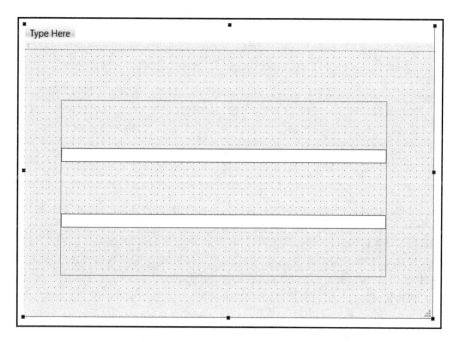

5. Drag a horizontal layout, and drop it on the vertical layout in the object viewer.
6. Drag and drop four **Push** buttons on the horizontal layout you just added.

7. Resize the containing window so that the entire layout shows in the window.

8. Rename the buttons `plusButton`, `minusButton`, `timesButton`, and `divideButton`, using the **Property** browser in the lower-right area of the screen. As you do so, scroll down to the **text** property (under **QAbstractButton**) and give each button a logical label, such as +, −, *, and /.

9. Select the top-line input, and name it `argument1Input`.

10. Select the bottom-line input, and name it `argument2Input`.

The next screenshot shows what you should see in the Qt Designer form editor pane so far. You can also manually arrange the buttons by breaking the layout and positioning them using the mouse, but that typically makes your layout less robust to window resizing and is generally not a good idea. The following screenshot depicts our calculator user interface:

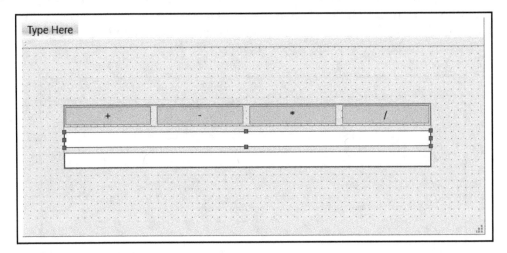

So far, this is pretty straightforward. We used a vertical layout and a horizontal layout to lay out the various controls; this takes advantage of Qt's dynamic constraints on widget layout and sizing. All widgets have minimum and maximum size properties, which are used by layouts to determine the actual size a widget consumes. Some widgets are elastic; that is, they stretch to fill their contents. When specifying the actual size of a widget, you can specify that it takes one of the following values in each of the *x* and *y* axes:

- The minimum size of the widget.
- The maximum size of the widget.
- A fixed size between its minimum and maximum.
- An expanding size, expanding to fit the contents of the widget.

Qt provides four kinds of layouts, which you can mix and match, as we just did. You've encountered the vertical and horizontal layouts; there's also a grid layout, which lets you organize things in an *m x n* grid, and a form layout, which organizes widgets in a manner similar to how the native platform enumerates fields on a form.

Right now, our layout's a little bunched up. Let's add some spacers, to better fill the space in the window, and also, add a button for an about box:

1. Drag a vertical spacer and drop it between the input lines, and a second vertical spacer between the horizontal layout that contains the row of buttons and the input line.
2. Drag a **Push** button to the vertical layout, and add a spacer between the bottom line and the **Push** button.
3. Name the last **Push** button aboutButton, and give it the text About. We'll add an icon later.

The next screenshot shows the application as we've constructed it in the designer. If you click on the **Run** button, you should see the following:

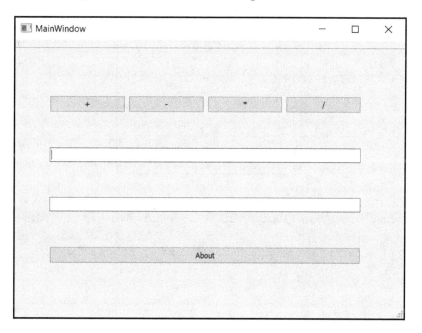

Now, let's make our result dialog. Right-click on the project and choose **Add New...**; then, follow these steps:

1. In the dialog that appears, choose **Qt** on the left, and then **Qt Designer Form** in the middle. Click on **Choose**.
2. Choose a dialog style for your dialog; choose **Dialog with Buttons Bottom**, and click on **Next**.
3. Name the file `resultdialog.ui`, and click on **Next**.
4. Click on **Finish**.
5. In the dialog that appears, drag out a form layout. Right-click on the dialog window (not the form layout) and choose **Lay out**, followed by **Lay Out Vertically**.
6. Add a label to the form layout. Change its text to read `Result`.
7. Drag out another label, and name it `result`. In the `objectName` field under `Property`, change the name to `result`.
8. Adjust the window size so that it's smaller, to make it look better.

You should have a dialog that looks like the following screenshot:

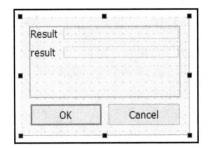

Now is a good time for you to experiment with layouts and spacers, and style the dialog any way you wish. To see how this happens, let's see how to use these resources.

Using application resources

Now, let's add an icon to the application for the **About** button. You can draw one, or download a free-to-use icon online. Icons can be in **Portable Network Graphics** (PNG), **Joint Photographic Experts Group** (JPEG), or other formats; a good choice is a **Scalable Vector Graphics** (SVG) format because SVG images are vector-based, and scale correctly to different sizes. Put the resource file in your project directory, and then perform the following steps:

1. Choose the **Edit** view in Qt Creator.
2. Right-click on the project, then choose **Add New....** In the **New File** dialog that opens, click on **Qt** under **Files and Classes**, and click on **Qt Resource file**.
3. Name the file resources.
4. Add it to the current project.
5. If resources.qrc isn't already open in the editor, double-click on it in the solution pane. The resource file editor will appear.
6. Click on **Add**, choose **Add prefix**, and make the prefix /.
7. Click on **Add** again, then on **Add Files**, and choose your icon.

Icons are loaded in the read-only segment of your application through the Qt resource compiler. You can access them anywhere you'd access a file, by prefixing the path and name of the resource with a colon. For example, we might place a text file in our application resources, and then open the file for reading, like this:

```
QFile file(":/folder/fileName.txt");
file.open(QIODevice::ReadOnly | QIODevice::Text);

while (!file.atEnd()) {
    QByteArray line = file.readLine();
    processLine(line); // Calling your own function
}
```

Application resources are suitable for text and small media files, such as icons or images. However, you should avoid using them for larger items, such as movies and large sounds, because they'll needlessly bloat the size of your application binary. For these purposes, it's better to package media files with your application and load them directly from the disk.

In the next section, we'll use the resource you added, when we add our about box to the application.

Instantiating forms, message boxes, and dialogs in your application

Qt Designer generates an XML-based layout file (which ends in .ui) for each form you create in Designer. At compile time, Qt Creator compiles the layout into a header file that constructs the components for your user interface layout. The pattern typically used by Qt applications is to construct a private layout class that the main class instantiates. Here's how it works for the main window:

```
#ifndef MAINWINDOW_H
#define MAINWINDOW_H

#include <QMainWindow>

namespace Ui {
  class MainWindow;
}

class MainWindow : public QMainWindow
{
    Q_OBJECT
public:
    explicit MainWindow(QWidget *parent = nullptr);
    ~MainWindow();
private:
    Ui::MainWindow *ui;
};

#endif // MAINWINDOW_H
```

In mainwindow.cpp, we have the following:

```
#include "mainwindow.h"
#include "ui_mainwindow.h"
#include "resultdialog.h"
#include <QMessageBox>

MainWindow::MainWindow(QWidget *parent) :
    QMainWindow(parent),
    ui(new Ui::MainWindow)
{
```

```
    ui->setupUi(this);
}

MainWindow::~MainWindow()
{
    delete ui;
}
```

 Why is the constructor declared explicitly? This prevents the C++ compiler from providing implicit casts so that callers can't use anything but the MainWindow instances when referring to MainWindow. Qt provides this by default.

The Ui::MainWindow class is automatically constructed by Qt Designer; by including its declaration in mainwindow.cpp, we create an instance of it and assign that instance to the ui field. Once initialized, we call its setupUi function, which creates the entire user interface you sketched out in Qt Designer.

The controls we laid out in Qt Designer are accessible as field names. For example, we can modify mainwindow.cpp to invoke an about box, by adding a slot to mainwindow.h to handle the case when you click on the **About** button, and then, we can add the code to invoke an about box in the implementation of the slot. To do this, follow these steps:

1. Add a public slot declaration to mainwindow.h, along with a slot named aboutClicked. It should now read like the following code:

```
class MainWindow : public QMainWindow
{
    Q_OBJECT
public:
    explicit MainWindow(QWidget *parent = 0);
    ~MainWindow();
public slots:
    void aboutButtonClicked();

private:
    Ui::MainWindow *ui;
};
```

2. At the top of mainwindow.cpp, add an include statement for the QMessageBox class, as follows:

```
#include <QMessageBox>
```

3. Add the implementation of the `aboutClicked` slot to `mainwindow.cpp`. This code constructs `QMessageBox` on the stack and sets its icon to the icon you added in your resources earlier, the text of the dialog to `Lorem ipsum`, and the title of the message box to `About`. The `exec` method of the `QMessageBox` invocation opens the message box and blocks the application flow until you dismiss the message box. It should read something like the code that follows:

```
void MainWindow::aboutButtonClicked()
{
    QMessageBox messageBox;
    messageBox.setIconPixmap(QPixmap(":/icon.png"));
    messageBox.setText("Lorem ipsum.");
    messageBox.setWindowTitle("About");
    messageBox.exec();
}
```

4. In the `MainWindow` constructor, connect the signal from the **About** button to the slot you just created. Your constructor should now read as follows:

```
MainWindow::MainWindow(QWidget *parent) :
    QMainWindow(parent),
    ui(new Ui::MainWindow),
{
    ui->setupUi(this);
    QObject::connect(ui->aboutButton, &QPushButton::clicked,
                        this, &MainWindow::aboutButtonClicked);
}
```

If we build the application, we now have a fully functioning about box, including the application icon you chose. The `connect` call is just like the previous signal-slot connections we've seen; it connects the clicked signal of the main window user interface's `aboutButton` to your `aboutClicked` slot.

A word on naming signals and slots before we continue: a signal is typically named a verb in its past tense, denoting the semantics of the event that just occurred that it's trying to signal. A slot should somehow match those semantics, preferably including more detail as to how the signal is being handled. So, Qt names the button's clicked signal logically, and I expand on this by giving a slot named `aboutClicked`. Of course, you can name your signals and slots whatever you like, but this is a good practice to follow.

Before we wire up the other buttons and implement our calculator logic, we need to set up the class for our results dialog. Qt creates this class automatically using the **user interface compiler** (**uic**), which compiles forms into classes. We'll follow the pattern of the MainWindow class, creating a private ui member containing an instance of the compile-time generated object that constructs the user interface for the results dialog. You can create the ResultDialog class, using the **New File** wizard available, by right-clicking on the project; choose **C++ Class**, and name it ResultDialog. The class itself should inherit from QDialog. The header file should look like this:

```cpp
#ifndef RESULTDIALOG_H
#define RESULTDIALOG_H

#include <QDialog>

namespace Ui {
    class Dialog;
}

class ResultDialog : public QDialog
{
    Q_OBJECT
public:
    explicit ResultDialog(QWidget *parent = nullptr);
    ~ResultDialog();

private:
    Ui::Dialog *ui;
};

#endif // RESULTDIALOG_H
```

The first thing we need to do is forward declare the Dialog class created by Qt Designer; we do this in the Ui namespace, so it doesn't conflict with any other code in the application, as follows:

```cpp
namespace Ui {
    class Dialog;
}
```

Then, we need to declare a pointer to an instance of that class as a private member variable; we name this pointer ui, as was done for the MainWindow class.

You can guess what our `ResultDialog` implementation looks like, and it's shown here:

```
#include "resultdialog.h"
#include "ui_resultdialog.h"

ResultDialog::ResultDialog(QWidget *parent) :
    QDialog(parent),
    ui(new Ui::Dialog)
{
    ui->setupUi(this);
}

ResultDialog::~ResultDialog()
{
    delete ui;
}
```

At construction time, it makes an instance of our `Ui:Dialog` class, and then invokes its `setupUi` method, to create an instance of the user interface at runtime.

Other than using the form file (`.ui`), you can also manually instantiate form widgets using just C++ code. Let's try it out. Before we start, check out `https://doc.qt.io/qt-5/qtwidgets-module.html` for all the Qt Widgets classes that you can use in your application.

Let's say you want to instantiate a push button manually to your program using C++. You must first include its header before you're able to access its properties and functionalities, as follows:

```
#include <QPushButton>
```

Then, you can proceed to instantiate the push button, like this:

```
QPushButton * button = new QPushButton("Click me", this);
```

In the preceding code, we declared a `QPushButton` object and set its caption as `Click me`. The second parameter is the parent object of the push button, for which we used the `this` keyword to indicate the parent object is the `MainWindow` object. If we want it to be something else, we can do it like this:

```
QPushButton * button = new QPushButton("Click me", this);
QPushButton * button2 = new QPushButton("Click me", button);
```

In the preceding code, we instantiated a second push button and made the first button its parent. Once a widget has been given a parent object, it will follow the parent object wherever it goes and will get deleted as well if the parent object gets deleted. An example of this can be seen in the following code block:

```
QPushButton * button = new QPushButton("Click me", this);
QPushButton * button2 = new QPushButton("Click me", button);
button->deleteLater();
```

Since we're deleting the button object, its child object button2 will also get deleted.

Now, post this instantiation, let us see how to wire the Qt Widgets logic for understanding its working.

Wiring the Qt Widgets application logic

The application logic for the calculator is simple: we add a property setter to ResultDialog that lets us set the result field of the dialog, and then we wire up some arithmetic, signals, and slots in MainWindow, to do the actual computation and show the dialog. Let's have a look at the following steps:

1. First, make the following change to ResultDialog:

```
void ResultDialog::setResult(float r)
{
    ui->result->setText(QString::number(r));
}
```

This method takes a float, the value to show in the dialog, and formats the result as a string, using Qt's default formatting. Qt is fully internationalized; if you do this in English-speaking locales, it will use a decimal point, whereas if you do it with a locale set to a region where a comma is used as the decimal separator, it will use a comma instead. The number method is a handy one, with overloads taking doubles and floats, as well as integers and arguments, to indicate the precision and exponentiation of the returned string.

2. Now, we move on to the modified `MainWindow` class. First, let's take a look at the revised class declaration, shown here:

```
#ifndef MAINWINDOW_H
#define MAINWINDOW_H

#include <QMainWindow>
#include <QPair>

namespace Ui {
    class MainWindow;
}

class ResultDialog;

class MainWindow : public QMainWindow
{
    Q_OBJECT
    typedef QPair<float, float> Arguments;
public:
    explicit MainWindow(QWidget *parent = nullptr);
    ~MainWindow();
    Arguments arguments();
signals:
    void computed(float f);
```

3. We continue to declare the slot functions and private variables of the class, as follows:

```
public slots:
    void aboutClicked();
    void plusButtonClicked();
    void minusButtonClicked();
    void timesButtonClicked();
    void divideButtonClicked();

    void showResult(float r);

private:
    Ui::MainWindow *ui;
    ResultDialog* results;
};

#endif // MAINWINDOW_H
```

In addition to the base class QMainWindow, we now include QPair, a simple Qt template that lets us pass pairs of values. We'll use the QPair template, a type defined as Arguments, to pass around a pair of arguments for an arithmetic operation.

4. We add a signal, computed, which the class triggers any time it performs an arithmetic operation. We also add slots for each of the arithmetic button clicks: plusButtonClicked, minusButtonClicked, timesButtonClicked, and divideButtonClicked. Finally, we add a showResult slot, which shows the result when a computation occurs.

5. The MainWindow constructor now needs to do a bunch of signal-slot wiring for all of our buttons, signals, and slots. Add the highlighted part of the code in mainwindow.cpp, as follows:

```
MainWindow::MainWindow(QWidget *parent) :
    QMainWindow(parent),
    ui(new Ui::MainWindow),
    results(0)
{
    ui->setupUi(this);
    QObject::connect(ui->aboutButton, &QPushButton::clicked,
                     this, &MainWindow::aboutButtonClicked);
    QObject::connect(this, &MainWindow::computed,
                     this, &MainWindow::showResult);
    QObject::connect(ui->plusButton, &QPushButton::clicked,
                     this, &MainWindow::plusButtonClicked);
    QObject::connect(ui->minusButton, &QPushButton::clicked,
                     this, &MainWindow::minusButtonClicked);
    QObject::connect(ui->timesButton, &QPushButton::clicked,
                     this, &MainWindow::timesButtonClicked);
    QObject::connect(ui->divideButton, &QPushButton::clicked,
                     this, &MainWindow::divideButtonClicked);

}
```

6. After connecting the **About** button to the slot that shows the about dialog, we
next connect the computed signal from `MainWindow` to its `showResult` slot.
Note that this signal/slot carries an argument, which is the value to show. The
remaining four connections connect each of the operation buttons with the code,
to perform a specific arithmetic operation.

The `showResult` slot creates a new `ResultDialog` if we don't already have one,
sets its result to the incoming value, and invokes the dialog, as shown in the
following code block:

```
void MainWindow::showResult(float r)
{
    if (!results)
    {
        results = new ResultDialog(this);
    }
    results->setResult(r);
    results->exec();
}
```

The `arguments` method is a helper method used by each of the arithmetic
functions, and fetches the values from each of the input lines, converts them from
strings to floating-point numbers, and does a little bit of error checking, to ensure
that the entries are valid floating-point numbers, as shown in the following code
block:

```
MainWindow::Arguments MainWindow::arguments()
{
    bool ok1, ok2;
    float a1 = ui->argument1Input->text().toFloat(&ok1);
    float a2 = ui->argument2Input->text().toFloat(&ok2);
    if (!ok1 || !ok2)
    {
        QMessageBox messageBox;
        messageBox.setIconPixmap(QPixmap(":/icon.png"));
        messageBox.setText("One of your entries is not a valid
number.");
        messageBox.setWindowTitle("Error");
        messageBox.exec();
    }
    return Arguments(a1, a2);
}
```

The `toFloat` method of `QString` does just that: it converts a string to a floating-point number, returning the number and setting the Boolean value passed in to `true` if the conversion was successful, or `false` otherwise. The code does this for both argument input lines, then it checks the resulting Boolean values and reports an error if either argument is malformed, before returning a `QPair` class of the arguments to the caller.

7. The remaining code actually performs the arithmetic, signaling that a computation has occurred when the operation is complete. For example, take the `plusButtonClicked` slot, as follows:

```
void MainWindow::plusButtonClicked()
{
    Arguments a = arguments();
    emit computed(a.first + a.second);
}
```

This obtains the arguments from the input lines using the `arguments` function, computes the sum, and then emits the computed signal with the summed value. As we connected the computed signal to the `showResult` slot, this triggers a call to `showResult`, which creates `ResultDialog` if necessary, and shows the dialog with the computed result. The `minusButtonClicked`, `timesButtonClicked`, and `divideButtonClicked` methods are all similar.

The end result looks something like the following screenshot:

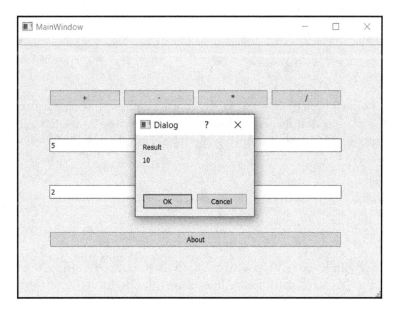

Let's see what more there is to it!

Learning more about Qt Widgets

There are whole books written about programming with the Qt Widgets widget set; it's a very rich widget set that includes just about everything you'd need to build the average Mac, Windows, or Linux application, and has the advantage that the user interface controls are familiar to most computer users.

We'll discuss it more in Chapter 5, *Developing Applications with Qt Widgets*, but you can also consult the Qt documentation at https://doc.qt.io/qt-5/qtwidgets-index.html.

Next, we will see how Qt Quick and syntax work with code interlude for programming.

Introducing Qt Quick's support for declarative user interface development

Most of the programming you do at the lowest level is imperative: you describe how an algorithm should work (take this value and square it; search for the first occurrence of this string and replace it; format this data this way; and so forth). With Qt Quick, your programming is largely declarative: instead of saying *how* you say *what*. For example, in C++ with Qt, we might write code like this to draw a rectangle:

```
QRect r(0, 0, 16, 16);
QPainter p;
p.setBrush(QBrush(Qt::blue));
p.drawRect(r);
```

This code creates a rectangle of 16 x 16 pixels, allocates a QPainter object that does the drawing, tells the painter that its brush should be colored blue, and then tells the painter to draw the rectangle. In QML, we'd simply write the rectangle code as follows:

```
import QtQuick 2.12
Rectangle {
    width: 16
    height: 16
    color: "blue"
}
```

The difference is obvious: we're just saying that there is a blue rectangle that's 16 x 16 pixels. It's up to the Qt Quick runtime to determine how to draw the rectangle.

Qt Quick's underlying language is QML. QML is based heavily on JavaScript, and, in fact, most things that you can write in JavaScript, you can also express in QML. Expression syntax is essentially unchanged; assignments, arithmetic, and so forth all are the same, and the name/value system is functionally the same, although object frames might be preceded by a type declaration (as you can see with the Rectangle example that I just showed you).

A key exception to the *what works in JavaScript works in QML rule* is the lack of a **document object model** (**DOM**), and things such as the document root for global variables because there's no root context or DOM on which other things hang. If you're porting a web application to QML, be prepared to refactor those parts of your application's architecture.

Objects in QML must be parented in the fashion of a tree; each QML file must contain an encapsulating object, and then can have child objects that have child objects. However, there must be a single root for the hierarchy at the top of the file. Often, this root is a Rectangle object, which draws a base rectangle on which its children are presented, or an Item object, which is a container for a more complex user interface element that doesn't actually draw anything. Each item can have a name, which is stored in its id property.

Most visible QML items can have states—that is, a collection of properties that apply when a particular state is active. This lets you do things such as declare the difference between a button's dormant and pressed state; pressing the button just toggles between the states, and the button's color, shadow, and so on can all change, with you not needing to change each individual property.

A key concept in QML that's not present in JavaScript is that of binding: if two QML object properties share the same value, changing one changes the other. Binding is a method that couples values with notifications about value changes; it's similar to how references work in C++, or how pass-by-reference works in other languages. This is very handy in coding things such as animations because you can use the value of one object as the value for another object, and when the underlying value changes in one place, both objects are updated.

QML files can depend on each other or include files of JavaScript for business logic. You've already seen one example of this at the top of every QML file: the import directive instructs the runtime to include the indicated file and version; so, when we write import QtQuick 2.12, the runtime finds the declaration of the Qt Quick module version 2.12 and includes its symbols when parsing the file. This is how you can encapsulate functionality. QML files in your project are included by default, while you can also include JavaScript files and assign them to a specific JavaScript variable.

For example, we can have a JavaScript file `calculatorLogic.js` that implements all of the functionality of our calculator. In the QML, write the following code:

```
import QtQuick 2.12
import "calculatorLogic.js" as CalculatorLogic
Item {
    // someplace in code
    CalculatorLogic.add(argument1, argument2);
}
```

The initial `import` statement loads the JavaScript file and assigns its value to the QML object `CalculatorLogic`; we can then dispatch methods and access properties of that object as if it were any other QML object.

Qt Quick declares a number of basic data types; these match closely with the data types you find in Qt when writing C++ code, although the syntax can differ. Some of the most important types you'll encounter are as follows:

- A point, with the x and y properties.
- A rectangle, with x, y, width, and height properties.
- A size, with width and height properties.
- A color, which is a quoted string in the HTML ARGB notation or a named color from Qt's lexicon of colors. (Most colors you can think of have names in QML.)
- A 2D, 3D, or 4D vector.
- Basic types, including Boolean values, strings, integers, and floating-point numbers.

 There are also a lot of visible types for user interface construction; in this chapter, there's only room to touch on a few. For a detailed list of all QML types and the documentation about those types, see https://doc.qt.io/qt-5/qmlreference.html.

QML is an alternative way to create Qt applications without using the C++ programming language. If you are familiar with web scripting languages such as JavaScript, learning QML is definitely an easy job for you. Next up, let us see how to build a Qt application.

Understanding the building of a Qt application

In `Chapter 1`, *Getting Started with Qt Creator*, you gained basic familiarity with Qt Designer for Qt Quick applications. Since we have created a calculator program using the C++ language in the previous example, as a comparison, we also create a calculator program in QML so that you can learn the differences.

Let's have another look before we recreate our calculator app in QML. The following screenshot shows the Qt Designer for the Qt Quick window:

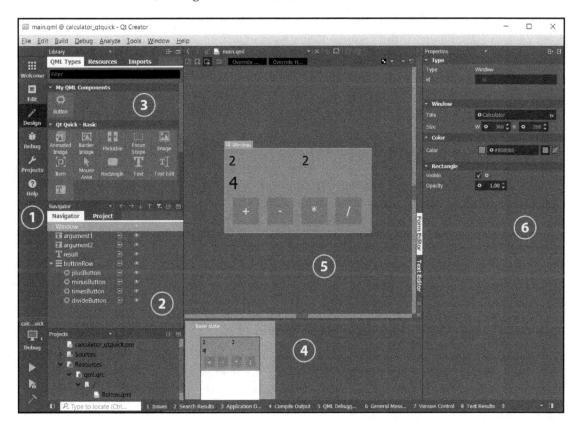

Working from the left again, we have the following components:

1. The view selector, showing that the Qt Designer view is active.
2. The object hierarchy for the file being edited, showing the parent-child relationship between visible items in that file.
3. Above the object hierarchy is a palette of the items you can drag out onto the QML editor pane.
4. Next to the object hierarchy is a summary of the states for the object.
5. Above the summary of the states is the object editor for the QML file.
6. Finally, there's a property editor that lets you adjust the properties of the currently selected QML item.

> Personally, I find it easier to just write QML than to use the designer. The syntax takes a little getting used to, but what the designer is good for is previewing the QML you've written by hand, and making minor adjustments to its layout.

Speaking of layout, before we see our sample code in detail, it's worth noting that QML has a rich dynamic layout system. Visible items have an anchor property, and you can anchor an item's sides against that of its neighbors or the parent view. You saw this briefly in `Chapter 1`, *Getting Started with Qt Creator*, where we made a `MouseArea` object as big as its parent. We'll use that too, to control the layout of the calculator argument input lines and operator buttons.

Let's start making our sample code now, by clicking on **New File or Project** from the **File** menu and walking through the wizard to create a Qt Quick 2.3 application. Name the application `QtQuickCalculator`.

Creating the Qt application

Our calculator has a button for each operation. While we could make each button a separate rectangle and `MouseArea`, it's far easier to make a single QML button that encapsulates the behavior of a button, including the change in appearance when you press on it, the placement of the button label, and so forth.

Create a new QML file by right-clicking on the project and choosing **Add New...**, and then, from the Qt items, choose **QML File (Qt Quick 2)**. The button is a `Rectangle` object that contains a second `Rectangle` object, a `Text` label for the button, and a `MouseArea` object that handles button clicks. Name the file `Button.qml`, and edit it so that it reads as follows:

```qml
import QtQuick 2.12

Rectangle {
    id: button

    width: 64
    height: 64
    property alias operation: buttonText.text
    signal clicked

    color: "green"

    Rectangle {
        id: shade
        anchors.fill: button;
        color: "black";
        opacity: 0
    }

    Text {
        id: buttonText
        anchors.centerIn: parent;
        color: "white"
        font.pointSize: 16
    }

    MouseArea {
        id: mouseArea
        anchors.fill: parent
        onClicked: {
            button.clicked();
        }
    }
    states: State {
        name: "pressed"; when: mouseArea.pressed == true
          PropertyChanges
        { target: shade; opacity: .4 }
    }
}
```

Working from the top of the code, we can see the following:

- Within the scope of this file, the button's ID is simply `button`.
- It's 64 pixels, in both width and height.
- The button has a single property configurable by its clients, the `operation` property. That property is actually an alias, meaning it's automatically setting the value of the `text` property of `buttonText`, instead of being a separate field.
- The button emits a single signal: the `clicked` signal.
- The button's color is green.
- There's a rectangle that fills the button that is colored black but has an opacity of zero, meaning in normal use it's not visible (transparent). As the button is pressed, we adjust the opacity of this rectangle, to shade the button darker when it's being pressed.
- The text label of the button is 16 points in size, colored white, and centered in the button itself.
- The `MouseArea` region that accepts clicks for the button is the same size as the button, and it emits the clicked signal.
- The button has two states: the default state, and a second state that occurs when the `mouseArea.pressed` property is true (because you are pressing the mouse button in `MouseArea`). When the state is pressed, we request a single `PropertyChanges` property, changing the share rectangle's opacity a bit to give a shadow over the button, darkening it.

You can actually see the two states of the button if you enter Qt Designer, as you can see in the next screenshot. A state is just a name, a `when` clause indicating when the state is active, and a collection of `PropertyChanges` property, indicating what properties should change when the state is active. All visible QML items have a `state` property, which is just the name of the currently active state.

 QML uses signals and slots similar to Qt in C++, but there's no `emit` keyword. Instead, you declare the signal directly, using the signal keyword and the name of the signal, and then, you invoke the signal as if it were a function call. For each QML item's signal, the slot is named on and the signal name. Thus, when we use the button, we write an `onClicked` handler for the `clicked` signal. Note that this is different from when writing slots in C++, where you can name a slot anything you want and connect it to a signal with `connect`.

The calculator's main view

In the previous section, we have successfully created our custom button object. Now, we want to make use of the button object in our calculator's user interface. Let's go back to the editor, and edit `main.qml` directly. We're going to declare our input lines, result line, and four operation buttons directly in code; you can do much of the same with the designer if you'd prefer, and then edit the code to match the following:

```qml
import QtQuick 2.12
import QtQuick.Window 2.12

Window {
    visible: true
    width: 360
    height: 200
    title: qsTr("Calculator")
    color: "grey"

    TextInput {
        id: argument1
        anchors.left: parent.left
        width: 160
        anchors.top: parent.top
        anchors.topMargin: 10
        anchors.leftMargin: 10
        anchors.rightMargin: 10
        text: "2"
        font.pointSize: 18
    }

    TextInput {
        id: argument2
        anchors.right: parent.right
        width: 160
        anchors.top: parent.top
        anchors.topMargin: 10
        anchors.leftMargin: 10
        anchors.rightMargin: 10
        text: "2"
        font.pointSize: 18
    }

    Text {
        id: result
        anchors.left: parent.left
        anchors.right: parent.right
        anchors.top: argument2.bottom
```

```
        anchors.topMargin: 10
        anchors.leftMargin: 10
        anchors.rightMargin: 10
        text: "4"
        font.pointSize: 24
    }
```

Then, we continue to add a `Row` layout, and place the operation buttons into the layout:

```
    Row {
        id: buttonRow
        anchors.bottom: parent.bottom
        anchors.bottomMargin: 20
        anchors.left: parent.left
        anchors.leftMargin: 20
        spacing: 20
        Button {
            id: plusButton
            operation: "+"
            onClicked: result.text = parseFloat(argument1.text) +
parseFloat(argument2.text)
        }

        Button {
            id: minusButton
            operation: "-"
            onClicked: result.text = parseFloat(argument1.text) -
parseFloat(argument2.text)
        }

        Button {
            id: timesButton
            operation: "*"
            onClicked: result.text = parseFloat(argument1.text) *
parseFloat(argument2.text)
        }

        Button {
            id: divideButton
            operation: "/"
            onClicked: result.text = parseFloat(argument1.text) /
parseFloat(argument2.text)
        }
    }
}
```

The view has two text input lines: a read-only text result line and the operation buttons, wrapped in a row item to give them a horizontal layout. The base view for the calculator is gray, which we set with the `color` property, and is in a 360 × 200 pixel window. The controls are positioned as follows:

- The first input line is anchored to the top left of the parent window, with margins of 10 pixels. It's 160 pixels long and has the default height of an 18-point text input field.
- The second input line is anchored to the right side of the parent, with a margin of 10 pixels at the top and right. It's also 160 pixels long and has the default height of an 18-point text input field.
- The result input line's top is anchored to the bottom of the input line and to the left of the parent rectangle. It also has 10 pixels of margins on each side.
- The buttons are spaced 20 pixels apart, in a row that's anchored to the bottom of the parent.

These anchors let the view reflow nicely if you resize the application window; the input lines spread across the width of the window, and the button bar on the bottom moves down as the window enlarges.

Each of the buttons has a `click` slot that obtains the floating-point interpretation of each of the input lines and performs the appropriate arithmetic operation. They're each an instance of `Button`; the QML class was the class that you wrote in the previous section. Note the use of the JavaScript function, `parseFloat`, in the `onClicked` handlers. As you'd expect from what was mentioned before, there's support for the functions in the JavaScript runtime in QML, so we can just invoke JavaScript functions directly.

The following screenshot shows the completed calculator application:

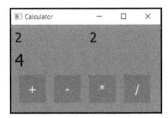

Note that when running the app, if you mouse over a button and press the mouse button, you'll see the shading darken (this isn't shown in the screenshot). This reflects the two states in the button that I showed you in the previous section.

Learning more about Qt Quick and QML

Qt Quick was designed to create fluid applications that don't have a lot of deep widget complexity. Media hubs, photo viewers, phone dialers, web browsers, and other sorts of applications that don't need to match the look and feel of the host platform (or are on embedded systems where the host platform is all written in Qt Quick) are good examples of applications suiting the Qt Quick paradigm.

 For more information about Qt Quick, with a plethora of examples that show you the breadth and power of the platform, see `https://doc.qt.io/qt-5/qtquick-touchinteraction-example.html`.

Summary

In the first half of the chapter, we successfully created a Qt application, using the C++ programming language. Then, we also learned how to create the same calculator program, using Qt Quick and the QML scripting language. Throughout these two examples, we have learned the differences between both methods, to allow us to decide which method is best suited for our project.

Qt comes with not one, but two, complementary **graphical user interface** (**GUI**) toolkits: Qt Widgets, which takes a traditional widget-based approach to GUI development, and Qt Quick, which provides a declarative approach better suited for platform-agnostic user interfaces for media boxes, some cell phone applications, automobile dashboards, and other embedded environments. For both, Qt offers Qt Designer, a drag-and-drop environment that lets you construct, configure, and preview your user interface as you build your application.

Next, we saw how core to Qt is the notion of signals and slots, Qt's answer to callbacks and events, to handle the late binding required of today's GUI applications. Qt objects can emit signals, which are type-safe function declarations, and other objects can connect to those signals, triggering method calls when the signals are emitted.

In the next chapter, you'll take a break from learning about Qt Creator and GUI development to focus on some fundamental capabilities provided by Qt, such as data structures, file I/O, networking with HTTP, and XML parsing.

4
Qt Foundations

Qt is truly one of the best cross-platform frameworks for building applications. As such, it has a large number of core classes to manage data, as well as wrappers around platform services such as threading, the filesystem, network I/O, and of course, graphics.

In this chapter, we discuss some of Qt's core classes that you will find especially handy while writing your applications. In this discussion, we will focus on the bits of Qt that are especially helpful when constructing the business logic for your application. We will begin with a discussion on a handful of useful data classes. After that, we will look at Qt's support for multithreading, a key tool in keeping applications feeling responsive. Next, we will look at accessing files as well as HTTP I/O, an important component in many applications. We will close with a look at Qt's XML parser, which you can use to create networked applications or use to load XML data from the filesystem.

We will cover the following topics in this chapter:

- Representing data using Qt's core classes
- Multithreading in Qt
- Accessing files using Qt
- Accessing HTTP resources using Qt
- Parsing XML using Qt
- Parsing JSON using Qt

Technical requirements

The technical requirements for this chapter include Qt 5.12.3 MinGW 64-bit, Qt Creator 4.9.0, and Windows 10.

Representing data using Qt's core classes

Probably the most common Qt core class you'll run into is Qt's `QString` container class for character strings. It has similar capabilities to the C++ STL `std::wstring` class. As with `wstring`, it's multibyte. You can construct one from a traditional C-style `char *` string or another `QString`.

`QString` has lots of helper methods, some of which are as follows:

- `append`: This appends one `QString` class onto another.
- `arg`: This is used to build up formatted strings (instead of `sprintf`).
- `at` and `operator[]`: These you can use to access a single character in a `QString`.
- `operator==`, `operator!=`, `operator<`, `operator>`, `operator<=`, and `operator>=`: These compare two `QStrings`.
- `clear`: This empties a `QString` and sets it to the null string.
- `contains`: This searches one string for another string or a regular expression.
- `count`: This counts the occurrences of a substring or character in a `QString`.
- `startsWith` and `endsWith`: These return true if a `QString` starts or ends with a specific string, respectively.
- `indexOf`: This returns the index of the first occurrence of a substring in a string, or −1 if the substring doesn't exist in the string.
- `insert`: This inserts another `QString` at a specific position in a `QString`.
- `lastIndexOf`: This returns the last index of a substring in a `QString`.
- `length`: This returns the length of a string in characters.
- `remove`: This removes all occurrences or a number of characters of a string from `QString`.
- `setNum`: This formats a number and replaces the value of the `QString` with the given number.
- `split`: This returns a list of `QString` objects (we'll discuss Qt lists in a moment) created by splitting the string at a specific separator character.
- `toDouble`, `toFloat`, `toInt`, and `toLong`: These return numeric representations of the string if a conversion is possible.
- `toLower` and `toUpper`: These return a copy of the string converted to lower- or uppercase.
- `truncate`: This truncates the string at a given position.

Qt also has a number of template collection classes. The most general of these is `QList<T>`, which is optimized for fast index-based access as well as fast insertions and deletions. There's also `QLinkedList<T>`, which uses a linked list structure to store its values, and `QVector<T>`, which stores its elements in a serial vector array, so the use of template classes is the fastest for indexed access, but is slow to resize. Qt also provides `QStringList`, which is the same as `QList<QString>` for all intents and purposes.

As you might imagine, these types provide `operator[]`, so you can access and assign any element of the list. Other `QList<T>` methods you'll find include:

- `append`: This appends an item to the list.
- `at`: This accesses an individual element of the list for read-only purposes.
- `clear`: This empties the list.
- `contains`: This searches the list for a specific element.
- `count`: This counts the number of times an element occurs in the list.
- `empty`: This returns true if the list is empty.
- `startsWith` and `endsWith`: These return true if the list begins or ends with the specified element.
- `first` and `last`: These return the first and last element of the list, respectively.
- `indexOf`: This returns the index of the first occurrence of an item if it's in the list, or −1 if the item is not found.
- `lastIndexOf`: This returns the last index of an item if it's in the list.
- `length`: This returns the length of the list.
- `prepend`: This prepends an item to the list.
- `push_back` and `push_front`: These push an element to the end or the beginning of the list, respectively.
- `removeAt`, `removeFirst`, and `removeLast`: These remove the ith, first, or last element of the list.
- `replace`: This replaces an element of the list.
- `swap`: This swaps two elements of the list at different indices.
- `toStdList`: This returns `std::list<T>` of the `QList`.
- `toVector`: This returns `QVector<T>` of the list.

A common thing you'll want to do with a list is iterate over its elements. QList provides iterators similar to how the C++ STL does, so you can iterate over the elements of a list like this:

```
QList<QString> list;
list.append("January");
list.append("February");
   ...
list.append("December");

QList<QString>::const_iterator i;
for (i = list.constBegin(); i != list.constEnd(); ++i)
    cout << *i << endl;
```

QList<T>::const_iterator and QList<T>::iterator provide read-only and mutable iterators over the list; you can obtain one by calling constBegin or begin, respectively, and compare it against constEnd or end to see when you're at the end of a list.

Now that we know how the core classes work, let us see how they work with key-value pairs.

Working with key-value pairs

A key-value pair, usually referred to as a map, is a type of container that allows you to easily sort and identify the data contained by it. If you've used other languages, you might know of it as a dictionary or a map. Every element in a map contains a pair of data – a key and a value. The key is an identifier that allows you to quickly look for the element, while the value is the actual data that will be returned to you.

For beginners who are just starting to learn about programming, you might find it hard to grasp the usage of a key-value pair. Let's use a simple example to illustrate the usefulness of a key-value pair. Imagine you're running a system for a school with a few thousand students and you're trying to look for one particular student with the name "John Smith". It would take ages for your program to look for this person if you're comparing the name with the full name list. Furthermore, there could be more than one student who is called John Smith.

To make things easier, we assign each and every student with a unique ID number. When we put all the students into a key-value pair, the ID number will become the `key`, and the student name will become the `value`. Thus, when we try and look for a particular student, we'll search for the ID number instead, which is a lot faster and easier to compare than just comparing names. Once we've found the ID number that we're looking for, we can then obtain its `value` and confirm whether it is the student we're looking for. A key-value pair is extremely efficient when searching a long list.

Qt provides four template classes for this: `QMap`, `QMultiMap`, `QHash`, and `QMultiHash`. They share interfaces, but `QHash` provides faster lookup, although its keys must provide the `==` operator and a global hash function, `qHash()`. This is because its underlying data structure uses a hash table for its data structure. `QMap`, on the other hand, stores key-value pairs as pairs in a list, so lookups are slower, but you have more flexibility in the key structure you choose. The `QMultiMap` and `QMultiHash` classes let you store multiple values for a single key, while `QMap` and `QHash` only store a single value for each key. Most of the time, it's fine to use `QMap` or `QMultiMap`; it's only if you're managing numbers of keys and values that `QHash` wins out in terms of access performance.

Here's an example of `QMap` with string keys and numeric values:

```
QMap<QString, int> map;
map["one"] = 1;
map["two"] = 2;
map["three"] = 3;
```

You can look up a value with `operator[]` or the `value` method. If you want to check to see whether a value is assigned to a given key, use the `contains` method. One thing to be aware of is that `operator[]` is not quite the same as `value`; if you use it and no value exists for the given key, it silently inserts a default value with the key you provide, which might not be what you intend. Other methods include:

- `clear`: This clears the dictionary.
- `empty`: This returns true if the dictionary is empty.
- `insert`: This inserts a key-value pair into the dictionary.
- `key`: This returns the first key that matches the value you pass in.
- `keys`: This returns a list of keys.
- `remove`: This removes an element for which you provide the key.

All of these container classes, including QString, are lightweight; they carry their data by reference when they can and are implemented using copy-on-write. So, let's create an instance of a class and assign it to a second instance, like this:

```
QString oneFish = "red fish";
QString twoFish = oneFish;
```

Both oneFish and twoFish point to the same data under the hood, and only when you begin to change the value of twoFish through its methods does it get its own memory buffer. This is an important way in which these classes differ from the STL classes and are key to Qt's better memory performance on low-memory platforms such as mobile devices.

Another lightweight data class you should be aware of is QByteArray, which abstracts a collection of bytes in memory for things such as I/O or other data manipulations. You can get a constant char * to a QByteArray by calling its constData method, or a mutable char * pointer by calling its data method. If you want to know its size, you can call its length method. As with QString, a QByteArray has lots of helper functions to search, append data, prepend data, and so forth. So, if you need to manipulate a raw collection of bytes, it's a good idea to look at QByteArray before rolling your own implementation with C-style functions.

 For more about these and other Qt core container classes, see https://doc.qt.io/qt-5/containers.html.

We have learned about some of the essential core classes provided by Qt. By understanding how to use these core classes, we will be able to use all other classes in Qt easily as they are all built on top of the core classes.

In the next section, we will learn how to create an application that utilizes Qt's multithreading feature.

Multithreading in Qt

A **thread** is a single line of execution within a single application. Nearly all of today's operating systems are multithreaded; that is, your application can have more than one concurrent line of execution at a time. Multithreading is a key way to improve the responsiveness of an application, because most processors today can execute multiple threads in parallel, and operating systems are optimized to share resources among multiple threads.

Qt supports multithreading over the host operating system through three key classes:

- QThread
- QSemaphore
- QMutex

The first, QThread, represents a single thread of execution, while the latter two are used to synchronize thread access to data structures.

By design, your application runs entirely on the user thread, a single thread of execution that starts when your application starts. You can create new threads of execution (which cannot manipulate the user interface) by subclassing QThread and overriding the run method. Then, when you need to perform an expensive operation, you just create an instance of your QThread subclass and call its start method. (This is similar to Java, if you're familiar with threading in Java.) In turn, this method calls your run method, and the thread runs until run exits. Once run exits, it emits its completion using the finished signal.

You can connect a slot to that signal to observe task completion. This is especially handy when you use threads to perform background work such as network transactions; you perform the network transaction in the background on the thread, and you'll know when the I/O is complete because your thread will complete and emit the finished method. We will see an example of this in the *Accessing HTTP Resources using Qt* section, later in this chapter.

Here's the simplest of thread examples:

```
class MyThread : public QThread
{
    Q_OBJECT
    void run() Q_DECL_OVERRIDE
    {
        /* perform the expensive operation */
    }
};

void MyObject::startWorkInAThread()
{
    MyThread *myThread = new MyThread(this);
    connect(myThread, &MyObject::threadFinished, this,
        MyObject::notifyThreadFinished);
    connect(myThread, &MyThread::finished, myThread,
        &QObject::deleteLater);
    myThread->start();
}
```

Before we dive into the code, let me explain a little bit about why we're doing this. If you're dealing with heavy computation, file operations in bulk, or heavy network I/O, you should put them into a separate thread instead of running in the main thread. This is because these are very "expensive" operations that may stall your application while it is being processed by the CPU. In layman's terms, an "expensive" operation means a heavy process that will take a very long time for the CPU to complete the computational task, which is why you don't want these heavy processes to be run on the main thread.

Instead, we create a second thread and place these expensive operations into the thread's `run` method. The thread will run as long as `run` is executing; when it's done, it will emit the `finished` signal. To start one of these threads of execution, simply create a new instance of the thread and call its `start` method. You then connect two signal handlers to the thread's `finished` method; the first simply deletes the thread when it completes, and the second (not shown) updates the UI with the results of the thread's execution.

Multithreaded programming can be tricky because you need to be aware of cases where one thread is writing to a data structure while another wants to read from the data structure. If you're not careful, you can end up with the reading thread receiving garbage, or half-updated data, leading to hard-to-reproduce programming errors. Qt provides two threading primitives, `QMutex` and `QSemaphore`, to let you block a thread's execution on a resource, such as a data structure, letting a thread have exclusive access to that resource while the thread is running.

A `QMutex` class has two methods:

- `lock`
- `unlock`

To ensure that only one thread has access to a block of code at a time, create a mutex and call its `lock` method. When execution finishes, you must call `unlock`; otherwise, no other thread can run that code. There's also the `tryLock` method, which tries to acquire a lock and immediately returns if it's unable to get the lock in the specified timeout, letting you do something else instead of waiting until your thread gets a lock on the mutex.

`QSemaphore` is a generalized version of `QMutex` and lets you manage a pool of *n* items; instead of blocking execution on a single mutex, your thread blocks until it can obtain the number of resources you specify when you invoke its `acquire` method. When you're done with a number of resources, you call the `release` method, indicating the number of items you're releasing. `QSemaphore` also has a `tryAcquire` method, which immediately returns if the resource acquisition fails in the desired timeout, and an `available` method, which returns the number of resources presently available.

Following is some example code showing how to use the `QSemaphore` class:

```
const int bufferSize = 10;
QSemaphore sem(bufferSize); // sem.available() == 10

sem.acquire(6); // sem.available() == 4
sem.acquire(4); // sem.available() == 0
sem.release(7); // sem.available() == 7
sem.release(3); // sem.available() == 10

sem.tryAcquire(2); // sem.available() == 8, returns true
sem.tryAcquire(540); // sem.available() == 8, returns false
```

Even though Qt provides us with some classes to make the multithreading easier, multithreading itself is quite an advanced topic among the programming disciplines. However, you must be able to grasp the idea of multithreading before you can make use of classes such as `QThread` or `QMutex` to efficiently spread the computing workload to your CPU threads. Do note that multithreading is not the absolute solution for improving your application's performance. It could be the reverse if you do it incorrectly.

 Since version 5.3, Qt has also introduced some higher-level programming constructs with Qt Concurrent that are beyond the scope of this book. For more information on `QThread` and its supporting classes, or Qt Concurrent, consult the Qt documentation at `https://doc.qt.io/qt-5/ threads-technologies.html`.

We have learned how to run heavy operations in Qt by empowering multithreadings using classes such as `QThread`, `QSemaphore` and `QMutex`. Next, we will learn how to access files from our local storage using Qt.

Accessing files using Qt

Files are basically digital information stored in the form of byte stream that reside somewhere in your hard disk. If your program needs to save or load data, such as for word processing, image editing, media streaming, or program configuration, you will need to access the files stored on your local hard drive. Qt provides us with classes that allow us to easily access the filesystem regardless of the type of operating system.

Qt encapsulates the more generalized notion of byte streams in its QIODevice class, which is the parent class for QFile, as well as network I/O classes such as QTcpSocket. We don't directly create a QIODevice instance, of course, but instead create something such as a QFile subclass and then work with the QFile instance directly to read from and write to the file.

 Files and network access usually take time, and thus your applications shouldn't work with them on the main thread. Consider creating a subclass of QThread to perform I/O operations such as reading from files or accessing the network.

To begin working with a file, we first must open it using the open method. The open method takes a single argument, the manner in which the file should be opened, which is a bitwise combination of the following:

- QIODevice::ReadOnly: This is used for read-only access.
- QIODevice::WriteOnly: This is used for write-only access.
- QIODevice::ReadWrite: This is used for read-and-write access.
- QIODevice::Append: This is used to only append to the file.
- QIODevice::Truncate: This is used to truncate the file, discarding all previous contents before writing.
- QIODevice::Text: This is used to treat the file as text, converting new-line characters to the platform representation during reading and writing.
- QIODevice::Unbuffered: This is used to bypass any buffering of the input and output.

These flags can be combined using the bitwise binary, or the | operator. For example, a common combination is QIODevice::ReadWrite | QIODevice::Text to read and write a text file. In fact, QIODevice:ReadWrite is defined as QIODevice::Read | QIODevice::Write internally.

Once you open the file, you can read a number of bytes by calling the file's read method and passing the number of bytes to read; the resulting QByteArray object contains the data to read. Similarly, you can write QByteArray by calling write, or use the overloaded write method that takes a constant * char. In either case, write also takes the number of bytes to write. If all you want to do is read the entire contents of a file into a single buffer, you can call readAll, which returns QByteArray of the entire contents of the file.

Some `QIODevice` subclasses such as `QFile` are seekable; that is, you can position the read/write cursor at any point in the file, or determine its position. You can use the `seek` method to position the cursor at a particular position in the file, and `pos` to obtain the current location of the file cursor. Note that other `QIODevice` subclasses, such as those for network I/O, don't support `seek` and `pos` methods, but fail gracefully if you attempt to use them.

If you want to peek at the data without actually moving the cursor, you can call `peek` and pass the number of bytes to return; the result is a `QByteArray`. Calling `read` after `peek` returns the same data, because `peek` doesn't advance the cursor past the data you've peeked at. The `peek` method is handy when creating a complex parser that needs to know about incoming data in more than one place of its implementation; you can peek at the data, make a decision about how to parse the data, and then call `read` later to get the data.

To determine whether or not you're at the end of a file and there's no more data to read, you can call `atEnd`, which returns true if there is no more data to read. If you want to know how many bytes there are in the file, you can call `bytesAvailable`, which returns the number of bytes available for reading (if known; a network socket might not carry that information, of course).

When working with files, we often need to work with directories as well. The `QDir` class lets us examine the contents of a directory, determine whether a file or directory exists or not, and remove a file or directory. One thing to note is that, regardless of the directory separator path used by the host platform, Qt always uses a forward slash, `/` , to denote directories, so even if we're writing a Qt program for Windows, we use forward slashes, not backslashes. This makes it easy to write cross-platform compatible code that runs on both Windows and Linux without the need to use a special case for the directory handling code.

First, create an instance of `QDir` by passing a file path; after that, you can do the following with it:

- Get an absolute path to the directory by calling `absolutePath`.
- Switch to a different valid directory by calling `cd`.
- Get a list of files in the directory by calling `entryInfoList`.
- Determine whether a specific file or directory exists by calling `exists`.
- Determine whether the directory is the root of the filesystem by calling `isRoot`.
- Remove a file by calling `remove` and passing the name of the file to `remove`.

- Rename a file by calling `rename`.
- Remove an empty directory by calling `rmdir` and passing the name of the directory to `remove`.
- Compare two directories using the `==` and `!=` operators.

Of course, locations of files, such as application preferences and/or temporary files, differ from platform to platform; the `QStandardPaths` class has a static `standardLocations` method that returns a path to the kind of storage we're looking for. To use it, we pass a value from the `QStandardPaths::StandardLocation` enumeration, which has values such as:

- `DesktopLocation`: This returns the desktop directory.
- `DocumentsLocation`: This returns the documents directory.
- `MusicLocation`: This returns the location of music on the filesystem.
- `PicturesLocation`: This returns the location of photos on the filesystem.
- `TempLocation`: This returns the path to store temporary files.
- `HomeLocation`: This returns the path to the current user's home directory.
- `DataLocation`: This returns a path to an application-specific directory for persistent data.
- `CacheLocation`: This returns a path to where the application can cache data.
- `ConfigLocation`: This returns a path to where the application can store configuration settings.

Okay, enough of the theory part. Let's get going and start writing some code! First, let's look at how we can load a text file and read its contents:

```
QFile file("myFile.txt");
if (!file.open(QIODevice::ReadOnly | QIODevice::Text))
{
    return;
}
while (!file.atEnd())
{
    QByteArray line = file.readLine();
    qDebug() << line;
}
```

We started off by providing the name of a `myFile.txt` text file into a `QFile` object for initialization. Then, we called `open()` to ask Qt to open up the file and tell it to read only (not write) as a text file. The `open()` function will return `true` if the file has been successfully opened, or return `false` if it failed to open the file.

Once the file has been opened, we use a `while` loop to check whether the reading process has reached the end of the text file. If it doesn't, then we repeatedly call `readLine()` to read each and every line of the text file until it reaches the end. Then, we display the text we have just read using `qDebug()`.

Next, let's try something different:

```
QString fileName = QFileDialog::getOpenFileName(this, "Open Image", "",
"Image Files (*.png *.jpg *.bmp)", QStandardPaths::DesktopLocation);
QImage image = QImage(fileName);
```

The preceding code simply opens up a file selection dialog and lets the user select an image file. We called `getOpenFileName()` to initiate the file selection dialog. We also set the dialog's title as `Open Image` and limit the file types to **PNG**, **JPG** and **BMP**. Then, we set the default location to the user's desktop by using the `DesktopLocation` enumeration. Once the user has selected an image file, the full path of the image file will be stored in the `fileName` variable. We can then use the `fileName` variable to convert the image data into a `QImage` object.

For more information about files and network I/O, see the Qt documentation at `https://doc.qt.io/qt-5/io-functions.html`.

That's it, we have nailed down how to load files from the local storage using Qt classes. Let's move on to the next section and learn how to access HTTP resources using Qt.

Accessing HTTP resources using Qt

A common thing to do in today's networked world is use the **HyperText Transfer Protocol** (**HTTP**) to access a remote resource or service on the web. To do this, your application should first use Qt's support to select a bearer network to make the HTTP request. Then, it should use its support for HTTP to make one or more HTTP requests across the network connection that the bearer network service opened.

To begin with, you need to be sure that you include the network module in your Qt declaration by editing your project's (`.pro`) file to include the following:

```
QT += network
```

Today's computing devices support multiple ways to access the network. For example, an Android tablet can have a built-in 4G wireless **wide area network** (**WAN**) adapter as well as a Wi-Fi radio with multiple network configurations for different access points. The Android platform contains sophisticated code to bring up the appropriate network interface based on the wireless network that provides the best bandwidth at the best cost, or prompts the user to select a desired Wi-Fi network. Various Linux distributions have similar features, as do Microsoft Windows and macOS X. To encapsulate this functionality, Qt provides the bearer network module that wraps the platform's underlying support to prompt the user which network connection to use, how to start a network connection, stop a network connection, and so forth.

If you're writing a networked application, to determine how to connect to the network, you'll want to use this module to prompt the user before your first attempt to use the network . The easiest way to do this is with a snippet of code such as this:

```
bool OpenNetworkConnection()
{
    QNetworkConfigurationManager manager;
    const bool canStartIAP = (manager.capabilities() &
QNetworkConfigurationManager::CanStartAndStopInterfaces); // Is there
// default access point, use it
    QNetworkConfiguration cfg = manager.defaultConfiguration();
    if (!cfg.isValid() || (!canStartIAP && cfg.state() !=
        QNetworkConfiguration::Active))
    {
        QMessageBox::information(this, tr("Network"), tr("No Access
            Point found."));
        return false;
    }
    QNetworkSession* session = new QNetworkSession(cfg, this);
    session->open();
    return session->waitForOpened(-1);
}
```

This code does the following:

- It creates an instance of the network configuration manager.
- It determines whether the manager can start and stop the network interfaces on the system.
- It gets the default configuration for network connectivity.
- If the default configuration is invalid, or the configuration manager can't start the network configuration and no network connection is up, it pops up a dialog box indicating that the application cannot start a new network connection and returns false to inform the caller that no network connection was established.

- If the default configuration is valid, the code gets a network session configured by the default configuration, opens it, and waits until the connection is opened. Under the hood, the platform might prompt the user for a desired network connection, manage one or more radios, and so forth. Once the session is configured, the network is available for your application to use.

Once you establish a connection to the network, you're able to issue network requests, or create low-level communication for TCP or UDP access. Next, we will see how HTTP requests work when online communications are required.

 Further information about low-level networking will not be discussed in this book; if you're curious, you can see the Qt documentation at `https://doc.qt.io/qt-5/qtnetwork-index.html`.

Performing HTTP requests

Qt provides three key classes to perform HTTP requests: QNetworkAccessManager, QNetworkRequest, and QNetworkReply. HTTP requests are very important to applications that require online communications with a server, for instance: user login, data entry, news feed, notification, and so on.

We use the QNetworkAccessManager request to configure the semantics of an HTTP request, configuring things such as proxy servers as well as to actually issue a request. The easiest thing to do is simply to create one, connect its finished signal to a slot you want to have it call when a request is finished, and then call its get method, like this:

```
mNetManager = new QNetworkAccessManager(this);
connect(mNetManager, &QNetworkAccessManager::finished, this,
&MainWindow::handleNetFinished);

// later, when you want to make a request
QNetworkReply *reply = mNetManager->get(QNetworkRequest(QUrl(url)));
```

The QNetworkAccessManager class has methods for each of the HTTP GET, POST, DELETE, HEAD, and PUT methods, aptly named get, post, delete, head, and put, respectively. For most transactions, to simply fetch data, you'll use get, the standard HTTP method to get a remote network resource. If you want to trigger a remote procedure call through the put method, invoke the put method of the QNetworkAccessManager class, passing a QNetworkRequest object and a QByteArray or QIODevice pointer to the data to be put to the server.

If you need to configure a proxy server as part of your request, you can do so using the `setProxy` method of `QNetworkAccessManager`. Note that Qt will configure itself with whatever system the HTTP proxy is by default, so you should only need to override the proxy server settings if you're working with an application-specific proxy server for your application.

The `QNetworkAccessManager` class uses the `QNetworkRequest` class to encapsulate the semantics of a request, letting you set HTTP headers that accompany the request by calling its `setHeader` or `setRawHeader` methods. The `setHeader` method lets you set specific HTTP headers such as the `User-Agent` header, while `setRawHeader` lets you provide custom HTTP header names and values as `QByteArray` values.

Once you issue a request, the `QNetworkAccessManager` class takes over, performing the necessary network I/O to look up the remote host, contact the remote host, and issue the request. When the reply is ready, it notifies your code with the `finished` signal, passing the `QNetworkReply` class associated with the request. Using the `QNetworkReply` class, you can access the headers associated with a reply by calling `header` or `rawHeader`, to fetch a standard or custom HTTP header, respectively. `QNetworkReply` inherits from `QIODevice`, so you can simply use the `read` or `readAll` methods to read from the response as you see fit, like this:

```cpp
void MyClass::handleNetFinished(QNetworkReply* reply)
{
    if (reply->error() == QNetworkReply::NoError)
    {
        QByteArray data = reply->readAll();
    }
    else
    {
        qDebug() << QString("net error %1").arg(reply->error());
    }
}
```

For more information about bearer network configuration, see the Qt documentation at `https://doc.qt.io/qt-5/bearer-management.html`. For more information about all of Qt's support for networking, see the Qt documentation at `https://doc.qt.io/qt-5/qtnetwork-index.html`. There are also some good network samples at `https://doc.qt.io/qt-5/examples-network.html`.

We have learned how to allow our application to communicate with an online server through HTTP requests. Next, we will be looking into how we can parse XML data using Qt.

Parsing XML using Qt

Earlier versions of Qt had a number of XML parsers, each suited to different tasks and different styles of parsing. Each XML parser was used for different formats in older versions of Qt. Fortunately, in Qt 5, this has been streamlined; currently, you only need a single XML parser to parse XML data. The key XML parser to use in the latest Qt version is the QXmlStreamReader class (see https://doc.qt.io/qt-5/qxmlstreamreader.html for details). This class reads from a QIODevice subclass and reads XML tags one at a time, letting you switch on the type of tag the parser encounters. Thus, our parser looks something like this:

```
QXmlStreamReader xml;
xml.setDevice(input);
while (!xml.atEnd())
{
    QXmlStreamReader::TokenType type = xml.readNext();
    switch(type)
    {
        ... // do processing
    }
}
if (xml.hasError())
{
    ... // do error handling
}
```

The QXMLStreamReader class reads each tag of the XML in turn, each time its readNext method is called. For each tag read, readNext returns the type of the tag read, which will be one of the following:

- StartDocument: This indicates the beginning of the document.
- EndDocument: This indicates the end of the document.
- StartElement: This indicates the beginning of an element.
- EndElement: This indicates the end of an element.
- Characters: This indicates that some characters were read.
- Comment: This indicates that a comment was read.

- `DTD`: This indicates that the document type declaration was read.
- `EntityReference`: This indicates that an entity reference that could not be resolved was read.
- `ProcessingInstruction`: This indicates that an XML processing instruction was read.

After understanding these basics of parsing XML with Qt, let us see how to use them.

Using XML parsing with HTTP

Let's put together the multithreading, HTTP I/O, and XML parsing with some example code using `WorkerThread` that fetches a flat XML document with unique tags from a remote server and parses selected tags from the XML, storing the results as name-value pairs in a `QMap<QString, QString>`.

A flat XML file is one with no nested elements, that is, an XML document in the following form:

```
<?xml version="1.0"?>
<document>
    <tag>Value</tag>
    <tag2>Value 2</tag2>
</document>
```

We'll begin with the `WorkerThread` class header:

```
#include <QMap>
#include <QThread>
#include <QXmlStreamReader>
#include <QNetworkAccessManager>
#include <QNetworkReply>

class WorkerThread : public QThread
{
    Q_OBJECT

public:
    WorkerThread(QObject* owner);
    void run();

    void fetch(const QString& url);
    void cancel();

signals:
```

```
    void error(const QString& error);
    void finished(const QMap<QString, QString>&);

private slots:
    void handleNetFinished(QNetworkReply* reply);

private:
    bool mCancelled;
    QNetworkAccessManager* mNetManager;
    QNetworkReply* mReply;
}
```

This class extends `QThread`, so it's a `QObject`. Its slot is private, because it's only used within the scope of this class and not available as part of its public interface. To use one, you create it and call its `fetch` method, passing the URL to fetch. It does its thing, signaling a successful result, passing the dictionary of name-value pairs from the XML via the `finished` signal, or a string with an error message if the request failed via the `error` signal. If we start a request and the user wants to cancel it, we simply call the `cancel` method.

The class carries very little data: a `mCancelled` cancellation flag, the `QNetworkAccessManager` instance it uses to perform the I/O, `mNetManager`, and the `QNetworkReply` request from the request, `mReply`. Next we will see how to implement `WorkerThread` to parse XML.

Implementing WorkerThread

Now that we know how parsing works in XML, we can see what the implementation of the core of `WorkerThread` looks like, as follows:

1. The following code shows the implementation of `WorkerThread`:

```
WorkerThread::WorkerThread(QObject* owner)
{
    this->setParent(owner);
    mNetManager = new QNetworkAccessManager(this);
    connect(mNetManager, &QNetworkAccessManager::finished, this,
&WorkerThread::handleNetFinished);
}

void WorkerThread::run()
{
    QXmlStreamReader xml;
    QXmlStreamReader::TokenType type;
```

```
QString fieldName;
QString value;
QString tag;
bool successful = false;
bool gotValue = false;
QMap<QString, QString> result;

xml.setDevice(mReply);
```

2. Then, we continue to write our code, and start parsing the XML data by looping through the file and reading every single XML element:

```
while(!xml.atEnd())
{
    // If we've been cancelled, stop processing.
    if (mCancelled) break;

    type = xml.readNext();
    bool gotEntry = false;
    switch( type )
    {
        case QXmlStreamReader::StartElement:
        {
            QString tag = xml.name().toString().toLower();
            fieldName = tag;
            gotValue = false;
            qDebug() << "tag" << tag;
        }
        break;
```

3. We continue to check for the type of XML element and save its value accordingly:

```
        case QXmlStreamReader::Characters:
        // Save aside any text
        if (!gotValue)
        {
            value = xml.text().toString().simplified();
            if (value != "")
            {
                gotValue = true;
                qDebug() << "value" << value;
            }
        }
        break;
        case QXmlStreamReader::EndElement:
        // Save aside this value
        if (gotEntry && gotValue)
```

```
        {
            result[fieldName] = value;
        }
        gotEntry = false;
        gotValue = false;
        break;
        default:
        break;
    }
}
```

4. Then, we check whether the parsing is successful. We trigger the `finished` signal if it is successful, or call the `error` signal if it isn't:

```
successful = xml.hasError() ? false : true;

if (!mCancelled && successful) {
    emit finished(result);
} else if (!mCancelled) {
    emit error(tr("Could not interpret the server's
response."));
    }
}
```

5. After that, we write the `fetch` and `handleNetFinished` functions to obtain data from the server. We also write the `cancel` function for cancelling the request:

```
void WorkerThread::fetch(const QString& url)
{
    // Don't try to re-start if we're running
    if (isRunning()) { this->cancel(); }

    QNetworkReply *reply = mNetManager->get(QNetworkRequest
        (QUrl(url)));

    if (!reply) { emit error(tr("Could not contact the server."));
}
}

void WorkerThread::cancel()
{
    mCancelled = true;
    wait();
};

void WorkerThread::handleNetFinished(QNetworkReply* reply)
{
```

```
        // Start parse by starting the thread.
        if (reply->error() == QNetworkReply::NoError)
        {
            if (!this->isRunning())
            {
                mReply = reply;
                start();
            }
        }
        else
        {
            emit error(tr("A network error occurred."));
            qDebug() << QString("net error %1").arg(reply->error());
        }
    }
```

There's a lot of code here (and the full class is shown in the download that accompanies this book), so let's take it method by method:

- The constructor initializes each of our member fields and connects the `finished` signal of `QNetworkAccessManager` to our `handleNetFinished` slot. (The constructor is omitted here, but is provided in the sample code that accompanies this book.)
- The `run` method is the heart of the class, responsible for reading and parsing the XML response. We put `read` and parse in the `run` method because it's likely to take the most time, and this way it can run on a background thread so it doesn't block the user interface.

The `run` method does the following:

- Initializes the `QXMLStreamReader` class with our network response, `mReply`.
- Loops over the tags found in the XML document it's reading. For each tag:
  - If the tag is a start element, it fetches the name of the tag and notes that it has received a new start element.
  - If the tag is a character string, it saves aside the character string and notes that it has a value for a tag.
  - If it's the end of an XML element and it has both a name of a tag and a value, it assigns the value of the tag to the named slot in the result hash.

- Once all the tags have been read or an error occurs, the code first tests for an error.
- If the parse wasn't cancelled and was successful, the code emits the `finished` signal, passing the resulting `QMap` with the names and values from the XML document.
- If the parse encountered an error, the code signals an error.
- The `fetch` method simply cancels the request if one is pending, before making an HTTP GET request on using `QNetworkAccessManager`.
- The `cancel` method sets the cancellation flag checked by the `run` method and waits for the thread to finish, ensuring that cancellation occurs before `cancel` returns.
- The `handleNetFinished` method is invoked by `QNetworkAccessManager` when the HTTP GET request returns, saves aside the resulting network request, starts the thread to read from the remote server, and parses the result. If an error occurs, it signals the error with the error signal and logs the HTTP error message to the debugger console.

We have now learned how to obtain XML data through HTTP web requests and then parse XML data using Qt. Next, we will learn how to parse another popular format called JSON.

Parsing JSON using Qt

JSON is a popular data-transmitting format after XML. It was first standardized in 2013 and has become the most popular format used on the web ever since. JSON data looks something like this:

```
{
"firstName": "John",
"lastName": "Smith",
"age": 42,
"address": {
"streetAddress": "14 2nd Street",
"city": "New York",
"state": "NY",
"postalCode": "10021-3100"
},
"phoneNumbers": [{
"type": "home",
"number": "212 686-7890"
},
{
```

```
    "type": "mobile",
    "number": "321 456-7788"
  }]
}
```

As you can see, it is completely different from the XML format. The main reason why it is so popular is because of how human-readable it is and how shorter it is compared to XML, without all the opening and closing tags.

To parse JSON data using Qt, let's start writing some code:

1. First, we must include the headers related to JSON classes:

   ```cpp
   #include <QJsonDocument>
   #include <QJsonObject>
   #include <QVariantMap>
   ```

2. After that, we will try and parse the preceding JSON data, which looks something like this when converted into `QString` format:

   ```cpp
   QString jsonString = "{\"firstName\": \"John\",\"lastName\":
   \"Smith\",\"age\": 42,\"address\": {\"streetAddress\": \"14 2nd
   Street\",\"city\": \"New York\",\"state\": \"NY\",\"postalCode\":
   \"10021-3100\"},\"phoneNumbers\": [{\"type\": \"home\",\"number\":
   \"212 686-7890\"},{\"type\": \"mobile\",\"number\": \"321
   456-7788\"}]}";
   ```

3. Next, we will parse the data by first converting it into a `QJsonDocument` object, then obtain the `QJsonObject` object by calling the `QJsonDocument::fromJson()` function.

4. Then, we convert the `QJsonObject` into a `QVariantMap` before we are able to obtain the data we need from it:

   ```cpp
   QJsonDocument doc = QJsonDocument::fromJson(jsonString.toUtf8());
   QJsonObject obj = doc.object();         // Get the json object
   QVariantMap map = obj.toVariantMap();   // Convert json object to
   variant map

   qDebug() << map["firstName"].toString();  // Obtain firstName data
   ```

5. The preceding code produces the following result:

```
John
```

As you can see, the code is straightforward and simple. We also made use of the knowledge we learned from the beginning of this chapter regarding the key-value pair to obtain the `firstName` data from our JSON variant map.

6. Next, we will look at how we can obtain data from a JSON array, for example:

```
{
"name":"John",
"age":30,
"cars":[ "Ford", "BMW", "Fiat" ]
}
```

7. The `cars` data consists of three individual data items wrapped in an array format. Let's start writing some code to parse the JSON data. Again, we'll convert the preceding JSON text into `QString` format:

```
QString jsonString = "{\"name\":\"John\",\"age\":30,\"cars\":[
\"Ford\", \"BMW\", \"Fiat\" ]}";
```

8. Then, we must add two new headers at the top of our code, namely `QJsonArray` and `QJsonValue`:

```
#include <QJsonArray>
#include <QJsonValue>
```

9. After that, we start parsing the JSON data like this:

```
QJsonDocument doc = QJsonDocument::fromJson(jsonString.toUtf8());
QJsonObject obj = doc.object();        // Get the json object
QJsonValue value = obj.value("cars");  // Get cars data in
QJsonValue format
QJsonArray array = value.toArray();    // Convert it to QJsonArray
```

10. Once the `cars` data has been converted to a `QJsonArray` format, we can then loop through it just like any ordinary C++ array:

```
for (int i = 0; i < array.size(); i++)
{
    qDebug() << array.at(i).toString(); // Get data
}
```

The preceding code produces the following result:

```
Ford
BMW
Fiat
```

Again, the code is very short and straightforward. Qt makes it really easy to parse JSON data through the following `QJsonDocument`, `QJsonObject`, `QJsonValue`, and `QJsonArray` classes.

 For more information about JSON support in Qt, please refer to the link here: `https://doc.qt.io/qt-5/json.html`.

In this chapter, we have learned how to use the core functionality of Qt. We have also learned how to parse XML data and JSON data using Qt classes. In the following chapter, we will learn how to create form applications using Qt Widgets.

Summary

We've covered a lot of ground in this chapter, from data structures, to files, to networking. You've learned how you can use fundamental Qt core and networking classes to build the backend logic, which can help you in building the business logic for your application.

Not only that, we've also learned how to make use of multithreading to spread the workload to different CPU threads for speeding up the process. This is especially useful if you're creating an application that does heavy computation and you don't want it to become unresponsive while the computation is still going on. This will severely affect the user experience and ultimately affect your reputation as a brand or company.

Other than that, we've also learned how we can make use of HTTP requests to communicate with a remote server and obtain data from it. Qt makes this process easier by providing its own classes that are well implemented behind the scene. This is very favorable to developers who want to build modern applications that empower the cloud architecture and provide dynamic contents to its users.

We have also learned how to parse different types of data formats, such as XML and JSON, which are both very popular and commonly used in web and desktop applications alike. By incorporating these features into your application, you will be able to make it compatible with any third-party system in the market, thus improving its value.

In the next chapter, we'll start looking at the Qt support to build your presentation logic. We'll take a break from these fundamentals and review the key Qt Widget classes for building desktop applications. You'll learn about the plethora of the basic Qt Widget classes available for your application, how Qt's support for the model-view-controller paradigm works, and finally how to render web content in your application using QWebEngineView – Qt's integrated web engine-based browser for application development.

Developing Applications with Qt Widgets

5

Qt has a long history in cross-platform GUI development. With controls for all aspects of GUI design that closely mimic the native platform's controls (or, in many cases, wrap the native platform's controls), it's a versatile choice for any cross-platform development project. For many people, the best way to get started with Qt Widgets is to fool around in Qt Creator's Designer pane, as we did in Chapter 3, *Designing Your Application with Qt Designer*. If you're the type that likes to read the documentation before you unpack a new toy, this chapter is for you.

In this chapter, you get a whirlwind tour of GUI programming using Qt Widgets. This isn't an exhaustive introduction, but will orient you with Qt Designer and the Qt documentation, helping you get a high-level understanding of what you can do as you set out to build your application. You will learn basic application management, how to create dialogs and error popups, and see some of the major GUI elements you can create using the designer.

Next, you will learn how to manage the layout of these GUI elements using Qt's flexible layout system, an important part of application development if you're going to target more than one screen size in your application. After that, you will learn about the **Model-View-Controller** (**MVC**) paradigm and how it's used in Qt for complex controls such as lists and tree views. The chapter will close with a quick peek at Qt's support for WebEngine, which lets you integrate rich web content into your application UI using the QWebEngineView control.

We will cover the following topics:

- Your main application and its menus
- Creating simple Qt Widgets
- Managing the widget layout with layouts
- MVC programming with Qt

- Rendering web content using `QWebEngineView`
- Using the model editor
- Enabling LSP on your Qt Creator

Technical requirements

The technical requirements for this chapter include Qt 5.12.3, MinGW 64-bit, Qt Creator 4.9.0, and Windows 10.

Your main application and its menus

In order to use Qt Widgets, you need to do two things. First, you need to ensure that you include the widgets module in your project by adding the following line in your project's `.pro` file:

```
QT += widgets
```

Second, any file using Qt Widgets should include the `QWidgets` header as one of its headers. You might also need to include the header files for individual widgets, such as `QButton` and `QMenuBar`:

```
#include <QWidgets>
```

Qt provides the `QGuiApplication` class (a subclass of `QCoreApplication`) to manage your application's life cycle, including the event loop required by today's GUI platforms. You've already seen `QCoreApplication`, which we used for our console application in `Chapter 1`, *Getting Started with Qt Creator*.

You probably won't do much with `QGuiApplication`, but there are two signals it offers that are good for you to know about:

- `QGuiApplication::applicationStateChanged()`: This emits the `applicationStateChanged` signal when the application state changes, notifying you as to whether an application is suspended, hidden, inactive, or active. It's a good idea to watch this signal on mobile platforms, where you should do a minimum of processing when your application is hidden or inactive.
- `QGuiApplication::lastWindowClosed()`: This emits the `lastWindowClosed` signal when your application's primary or parent window has closed and it's about to exit.

In addition to these signals, QGuiApplication has a few static methods that can come in handy to determine things such as the application's display name, whether the locale mode shows the text left-to-right or right-to-left, and the platform name. For a complete list, refer the interface documentation at https://doc.qt.io/qt-5/qguiapplication.html, or Qt Creator's Help documentation for QGuiApplication.

The main window of QGuiApplication includes a menu bar into which you can add menu items. On Microsoft Windows, the menu bar is a part of the window; on macOS X, it's the menu bar at the top of the screen; while X-Windows-based applications, such as Linux, put them where the window manager dictates. Qt provides the QMenuBar class to implement the functionality of a horizontal menu bar; this class has zero or more QMenu instances associated with it, each corresponding to a single menu (such as **File**, and **Edit**). Menu items themselves are represented as actions, implemented in Qt as instances of the QAction class. It's easiest to understand the flow if we work bottom-up, from actions to menus to menu bars.

A QAction class is an abstract user interface action that can be embedded in Qt Widgets such as menus. An action can have the following properties:

- enabled: This is a Boolean flag indicating whether the action is enabled (selectable).
- font: This is used to show any text associated with the action.
- icon: This is to represent an action.
- iconVisibleInMenu: This is a flag that is used to check whether an icon is visible in a menu.
- shortcut: This is a keyboard shortcut associated with an action.
- text: This is a textual description of the action.
- toolTip: This is a tooltip for the action.
- visible: This shows whether the action is visible.

Actions have a trigger signal that fires when the action is triggered, such as when the user selects the corresponding menu item. (Their properties also have change signals, so you can monitor when they change, but that's a less common thing to do.) If you need to have an action trigger its events as if it were invoked, call its activate method. For more information, check out the documentation at https://doc.qt.io/qt-5/qaction.html.

An instance of QMenu groups one or more logically related actions; you can use it as either a pull-down menu, as part of a menu bar, or as a context menu. QMenu provides the following methods you can use to build up a menu hierarchy:

- addAction and removeAction: These methods add and remove a single QAction instance, respectively.
- clear: This method removes all actions.
- addSeparator: This method adds a menu separator between two actions.
- addMenu: This method adds a submenu to a menu.

Finally, QMenuBar groups all of the drop-down menus; it has the addMenu and insertMenu methods to add and insert menus after and before their specified menu argument. You can check out the documentation regarding QMenu at https://doc.qt.io/qt-5/qmenu.html and QMenuBar at https://doc.qt.io/qt-5/qmenubar.html.

Once you add or insert a menu to a menu bar, you can't remove the menu itself. This is consistent with how most GUIs behave; they don't let you remove menus entirely from the main menu bar.

In practice, all of this is far simpler than it sounds because you can use Qt Creator Designer to build your application menus.

By opening up the user interface form for your application's main view (ones based on the main window template, MainWindow), you can click on the **Type Here** text and create a new QMenu instance. Clicking on the new menu bar instance results in the menu bar dropping down and the first menu item being labeled as **Type Here**. To try this, go back to the Qt Widgets sample application in Chapter 1, *Getting Started with Qt Creator* (or the calculator example in the previous chapter) and try clicking on the menu bar in Qt Designer. Again, typing over the menu item with a label creates a menu action; you can then name the action in the **Property** editor.

The following screenshot shows this behavior of Qt Designer:

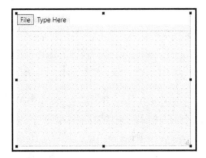

Once you name an action, you just need to connect its triggered signal to a slot in your application. Typically, we do this in our main window's constructor, like this:

```
MainWindow::MainWindow(QWidget *parent) :
    QMainWindow(parent),
    ui(new Ui::MainWindow)
{
    ui->setupUi(this);
    connect(ui->actionAbout, &QAction::triggered, this, &MainWindow:
      :handleAbout);
}
```

> For more information about using menus, refer to Qt's menu sample at `https://doc.qt.io/qt-5/qtwidgets-mainwindows-menus-example.html`.

We have learned how to create an application menu and link it to a function using the signals and slots mechanisms. Let's now proceed to the next section and learn about different widgets!

Creating simple Qt Widgets

Playing with the widgets in Qt Creator is the best way to get a feel for what's available, but it's worth commenting on a few of the classes you're likely to use the most. We've already talked about menus; next, let's look at buttons, text input, and combo boxes. If you're curious what any of these widgets look like, fire up Qt Designer and make one:

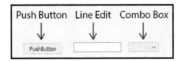

Qt's button classes that implement push-buttons, checkboxes, and radio buttons all inherit from the QAbstractButton class. You can drag out any of the concrete subclasses of QAbstractButton in Qt Creator's Designer or instantiate them programmatically. Through QAbstractButton, all buttons have the following properties:

- checkable: This is a Boolean flag indicating whether the button has a checkbox behavior. By default, the value for this property is false.
- checked: This indicates whether or not the button is presently checked.
- down: This is a type of Boolean indicating whether or not the button is currently in the pressed state.
- icon: This property holds the icon shown on the button.
- shortcut: This property holds the mnemonic associated with the button.
- text: This property holds the text shown on the button.

Buttons offer the following signals that you can wire to slots in your application to detect user input:

- The button emits the clicked signal when the button is clicked.
- The button emits the pressed signal when the button is pressed (that is, receives a mouse or pen-down event).
- The button emits a released signal when the button is released (that is, receives a mouse or pen-up event).
- The button emits the toggled signal when it changes the state from checked to unchecked or vice versa.

You can group multiple buttons in a parent container, such as QFrame, to control exclusive behavior; this is how radio buttons work. A good choice of container is the QGroupBox widget, which frames its contents and provides a title for the collection. By placing multiple buttons such as QRadioButtons in a single QFrame container and ensuring that their autoExclusive property is true (the default for QRadioButtons), clicking one radio button checks that button while unchecking all of the others.

Let's see how we can create a push-button using C++ code:

```
QPushButton* button = new QPushButton("Some default text", ui->
    centralWidget);
button->setText("Click me!");
```

The preceding code is the minimal code for creating a push-button. You can also achieve this by simply dragging a push-button from Qt Designer to the canvas. The result is shown as follows:

 Don't forget that you should use radio buttons for options that have exclusive behavior (that is, only one item can be selected) and checkboxes for items where multiple items can be selected.

I've mentioned icons twice now, once in discussing menus, and once in discussing buttons, without really describing how they work in Qt. Of course, you can manipulate bitmaps directly (we will discuss this further in Chapter 6, *Drawing with Qt*), but for most user interface elements, you need a container that can represent an icon in its various modes and states (such as pressed, released, and highlighted). In Qt, that container is QIcon.

Using QIcon is easy; you can simply instantiate one from a pixmap or resource. For example, to set a button's icon to a particular image in your application resource, you need to only write this:

```
button->setIcon(QIcon(":/icon.png"));
```

Under the hood, the `QIcon` class creates three additional icons for different states for you. This is because an icon can actually be in one of the four modes: normal, active, disabled, or selected. You can apply multiple images to `QIcon` and different images will be displayed for different modes. To better understand this, I have prepared a chart for comparison purposes, shown as follows:

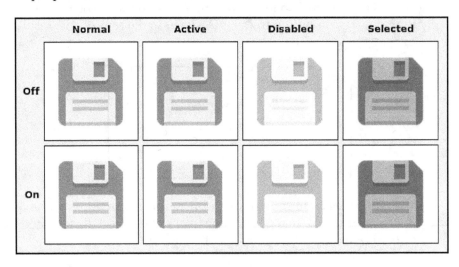

Each of the modes can be in two states: **On** or **Off**.

In addition, `QIcon` will scale the icon to fit the user interface element the icon is associated with, so you can create icons at the largest resolution your user interface requires and rely on `QIcon` to do the scaling to fit the various elements of your interface.

Let's move on to text. By far the most common and easy-to-use text container in Qt Widgets is the `QLabel` class, which is just a label. `QLabel` can actually display either text or an image; you set its text using its `setText` method and its image using its `setPixmap` or `setPicture` method. The text can be either plain or rich text; rich text is a subset of the HTML4 markup, so you can do simple things such as have bold text, underlined text, or even hyperlinks. If you use a hyperlink with a `QLabel` class, you should be prepared to catch a user click by connecting to the label's `linkActivated` signal, which the label emits if the user clicks a link, sending the URL for the link as the signal's argument.

By default, labels display left-aligned, vertically centered content; you can change this by calling the label's `setAlignment` method, or by setting the alignment property in Qt Creator Designer. You can also control word wrapping for a label by setting whether or not word wrapping occurs by calling `setWordWrap` and passing `true` to enable word wrap, or `false` to disable it.

Let's see how the code looks for creating `QLabel` in C++:

```
QLabel* label = new QLabel("This is some text", ui->centralWidget);
```

The result looks something like this:

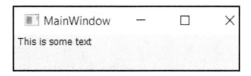

Next in complexity is a text entry; Qt provides the `QLineEdit` element for single-line text entry and a `QTextEdit` for multi-line entry. Support for editing functionality is provided by whatever the host platform is, so you usually get undo and redo, copy and paste, and drag and drop functionalities for free using `QLineEdit` and `QTextEdit`.

Let's talk about `QLineEdit` first, because it's a little simpler. It's a widget that lets the user edit a single line of text. `QLineEdit` has the following properties, which you can set either using Qt Creator Designer or in the source code:

- `alignment`: This controls the alignment of the text as it's displayed.
- `cursorPosition`: This indicates the current cursor position.
- `displayText`: This shows the text displayed to the user (which can be different depending on the `echoMode` property).
- `echoMode`: This can be used to control password-blanking or conventional input line behavior.
- `hasSelectedText`: This property is `true` if the text field has selected text.
- `inputMask`: This controls input validation (which I'll say more about in a moment).
- `maxLength`: This specifies the maximum length of the input line in characters.
- `placeholderText`: This is shown as grayed-out text when the text field is empty.
- `readOnly`: When `true`, this flag indicates that the text field can't be edited.
- `selectedText`: This contains the currently selected text in the text field.
- `text`: This field contains the entire text of the input line.

`QLineEdit` has the following signals:

- `cursorPositionChanged`: This is emitted by the line editor when the cursor moves.
- `editingFinished`: This is emitted by the line editor when the user has finished editing a text field and moved focus to the next focusable element.
- `returnPressed`: This is emitted by the line editor when the user presses the *Return* or *Enter* key on the keyboard.
- `selectionChanged`: This is emitted by the line editor when the selected text changes.
- `textChanged`: This is emitted by the line editor when the text in the field changes, passing the new text of the field.
- `textEdited`: This is emitted by the line editor when the user changes the text in the field (not when the text changes programmatically), passing the new text of the field.

Let's check out the minimal C++ code for creating `QLineEdit`:

```
QLineEdit* lineEdit = new QLineEdit(ui->centralWidget);
```

The preceding code produces the following result:

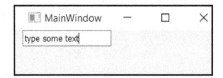

`QLineEdit` instances can perform input validation; you can go about this in two ways: either by setting an input mask or by providing a validator. Input masks are simple and useful for basic tasks such as validating IP addresses or numeric entry. An input mask is a string of characters that indicates the allowable character class for each position in the string. `QLineEdit` defines the following character classes for input masks:

Character in input mask	Character class
A	An ASCII alphabetic character is required: A-Z, a-z.
a	An ASCII alphabetic character is permitted but not required.

N	An ASCII alphanumeric character is required: A-Z, a-z, 0-9.
n	An ASCII alphanumeric character is permitted but not required.
X	Any character that is required.
x	Any character is permitted but not required.
9	An ASCII digit is required: 0-9.
0	An ASCII digit is permitted but not required.
D	An ASCII digit is required: 1-9.
d	An ASCII digit is permitted but not required (1-9).
#	An ASCII digit or plus/minus sign is permitted but not required.
H	A hexadecimal character is required: A-F, a-f, 0-9.
h	A hexadecimal character is permitted but not required.
B	A binary character is required: 0-1.
b	A binary character is permitted but not required.
>	All alphabetic characters following this character are uppercased.
<	All alphabetic characters following this character are lowercased.
!	Switch off case conversion.
\	Use \ to escape the special characters listed previously to use them as separators.

For example, you can set an input mask for IP addresses by using the string
`000.000.000.000;`. This restricts input to three sets of four numeric digits, bracketed by periods.

For more complex validation tasks, you can specify a validator, which is an instance of a class such as QIntValidator, QDoubleValidator, or QRegExpValidator that QLineEdit invokes each time the user changes the text, validating the input. Of these, the most flexible is QRegExpValidator, which takes a regular expression and validates the input against the regular expression.

For larger blocks of text, you'll want to use QTextEdit instances. Unsurprisingly, QTextEdit shares a lot of its interface with QLineEdit. Differences include the following:

- You can't mask input for passwords as you might with QLineEdit.
- If the acceptRichText flag of QTextEdit is true, the field can accept rich text represented as a subset of HTML4.
- The rich text of QTextEdit is available as an HTML property, while the parsed text is available as a text property.

Finally, there's QComboBox, which combines an input line with a drop-down menu to prompt the user with a selection of canned text. As you might imagine, its interface is similar to both menus and input lines; you can append and insert items of text to the combo box using addItem and insertItem. You'll want to connect to its highlighted and editTextChanged signals, which it emits when the user selects a menu item or changes the text input line.

Let's write some code!

```
QComboBox* cbox = new QComboBox(ui->centralWidget);
cbox->addItem("Option 1");
cbox->addItem("Option 2");
cbox->addItem("Option 3");
```

The preceding code produces the following result:

So far, we have learned how to create push-buttons, text input fields, and combo boxes using C++ code in Qt. You can use a similar method to create other types of widgets and place them in your application. However, the widgets are not properly placed without a layout. Let's proceed to the next section and learn how we can manage widget positioning using layouts.

Managing the widget layout with layouts

Qt Widgets includes a robust layout system to control the presentation of widgets on the display. Layouts are basically similar to widgets; they can be placed on an application, get named, become a parent to other widgets, and many others.

However, unlike widgets, their sole purpose is for managing the widgets and their positions in your application. The following screenshot illustrates the purpose of layouts. Do note that we're only showing one type of layout here (a vertical layout), and there are many other types of layouts that we will talk about later:

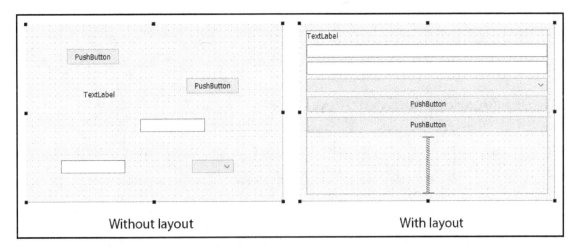

In Qt Creator Designer, you can pick from the following layouts:

- QBoxLayout: This lays out its view children horizontally or vertically.
- QHBoxLayout: This lays out its view children horizontally.
- QVBoxLayout: This lays out its view children vertically.
- QFormLayout: This lays out pairs of widgets (such as labels and textboxes) side by side and then tiles those pairs vertically, giving the appearance of a form.
- QGridLayout: This lays out widgets in a grid.
- QStackedLayout: This shows only a single widget at a time.

Using one of these layouts is easy: simply choose the appropriate layout in Qt Creator Designer and drag it to the widget or window you're building. If you're constructing a hierarchy of widgets in the code, you add the widgets to the layout and set the parent widget's layout, like this:

```
QWidget *window = new QWidget();
QPushButton *button1 = new QPushButton("One");
QPushButton *button2 = new QPushButton("Two");
QPushButton *button3 = new QPushButton("Three");

QHBoxLayout *layout = new QHBoxLayout;
layout->addWidget(button1);
layout->addWidget(button2);
layout->addWidget(button3);

window->setLayout(layout);
window->show();
```

The preceding code produces the result as shown:

Layouts work in conjunction with a widget's `sizePolicy` and `sizeHint` properties. These properties provide information to the layout and layout manager about how the widgets should be laid out. The `sizePolicy` property is an instance of the `QSizePolicy` class and controls layout preferences to choose between layouts in both the horizontal and vertical directions, offering the following choices in each direction:

- `QSizePolicy::Fixed`: Here, the widget's `sizeHint` property is the only size the widget should be.
- `QSizePolicy::Minimum`: Here, the widget's size is the minimum it can be, and there's no advantage to it being larger.
- `QSizePolicy::Maximum`: Here, the widget's size is the maximum size it can be; it can be smaller, but should be no larger.
- `QSizePolicy::Preferred`: Here, the widget's `sizeHint` property is respected if it can be.
- `QSizePolicy::Expanding`: This is used to indicate that the `sizeHint` property is a recommendation, but that more space can be used if it's available.
- `QSizePolicy::MinimumExpanding`: This is used to indicate that `sizeHint` is minimal and sufficient, but that more space can be used if it's available.

Widgets in Qt Widgets have size policies that make sense for the general UI constraints of the target platform, and you typically won't need to change the policy with `QSizePolicy::setVerticalPolicy` or `QSizePolicy::setHorizontalPolicy`.

Use the layout classes and their defaults as much as you can in your application to ensure cross-platform compatibility and proper layout on screens of different sizes. If you're worried about individual pixel placement for your widgets, you're likely doing something wrong and will end up with a user interface that doesn't look like what you expect on at least some systems some of the time.

For more information about managing widget layouts with the layout classes, refer to the Qt documentation at `https://doc.qt.io/qt-5/layout.html`.

We have learned how to use different types of layouts to manage widgets in our Qt application. Let's proceed to learn model-view-controller programming in the following section.

Model-View-Controller programming with Qt

Writing software is an exercise in managing abstractions. The more you can reason abstractly about your software system, the better off you are. A key abstraction that's been around in the GUI world since the 1970s is the **Model-View-Controller** (**MVC**) paradigm. I'll discuss MVC briefly here, but there's a lot written about it on the web, so if it's new to you, you should definitely head over to your favorite search engine and look it up.

In MVC, you divide the code that concerns your user interface into three logical components:

- **Model**: This is responsible for storing the data to show to the user. It's a container of some kind and has no knowledge of your user interface, how things should be drawn, or which events or methods should be triggered by the user when they interact with your application.
- **View**: This is responsible for drawing the model's contents on the display.
- **Controller**: This is responsible for manipulating the contents of the model and view in response to individual user actions.

Each of these separate logical components only communicates with the next through well-defined interfaces, as follows:

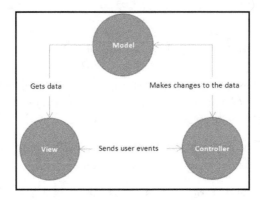

In Qt, the view and controller are combined simply into the view, an arrangement called the **model/view** pattern. To make user interface development as general as possible, Qt also introduces a delegate that makes it easy to switch in and out different user event handlers while sharing the same view and model. Common to both MVC and the model/view pattern is the notion that data and view are separate, which lets you use the same data model for different views, or different models with the same view. Models and their views communicate through signals and slots, as you'd expect.

Qt uses the model/view pattern to manage its more complex user interface elements such as list views, table views, and tree views. The view classes that use Qt's model classes are as follows:

- QListView: This shows a sequential list of items.
- QTreeView: This shows a tree view of items in their hierarchy.
- QTableView: This shows a table view of items.

All of these views accept one of Qt's model classes to store the data that Qt presents to the user; these model classes provided by Qt all inherit from one of the following abstract base classes:

- QAbstractItemModel: This is flexible enough to handle views that present data in the form of tables, lists, and trees.
- QAbstractListModel: This is a more specialized model superclass optimized to present data in list views.
- QAbstractTableModel: This is a more specialized model superclass optimized to present data in table views.

Most of the time, you don't need to roll your own model for your application. Qt provides several concrete model implementations that are good enough for many applications:

- QStringListModel: This can be used to store a sequential list of strings.
- QStandardItemModel: This can be used to store items in an arbitrary tree hierarchy.
- QFileSystemModel: This can be used as a data model over a filesystem.
- QSqlQueryModel, QSqlTableModel, and QSqlRelationalTableModel: These can be used over a SQL database.

If these classes don't meet your needs, you can implement a subclass of one of the abstract model classes and hook that to your view. Typically, you'd choose to do this for one of two reasons: either the existing implementation isn't performant enough for your needs (typically not a problem unless you're managing thousands of items in the model), or you're trying to put a model in front of a new data source other than memory, the filesystem, or SQL.

For example, if you were building a database browser over a MongoDB database, you might want to create a model that queries and updates the MongoDB database directly. If this is an option you need to pursue, be sure to see the Qt documentation on the topic at https://doc.qt.io/qt-5/model-view-programming.html#creating-new-models.

Analyzing a concrete model subclass

Let's look for a moment at a concrete model subclass and see how you'd move data in and out of it. By far and away the most common model you'll use is QStandardItemModel, which stores its items as a two-dimensional array of QStandardItem instances. Each QStandardItem instance can store the following:

- The data associated with the item in the model. This is usually a string, but can also be a number or Boolean value. You access this with the data method and set it with the setData method.
- The font used to render the item in the view. You access this with the font method and set this with the setFont method.
- An optional icon associated with the item. You access this with the icon method and set this with the setIcon method.

- Whether or not the item can be marked with a checkmark, and if so, whether the item is checked. You use the `checkable` and `setCheckable` methods to indicate whether or not the item can be marked and `checked` and `setChecked` to actually set the check state of the item.
- Whether or not the item can be dragged from or dropped to. You use the `dragEnabled`, `dropEnabled`, `setDragEnabled`, and `setDropEnabled` methods to get and set these options.
- Whether or not the item is editable. You use the `editable` and `setEditable` methods to get and set the editable state of the item.
- Whether or not the item is selectable. You use the `selectable` and `setSelectable` methods to get and set the selectable state of the item.
- A tooltip for the item. You use the `toolTip` and `setToolTip` methods to get and set the tooltip for the item.

Each `QStandardItem` method can also have its own rows and columns, giving it the ability to store a tree structure. You can manipulate rows and columns by calling `appendRow`, `appendColumn`, `removeRow`, or `removeColumn`. For example, to create a simple model that represents a tree, you might write the following:

```
QStandardItemModel model;
QStandardItem *parentItem = model.invisibleRootItem();
for (int i = 0; i < 4; ++i)
{
    QStandardItem *item = new QStandardItem(QString("node %0").arg(i));
    parentItem->appendRow(item);
    parentItem = item;
}
```

This creates a model with a root element with four child elements, each in their own row. With this model in hand, you can create a tree view that shows the model like this:

```
QTreeView *treeView = new QTreeView(this);
treeView->setModel(myStandardItemModel);
```

Of course, you'll want to know when an item is clicked; the `QTreeView` method emits a `clicked` signal when the user clicks an item, so you can connect this signal to a slot in your class:

```
connect(treeView, &QTreeView::clicked, this, &MainWindow::clicked);
```

Qt model/view views use the `QModelIndex` class to indicate the index of an item in a model; `QStandardItem` is never passed around between the model and the view. `QModelIndex` offers the `itemFromIndex` method to return `QStandardItem` at the indicated position in the model. Note that you shouldn't cache `QModelIndex` instances in your application for any length of time, because if the model changes underneath you, the indexes to a given piece of data will change. Similarly, if you need the index of an item in its model, call the item's `index` method, which returns `QModelIndex` of the item in the model.

Using the MVC model on Qt Creator

While the preceding example showed how we can apply the MVC model to a tree view entirely in C++, let's check out how we can do the same with the widgets in Qt Designer. There are several widgets in Qt Creator that can be used with the MVC design pattern; they are called the model-based item views:

- **List View**
- **Tree View**
- **Table View**
- **Column View**
- **Undo View**

They are all very similar, except the way they are presented to the user. These widgets are where the controller and view are implemented. The controller (or sometimes called **delegate**) is where the logic is applied, such as the rules of interaction between the presentation layer (view) and the data layer (model). For example, we can make a table editable via the delegate and update the data in the model when the user is done editing. The view will provide the user with the UI, and the delegate will handle the logic behind the rendering and editing of the view. Lastly, the model is the actual container that stores the data. You can apply the same model to different delegates and views since they are separated. This is the advantage of using the MVC design pattern, which gives you a lot of flexibility.

In Qt Designer, you can find the built-in widgets in the widget box. For this example, we don't use the item-based widgets in the **Item Widgets** category, as the widgets have built-in models and can't be modified:

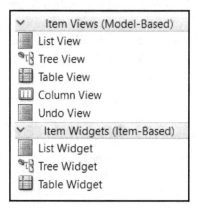

For the GUI design, it's very simple. First, we delete the menu bar, toolbar, and status bar as we don't need those extra panels. Then, we place a table view onto the central widget, as follows:

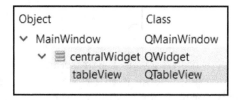

Then, select the central widget and click **Lay Out Vertically** located above the canvas. The table view will now fill up the entire main window:

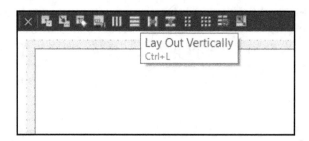

Since the `QTableView` already handled the view and delegate, we only need to take care of the model by ourselves. There are many types of models supported by Qt, such as the following:

- `QStandardItemModel`
- `QStringListModel`
- `QSqlTableModel`
- `QDirModel`

You can even make your own model by inheriting one of the abstract model classes if you want to:

- `QAbstractProxyModel`
- `QAbstractListModel`
- `QAbstractTableModel`

Some of these built-in models are designed for single-column data structures, while some others support multiple columns or even recursive tree-like structures. For our case, we need a model that supports multiple columns to accommodate our table view.

Therefore, in our `MainWindow` class' constructor, we create a `QStandardItemModel` object, which offers a lot of flexibility for creating multiple columns and rows for our table. For testing purposes, we set the column count to 5 and the row count to 10:

```
MainWindow::MainWindow(QWidget *parent) : QMainWindow(parent), ui(new
Ui::MainWindow)
{
    ui->setupUi(this);

    QStandardItemModel* model = new QStandardItemModel(this);
    model->setColumnCount(5);
    model->setRowCount(10);
```

After that, we use two `for` loops to insert some dummy data in the standard model. We loop through every single column and row, and then create a `QStandardItem` object with the words `"row #, column #"` (# represents the row number and column number) and attach it to its respective position. Do note that I added 1 to both row and column numbers so that they don't start from zero:

```
for (int row = 0; row < model->rowCount(); row++)
{
  for (int column = 0; column < model->columnCount(); column++)
    {
        QStandardItem *item = new QStandardItem(QString("row %0,
```

```
        column %1").arg(row + 1).arg(column + 1));
      model->setItem(row, column, item);
    }
  }
```

Finally, we call `setModel` on our table view and apply the model to it:

```
  ui->tableView->setModel(model);
}
```

Also, don't forget to include the required headers at the top:

```
#include <QStandardItemModel>
#include <QMessageBox>
```

If you build and run the program now, you should see something like this:

	1	2	3	4	5
1	row 1, column 1	row 1, column 2	row 1, column 3	row 1, column 4	row 1, column 5
2	row 2, column 1	row 2, column 2	row 2, column 3	row 2, column 4	row 2, column 5
3	row 3, column 1	row 3, column 2	row 3, column 3	row 3, column 4	row 3, column 5
4	row 4, column 1	row 4, column 2	row 4, column 3	row 4, column 4	row 4, column 5
5	row 5, column 1	row 5, column 2	row 5, column 3	row 5, column 4	row 5, column 5
6	row 6, column 1	row 6, column 2	row 6, column 3	row 6, column 4	row 6, column 5
7	row 7, column 1	row 7, column 2	row 7, column 3	row 7, column 4	row 7, column 5
8	row 8, column 1	row 8, column 2	row 8, column 3	row 8, column 4	row 8, column 5
9	row 9, column 1	row 9, column 2	row 9, column 3	row 9, column 4	row 9, column 5
10	row 10, column 1	row 10, column 2	row 10, column 3	row 10, column 4	row 10, column 5

You can even double-click any of the data blocks and edit the data on the fly. This is the default behavior of the delegate within the `QTableView` class, which can be disabled via Qt Designer (or C++ code, if you want to). Let's try and disable it by selecting the table view and setting its **editTriggers** property to **NoEditTriggers**:

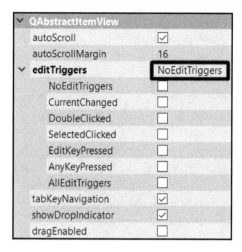

We want to change the double-clicking behavior to something else instead. Let's right-click on the table view on Qt Designer and select **Go to slot** on the pop-up menu. Then, select the **doubleClicked(QModelIndex)** signal and press **OK**:

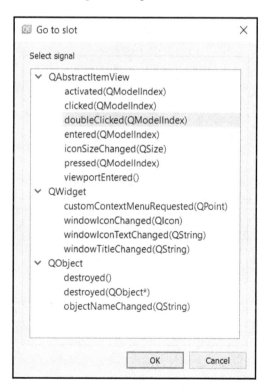

A slot function will be created for you. Let's just pop out a message box and display the data in the data block when double-clicking on it:

```
void MainWindow::on_tableView_doubleClicked(const QModelIndex &index)
{
    QMessageBox::information(this, "Data", index.data
        (Qt::DisplayRole).toString());
}
```

In the preceding code, we prompted an information message box with the title "Data", and the data as the message. We used DisplayRole to specify that we want to obtain the text instead of the **DecorationRole** icon or the **ToolTipRole** tooltip. The following screenshot, taken from the official documentation, clearly shows the distinction between the different roles:

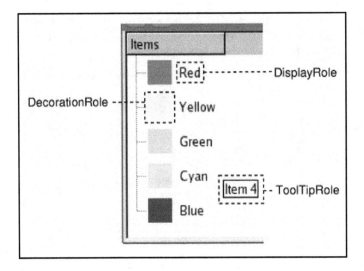

If we build and run the program again, we should get the following result when double-clicking on the table:

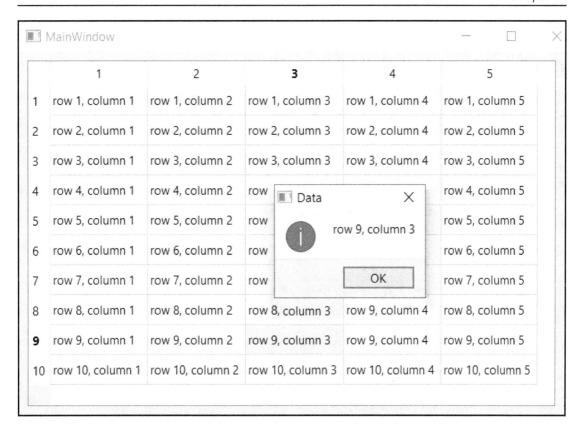

From the preceding example, we have learned how we can implement our own model and apply it to the table view we created using Qt Designer. Once again, these are the built-in MVC design patterns of Qt, which always try to make things easier by removing some of the controls from the user. For example, Qt's MVC only applies to one data structure and has a simpler view structure with the controller built in. If you want a more **proper** MVC design pattern for your program, you can always write your own, which, to be honest, is quite a complex task.

For more information about Qt's application of the model/view pattern, see https://doc.qt.io/qt-5/model-view-programming.html.

We have learned how to make use of model-view-controller programming to display data dynamically. Next, we will learn how to display web content using QWebEngine.

Rendering web content with QWebEngineView

Qt includes a port of WebEngine, the popular browser implementation behind Chromium and several open source browsers, in its Qt WebEngine module. Using the Qt WebEngine module, your application can display rich HTML, or even be a full-fledged web browser on its own. It's very easy to create hybrid applications that incorporate both features of native applications and the ability to display web content from local resources, the local filesystem, or the internet.

 Do note that the Qt WebEngine module only works on MSVC compilers. You will get an error if you use other compilers.

To use the Qt WebEngine module, you must include it in your application by adding the following to your PRO file:

```
QT += webenginewidgets
```

Any source file that accesses the Qt WebEngine widget's classes should also include the interfaces with the following `#include` statement:

```
#include <QtWebEngineWidgets>
```

The key class for web page presentation that this module exposes is `QWebEngineView`; using it is as easy as adding it to a layout in Qt Creator Designer and then telling it to open a document, like this:

```
QWebEngineView *view = new QWebEngineView(ui->centralWidget);
view->load(QUrl("http://www.zhieng.com"));
```

The preceding code produces the following result:

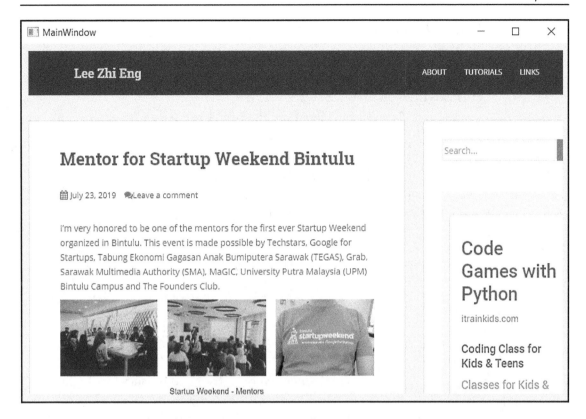

The `load` method starts the process of firing up the network layer, resolves the URL, fetches the content, and renders the results. You can also use the `setUrl` method of `QWebEngineView` to set its `url` property, which triggers the same flow, or if you have the HTML locally (say, you built it up programmatically or fetched it from a resource), you can just call its `setHtml` method.

While `QWebEngineView` is in the process of loading the page, it emits three signals:

- `loadStarted`: This is emitted when the page starts to load.
- `loadProgress`: This is emitted for each element of the web view as that element finishes loading.
- `loadFinished`: This is emitted once the page finishes loading.

`QWebEngineView` has the following properties:

- `hasSelection`: This is `true` if the user has selected a region in `QWebEngineView`.
- `icon`: This is the icon for `QWebEngineView`.
- `selectedText`: This contains the unmarked-up text the user has selected in `QWebEngineView`.
- `title`: This contains the document's title.
- `url`: This contains the document's URL.
- `zoomFactor`: This is a real number that indicates how much the page should be zoomed when being rendered. The default value, `1.0`, indicates that no scaling should occur.

`QWebEngineView` contains an instance of `QWebEnginePage`, available through the `page` method. The `QWebEnginePage` method itself is what performs the actual rendering and has several additional signals you can monitor to observe the behavior of the rendering engine itself:

- `loadStarted`: This is emitted when `QWebEnginePage` starts loading the document.
- `loadFinished`: This is emitted when `QWebEnginePage` finishes loading the page.
- `urlChanged`: This is emitted when `QWebEnginePage` is about to change its URL before loading a new web page. This signal passes the new URL to the slots connected to the signal.

When you create hybrid applications, you might want to access application data in your C++ application from your application's JavaScript. The `QWebChannel` class provides the `registerObject` method, which lets you bind a `QObject` instance to a slot as a child of the web page's `window` object. For example, let's write the following code snippet:

```
QWebEnginePage *page= myView->page();
QWebChannel *channel = new QWebChannel(page);
page->setWebChannel(channel);
channel->registerObject(QString("TheNameOfTheObjectUsed"), this);
```

Properties of your object are available as slots in the exposed object in JavaScript, so you can share data across the C++/JavaScript boundary. The bridge also lets you extend script invocations across the boundary by invoking signal functions on your JavaScript object in JavaScript; this will cause any slots connected to that signal to execute. Similarly, your JavaScript object supports a `connect` method that lets you connect named slots to JavaScript code, so invoking the signal from C++ invokes the JavaScript methods connected to that slot.

 For more information about `QWebEngineView` and Qt's support for the WebEngine browser, refer to the Qt documentation at `https://doc.qt.io/qt-5/qtwebengine-overview.html`.

We have learned how to display web content using QWebEngineView and created a mini web browser of our own. In the next section, we will learn how to use the model editor in Qt Creator.

Using the model editor

The model editor is a new addition to Qt's toolset. You can use it to create **Universal Modeling Language** (**UML**)-style models to visualize how your application would behave. This is one of the good ways to communicate with your programmers or to present your idea to your team. Currently, the model editor is still in the beta testing phase and will be subject to changes in later versions. At the moment, you need to enable it in Qt Creator before you're able to use it. To do this, try the following steps:

1. Go to **Help | About Plugins** to open up the **Installed Plugins** window. Make sure that the **ModelEditor** option has been checked.

2. After that, you can create a new model file by going to **File| New File or Project** and select either the **Model** or **Scratch Model** options under **Files and Classes | Modeling**. The other option, **State Chart**, is for state machine editing so it's not related to our current topic. Refer to the following screenshot for better understanding:

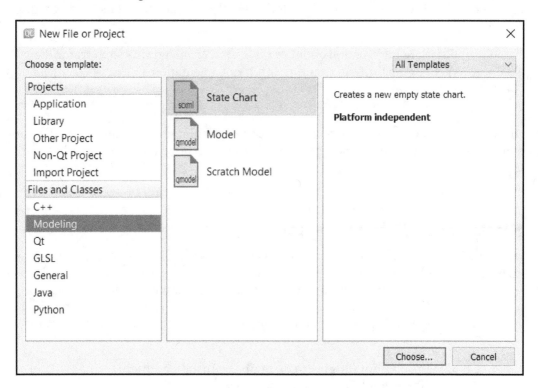

3. Once you have created the model files, let's open them up with Qt Creator. You will see a brand-new user interface specially designed for model editing:

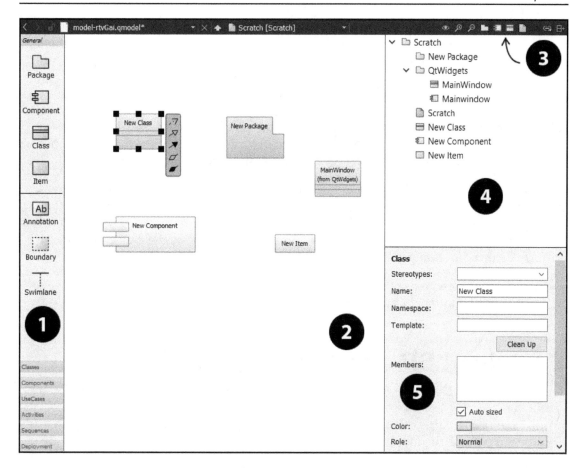

The user interface contains five different sections described as follows:

1. Element toolbar: You can drag and drop elements from this toolbar to the model editor.
2. Model editor: This is where your model is visualized. You can edit your model in this editor view.
3. Toolbar buttons: You can find some shortcut buttons here, such as zoom in, zoom out, zoom to original size, add package, add component, add class, and add canvas diagram.

4. Element tree: The element tree displays all the elements that you have added to the model editor in tree diagram format. You can select or delete an element here other than doing it at the model editor.

5. Properties editor: This is where you edit the properties of the element that you have just selected.

Just like any other UML modeling software, you can place different types of diagrams to the editor view and edit its name, color, role, and other properties of the diagram element. You can also link different elements together to visualize their relationship.

Once you are satisfied with the result, you can go to **File** | **Export Diagram** to save the diagram as an image. Other than this method, you can also select all the elements in the editor view and press *Ctrl + C* on your keyboard to convert them into a 300 dpi image before storing it in your clipboard. You may press *Ctrl + V* to paste the image onto your preferred word processing software or image editing software.

We have learned how to use the model editor provided by Qt Creator suite. Let's move on to the next section for enabling LSP on your Qt Creator.

Enabling LSP on your Qt Creator

The **LSP** (short for **Language Server Protocol**) is one of the latest features added to Qt in recent versions. The LSP makes Qt even more powerful by adding supports for other programming languages other than C++ and QML. By providing a client for the LSP, Qt Creator can provide the following features for programming languages that support the LSP:

- Code autocompletion
- Highlighting a symbol when it has a mouseover event
- Code actions
- Inspecting code by viewing the document outline
- Integrating diagnostics from the language server
- Finding references to a symbol
- Navigate to a symbol definition

This extends the usefulness of Qt Creator and removes the barrier that keeps Qt within the C++ realm. You could even write your Python project using Qt Creator and execute the code directly without leaving Qt! So, to enable LSP in Qt Creators, go to **Help** | **About Plugins**. Then, in **Installed Plugins**, look for the **LanguageClient (experimental)** option and make sure it is checked. You may be required to restart Qt Creator after you have checked the option. The following screenshot shows this:

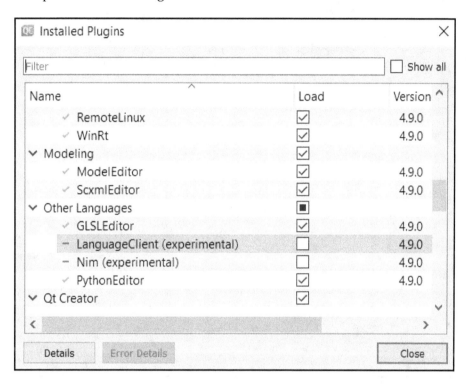

There are several things you need to do before you're able to use an alternative language in Qt Creator.

1. First, you must install the language server before Qt can use it. For example, if you're planning to use Python, then you must download the installer from `https://www.python.org` and install it to your computer.

2. Once you're done, you can start adding the language server to your Qt Creator by going to **Tools** | **Options...** | **Language Client**.
3. Then, click on the **Add** button. The following screenshot shows this:

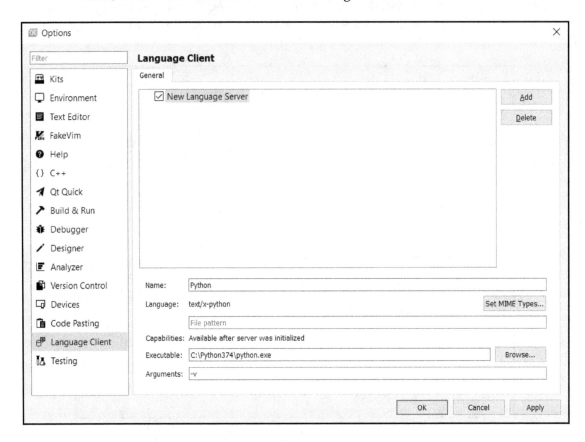

Fill in the information of the language before applying it:

- **Name**: The name of the language you're adding to Qt Creator.
- **Language**: The MIME types must be set correctly, because Qt Creator uses the MIME type to determine which language server to connect to when you're opening a file.
- **Executable:** This is the executable that acts as the language server in which Qt Creator will be communicating.
- **Arguments**: The arguments that the executable is expecting when communicating with it.

4. Once you're done, click **OK**. You're now able to start writing code in alternative languages that Qt doesn't support by default! The following screenshot is one such example:

```
1    # This Python file uses the following encoding: utf-8
2  ∨
3    # if__name__ == "__main__":
4    #      pass
5
6    fruits = ["apple", "orange", "banana"];
7  ∨ for x in fruits:
8        print(x)
9
10 ∨ def my_function():
11        print("Hello world!")
12
13    my_functio
     my_function
```

The preceding screenshot shows the code completion and syntax highlighting in action when writing Python with Qt Creator.

> Do note that currently, the LSP is still an experimental feature. It might not work very well on all languages since Python is the only language that has been fully tested. It is not recommended to use it on critical commercial projects.

We have learned how to enable LSP on Qt Creator in this section. I hope that you find this useful and that it enhances your work quality and improves productivity.

Summary

In this chapter, we took a whirlwind tour of the Qt Widgets module. We learned about some of the basic widgets available, and the signals, slots, and properties they provide. We also learned about Qt's application of the MVC paradigm and how, for complex widgets like such as and tree views, Qt separates concerns into a model and a view, letting us implement new data models for our applications, or create new views based on those data models. Then, we learned about Qt's support for the WebEngine browser, letting us build hybrid applications that incorporate the best of JavaScript and HTML with the best of Qt. Finally, we learned about the new additions to Qt Widgets and how they help in application development and language support.

In the next chapter, we move on from widgets to low-level drawing, which we can use to either implement our own widgets or basic pixel-based rendering applications.

Section 2: Advanced Features

In the second section of this book, we will look into a few advanced topics of Qt that will help us gain a better understanding of it, which also includes the working of sensors aside from some tools to work with Qt.

This section comprises the following chapters:

Drawing with Qt 6

While many applications can be built using only the built-in widgets, others require the ability to perform custom drawing—for example, when you need a custom widget or two, or maybe you're doing offscreen rendering to programmatically create images in graphics files, or else you're interested in building a radically different user interface. Qt provides support for all of these scenarios in C++, in addition to what you can do with Qt Quick.

In this chapter, we will see what is needed to know for general drawing in Qt. We begin by discussing `QPainter`, and how it uses `QPaintDevice` instances to abstract drawing functionality. We will see how this works in general terms, and then give concrete examples for offscreen drawing to bitmaps, as well as creating custom widgets that interoperate with Qt Widgets. In the last half of the chapter, we will turn to a newer and lower level of abstraction that Qt provides for graphics management: the graphics view/graphics scene architecture provided by `QGraphicsView` and `QGraphicsScene`, and how you can use this to build applications in C++ that interoperate with the Qt Widgets classes, yet encompassing a complex visual hierarchy.

In this chapter, we will cover the following topics:

- Starting to draw in Qt
- Drawing with `QPainter` on `QPaintDevice` instances
- Drawing off screen
- Creating custom widgets
- Introducing the Graphics View framework

> Throughout the chapter, don't forget you can always ask for Qt Creator's help when encountering an unfamiliar class or method. Qt Creator also comes with a number of examples you can look at; these are in the `examples` directory, under the directory in which you installed Qt.

Technical requirements

The technical requirements for this chapter include Qt 5.13.1 MinGW 64-bit, Qt Creator 4.10.0, and Windows 10.

The code files can be found at the following link: `https://github.com/PacktPublishing/ Application-Development-with-Qt-Creator-Third-Edition`

Starting to draw in Qt

All the material we cover in this chapter depends on the Qt GUI module, available as part of Qt. Even if you're writing a command-line tool (say, to process image files), you need to include that module in your project by adding the following code to your `.pro` file:

```
QT += gui widgets
```

Of course, in your C++ implementation, we also need to include the header files for the classes we're using. For example, if we're using `QImage`, `QBitmap`, and `QPainter`, be sure to include these headers at the top of your C++ file, like this:

```
#include <QImage>
#include <QPainter>
#include <QBitmap>
```

As Qt's painting implementation uses the underlying windowing system, any application that performs graphics operations must be built using `QGuiApplication`, which initializes the windowing system as part of its startup.

As we have added the required modules and headers to our project and enabled drawing in our Qt project, let's get started, to draw something in the next section!

Drawing with QPainter on QPaintDevice instances

At its core, graphics painting requires two things: something that knows how to paint, and something that can be painted on. Qt defines the QPainter class as the former, and the QPaintDevice as the interface for classes for the latter. You'll seldom instantiate each, but you use both of these classes a lot if you're doing graphics programming; typically, you'll have an instance of a subclass of QPaintDevice, ask it for its associated QPainter, and then use QPainter to perform your drawing. This can happen when you're writing a widget; you'll be passed a QPainter subclass, for example, when you need to paint the widget's contents.

There are several subclasses of QPaintDevice, as follows:

- QWidget: This class and its subclasses are used by the widget hierarchy.
- QImage: This is a container class for offscreen images that are optimized for input/output and individual pixel access.
- QPixmap: This is a container class for offscreen images that are highly optimized for interaction with the screen.
- QBitmap: This is a subclass of QPixmap that has a bit depth of 1, making it suitable for monochrome images.
- QPicture: This is a paint device that records QPainter drawing operations and can play them back.

QPaintDevice subclasses have the width and height methods that return the width and height of the paint device in pixels, respectively; the corresponding widthMM and heightMM methods return the width and height of the paint device in millimeters if known. You can also get the bit depth of the QPaintDevice class, by calling its depth method.

We'll discuss further how to get a QPaintDevice subclass in each of the following sections, as we see what we want to paint on (say, an offscreen bitmap or a custom widget). Let's turn to QPainter, which is the class we use to perform drawing.

QPainter encapsulates the notion of painting through the use of methods that draw specific shapes (points, lines, polygons, ellipses, arcs, and the like), and a number of settings that control how QPainter performs the actual painting you request.

The settings include the following:

- `brush`: This indicates how it should fill shapes.
- `backgroundMode`: This indicates whether the background should be opaque or transparent.
- `font`: This indicates the font it should use when drawing text.
- `pen`: This indicates how it should draw outlines of shapes.

You can also specify whether or not you have enabled a view transform, which lets you set the affine transforms that the `QPainter` instance will apply as it performs your drawing.

Qt lets you specify an arbitrary coordinate system for your `QPainter` instance that might differ in terms of scale, rotation, and origin from the coordinate system of the target `QPaintDevice` class. In doing so, it lets you specify the affine transformation between the drawing coordinate system as either a transformation matrix or by separate scale, rotation, and origin offset arguments. The default is no transformation, as you'd expect.

Discussing transformations is beyond the scope of this section; for more details, see the Qt documentation on this topic at `https://doc.qt.io/qt-5/qpainter.html#coordinate-transformations`.

The `QBrush` and `QPen` classes both take `QColor` instances to specify colors; using `QColor`, you can specify colors as RGB, HSV, or CMYK values, or by the color's name as one of the colors defined by a **Scalable Vector Graphics** (**SVG**) color name (see a list at `http://www.december.com/html/spec/colorsvg.html`). In addition to color, `QBrush` instances also specify a style, a gradient, and a texture; `QPen` instances specify a style, width, brush, cap style (used on the pen's endpoints), and join style (used when two strokes are joined). Both have simple constructors that set the various fields of the object, or you can specify them through the setter and getter methods. For example, we can create a green pen that is 3 pixels wide and made up of a dashed line with rounded caps and joins, using the following line of code:

```
QPen pen(Qt::green, 3, Qt::DashLine, Qt::RoundCap, Qt::RoundJoin);
```

Similarly, to create a `QBrush` that fills with solid green, you can write this code:

```
QBrush brush(Qt::green, Qt::SolidPattern);
```

QFont operates similarly, but, of course, there are more options for fonts than for brushes or pens. Typically, you pass the font family to the constructor for the font you want, along with the font size and weight. Qt has a robust font-matching algorithm that attempts to match the desired font family with what's actually available on the system, because it's notoriously hard to predict which fonts are available everywhere once you move away from the common staple of *Times New Roman, Helvetica,* and so forth. Consequently, the font you get might not be exactly the font you request; you can get information about a font by creating a QFontInfo method from the QFont you create, like this:

```
QFont serifFont("Times", 10);
QFontInfo serifInfo(serifFont);
```

Once you set the brush, pen, and font of QPainter, drawing is simply a matter of calling the various QPainter methods. Rather than enumerating all of them, I'll direct your attention to just a few here, and then show you an example that uses some of them:

- drawArc: This draws an arc, starting at an angle and spanning an angle in a rectangle. Angles are measured in sixteenths of a degree.
- drawConvexPolygon: This takes a list of points, and draws a convex polygon.
- drawEllipse: This draws an ellipse in a rectangle (to draw a circle, make the rectangle a square).
- drawImage: This draws an image (QImage), taking the target rectangle, the image, and the source rectangle.
- drawLine: This draws a single line; drawLines draws a series of lines.
- drawPicture: This draws a picture (QPicture).
- drawPixmap: This draws a pixmap (QPixmap).
- drawPoint and drawPoints: These draw a point or an array of points.
- drawPolygon: This draws a (possibly concave) polygon, giving its points as either an array of points or in a QPolygon.
- drawPolyline: This draws a polyline.
- drawRect: This draws a single rectangle; drawRects draws multiple rectangles.
- drawText: This draws a text string.
- fillPath: This fills a polygonal path with the brush you pass.
- fillRect: This draws a filled rectangle with the brush you pass.

To facilitate these methods, Qt defines helper container classes including QPoint, QLine, and QPolygon. These take integer coordinates; if you want a greater position when drawing (say, when drawing with a transform), you can use the floating-point variants, QPointF, QLineF, and QPolygonF.

Let's see how all of this stacks up in practice, by drawing a face. Given a QPainter class, we can write it as follows:

```
void MainWindow::paintEvent(QPaintEvent *event)
{
    QPainter painter(this);
    QPen pen(Qt::black, 2, Qt::SolidLine);
    QBrush whiteBrush(Qt::white, Qt::SolidPattern);
    QBrush blackBrush(Qt::black, Qt::SolidPattern);
    QRect faceOutline(0, 0, 100, 100);
    painter.setPen(pen);
    painter.setBrush(whiteBrush);
    painter.drawEllipse(faceOutline);
```

This preceding code begins by defining a solid black pen and solid black-and-white brushes, setting the pen to the pen we created.

Next, it creates a square of 100 pixels per side, into which it draws a white circle using drawEllipse. After that, we draw the mouth, which is a half-ellipse arc at the bottom of the circle. Next, we draw two eyes, each a filled circle, using a single rectangle. Finally, we draw a nose using two lines, defined by three points, as follows:

```
    QRect mouth(30, 60, 40, 20);
    painter.drawArc(mouth, 180 * 16, 180 * 16);   // Draw mouth
    QRect eye(25, 25, 10, 10);
    painter.setBrush(blackBrush);
    painter.drawEllipse(eye);   // Draw left eye
    eye = QRect(65, 25, 10, 10);
    painter.drawEllipse(eye);   // Draw right eye
    QPoint nosePoints[3] = {
        QPoint(50, 45),
        QPoint(40, 50),
        QPoint(50, 50) };
    painter.drawPolyline(nosePoints, 3);   // Draw nose
}
```

You can see the result in the following screenshot:

We have learned how we can draw a smiley face on the screen! Now, let's see how to use `QPainter` to draw off screen.

Drawing off screen

There are a number of reasons why you might like to draw off screen: you might want to compose a collection of images and show them one after another (this is called **double-buffering**, which you can do to avoid screen painting flicker when you draw on screen), or write a program that generates image files directly.

As I mentioned in the previous section, Qt provides several classes for offscreen drawing, each with different advantages and disadvantages. These classes are `QImage`, `QPixmap`, `QBitmap`, and `QPicture`. In normal circumstances, you need to choose between `QImage` and `QPixmap`.

> `QImage` is the class best suited for general-purpose drawing, where you're interested in loading the image from or saving the image to a file. If you're working with resources, combining multiple images, and doing a bit of drawing, `QImage` is the class you want to use.

On the other hand, if you're working primarily with offscreen rendering for the purposes of display performance or double-buffering, you'll want to use `QPixmap`. `QPixmap` is optimized to use data structures in the underlying windowing system and interoperates with the native windowing system more quickly than `QImage`. `QBitmap` is just a convenience subclass of `QPixmap` that defines a monochrome bitmap.

QPicture is an interesting beast that records drawing operations in a resolution-independent format that you can save to a file and replay later. You might want to do that if you want to create lightweight platform-independent vector images, but, typically, just using a **Portable Network Graphics** (**PNG**) format at the appropriate resolution is probably easier.

To get a painter for one of these classes, simply create an instance of the class, and then pass a pointer to the instance of a QPainter constructor. For example, to perform the drawing in the previous section to an offscreen image and save it to a PNG file, we'd begin by writing the following code:

```
QImage image(100, 100, QImage::Format_ARGB32);
QPainter painter(&image);
```

The first line creates an image that's 100 pixels square, encoding each pixel a 32-bit integer, 8 bits for each channel of opacity, red, green, and blue. The second line creates a QPainter instance that can draw on the QImage instance. Next, we perform the drawing you just saw in the previous section, and when we're done, we write the image to a PNG file, with the following line:

```
image.save("face.png");
```

QImage supports a number of image formats, including PNG and JPEG. QImage also has a load method, where you can load an image from a file or resource.

That's it; we have not only learned how to draw an image on screen, but also how to draw it off screen and save it into an image file. Next, we will proceed to learn how to create our own custom widgets in Qt.

Creating custom widgets

Painting with a custom widget is, at its heart, no different than offscreen painting; all you need is a widget subclass and a painter pointing to the widget, and you're all set. Yet, how do you know when to paint?

Qt's QWidget class defines an interface used by the rendering system to pass events to your widget: Qt defines the QEvent class to encapsulate the data about an event, and the QWidget class defines an interface that Qt's rendering system uses to pass events to your widget for processing. Qt uses this event system not just to indicate things such as mouse movements and keyboard input, but also for requests to paint the screen as well.

Let's look at painting first. QWidget defines the `paintEvent` method, which Qt's rendering system invokes, passing a `QPaintEvent` pointer. The `QPaintEvent` pointer includes the region that needs to be repainted and the bounding rectangle of the region because it's often faster to repaint an entire rectangle than a complex region. When you draw a widget's content with `QPainter`, Qt performs the necessary clipping to the region; however, you can use the information as a hint to what needs to be redrawn, if it's helpful.

Let's look at another painting example, this time, an analog clock widget. This example is from the sample code that comes with Qt; you can see it at `https://doc.qt.io/qt-5/qtwidgets-widgets-analogclock-example.html`.

I've included the whole `QWidget` subclass implementing an analog clock here. We'll pick through it in several pieces; first come the obligatory header inclusions, as follows:

```
#include "analogclock.h"
```

The constructor comes after the header inclusions, as follows:

```
AnalogClock::AnalogClock(QWidget *parent) : QWidget(parent)
{
    QTimer *timer = new QTimer(this);
    connect(timer, &QTimer::timeout, this, &AnalogClock::update);
    timer->start(1000);
    resize(200, 200);
}
```

The constructor creates a `timer` object that emits a timeout signal every `1000` milliseconds and connects that timer to the widget's `update` slot. The `update` slot forces the widget to repaint; this is how the widget will update itself every second. Finally, it resizes the widget itself to be `200` pixels on a side.

The `timeout` signal triggers the `update` slot function, which basically tells the parent `QWidget` class to refresh the screen, subsequently triggering the `paintEvent` function, as follows:

```
void AnalogClock::update()
{
    QWidget::update();
}
```

The next part is the paint event handler. This is a long method, so we'll look at it in pieces. The method can be seen in the following code block:

```
void AnalogClock::paintEvent(QPaintEvent *)
{
    static const QPoint hourHand[3] = {
        QPoint(7, 8),
        QPoint(-7, 8),
        QPoint(0, -40)
    };
    static const QPoint minuteHand[3] = {
        QPoint(7, 8),
        QPoint(-7, 8),
        QPoint(0, -70)
    };

    QColor hourColor(127, 0, 127);
    QColor minuteColor(0, 127, 127, 191);
    int side = qMin(width(), height());
    QTime time = QTime::currentTime();

    QPainter painter(this);
```

Before this is a declaration of stack variables, including the coordinate arrays and colors for the hour and minute hands, and getting a `QPainter` instance with which to paint.

Next is the code that sets up the painter itself. We request an antialiased drawing and use Qt's support to scale and translate the view, to make our coordinate math a little easier, shown as follows:

```
    painter.setRenderHint(QPainter::Antialiasing);
    painter.translate(width() / 2, height() / 2);
    painter.scale(side / 200.0, side / 200.0);

    painter.setPen(Qt::NoPen);
    painter.setBrush(hourColor);
```

We translate the origin to the middle of the widget. Finally, we set the pen and brush; we choose `NoPen` for the pen, so the only things drawn are fills, and we set the brush initially to the hour brush color.

After that, we draw the hour hand. This code uses Qt's support for rotation in rendering, to rotate the viewport by the right amount to place the hour hand (each hour takes 30 degrees), and draws a single convex polygon for the hand itself. The following code snippet shows this:

```
painter.save();
painter.rotate(30.0 * ((time.hour() + time.minute() / 60.0)));
painter.drawConvexPolygon(hourHand, 3);
painter.restore();
```

The code saves the configured state of the painter before doing the rotation and then restores the (unrotated) state after drawing the hour hand.

Of course, hour hands are better read with hour markings, so we loop through 12 rotations, drawing a line for each hour mark, as follows:

```
painter.setPen(hourColor);

for (int i = 0; i < 12; ++i) {
    painter.drawLine(88, 0, 96, 0);
    painter.rotate(30.0);
}
```

With the hour hand out of the way, it's time to draw the minute hand. We use the same trick with rotation to rotate the minute hand to the correct position, drawing another convex polygon for the minute hand, as follows:

```
painter.setPen(Qt::NoPen);
painter.setBrush(minuteColor);
painter.save();
painter.rotate(6.0 * (time.minute() + time.second() / 60.0));
painter.drawConvexPolygon(minuteHand, 3);
painter.restore();
```

Finally, we draw 60 tick marks around the face of the clock, one for each minute, as follows:

```
painter.setPen(minuteColor);

for (int j = 0; j < 60; ++j) {
    if ((j % 5) != 0)
        painter.drawLine(92, 0, 96, 0);
    painter.rotate(6.0);
}
}
```

As I hinted at earlier, custom widgets can also accept events; the `mousePressEvent`, `mouseReleaseEvent`, and `mouseDoubleClick` events indicate when the user presses, releases, or double-clicks on the mouse within the bounds of the widget. There's also the `mouseMoveEventmouseMoveEvent`, which the Qt system invokes whenever the mouse moves in a widget and a mouse button is pressed down. The interface also specifies events for key presses: there's the `keyPressEvent` that tells you when the user has pressed a key, along with the `focusInEvent` and `focusOut` events that indicate when the widget gains and loses keyboard focus, respectively.

The header file looks much simpler, as we can see in the following code block:

```
#include <QWidget>
#include <QTimer>
#include <QTime>
#include <QPainter>

class AnalogClock : public QWidget
{
    Q_OBJECT
public:
    explicit AnalogClock(QWidget *parent = nullptr);
    void paintEvent(QPaintEvent *);
signals:
public slots:
    void update();
};
```

The following screenshot shows the clock face in action:

 For more information about the `QWidget` interface and creating custom widgets, see the `QWidget` documentation at `https://doc.qt.io/qt-5/qwidget.html` and the Qt event system documentation at `https://doc.qt.io/qt-5/eventsandfilters.html`.

In this section, we have learned how to create a real-time analog clock display, using Qt's paint event. Let's move on to the next section, and learn how to create a simple 2D game, using Qt's Graphics View framework!

Introducing the Graphics View framework

Qt provides a separate view framework, the Graphics View framework, to draw hundreds or thousands of relatively lightweight customized items at once. You will choose the Graphics View framework if you're implementing your own widget set from scratch (although you might want to consider Qt Quick for this as well), or if you have a large number of items to display on the screen at once, each with their own position and data. This is especially important for applications that process and display a great deal of data, such as geographic information systems or computer-aided design applications.

In the Graphics View framework, Qt defines the scene, responsible for providing a fast interface to a large number of items. (If you remember our discussion of **Model-View-Controller** (**MVC**) from the previous chapter, you can think of the scene as the model for the view renderer.) The scene also distributes events to the items it contains and manages the state of individual items in the scene. QGraphicsScene is the Qt class responsible for the implementation of the scene. You can think of QGraphicsScene as a container of drawable items, each a subclass of QGraphicsItem.

Your QGraphicsItem subclass can be used to override the drawing and event handling for each item, and you can then add your custom items to your QGraphicsScene class by calling the addItem method QGraphicsScene. QGraphicsScene offers an items method that returns a collection of items contained by or intersecting with a point, a rectangle, a polygon, or a general vector path. Under the hood, QGraphicsScene uses a binary space partitioning tree (see Wikipedia's article on BSP trees at http://en.wikipedia.org/wiki/Binary_space_partitioning), for very fast searching of the item hierarchy by position.

Within the scene are one or more QGraphicsItem subclass instances, representing graphical items in the scene; Qt defines some simple subclasses for rendering, but you'll probably need to create your own. Qt provides the following:

- QGraphicsRectItem: This is used to render rectangles.
- QGraphicsEllipseItem: This is used to render ellipses.
- QGraphicsTextItem: This is used to render text.

Let us understand each here:

QGraphicsItem provides an interface you can override in your subclass to manage the mouse and keyboard events, drag and drop, interface hierarchies, and collision detection. Each item resides in its own local coordinate system, and helper functions provide you with fast transformations between an item's coordinates and the scene's coordinates.

The Graphics View framework uses one or more QGraphicsView instances to display the contents of a QGraphicsScene class. You can attach several views to the same scene, each with their own translation and rotation, to see different parts of the scene. The QGraphicsView widget is a scroll area, so you can also hook scroll bars to the view and let the user scroll around the view. The view receives input from the keyboard and the mouse, generating scene events for the scene, and dispatching those scene events to the scene, which then dispatches those same events to the items in the scene.

The Graphics View framework is ideally suited to creating games, and, in fact, Qt's sample source code is just that, a towers-and-spaceships sample application you can see at https:/ /wiki.qt.io/Towers_lasers_and_spacecrafts_example. The game, if you will, is simple, and is played by the computer; the stationary towers shoot the oncoming moving spaceships, as you can see in the following screenshot:

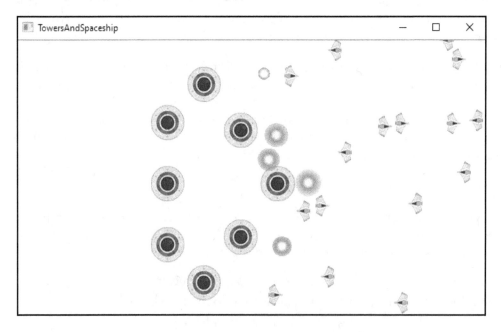

Let's look at bits from this sample application, to get a feel of how the Graphics View framework actually works.

The core of the game is a game timer that updates the positions of mobile units; the application's entry point sets up the timer, QGraphicsView, and a subclass of QGraphicsScene that will be responsible for tracking the state. For this, consider the following code:

```
#include "mainwindow.h"

#include <QApplication>
#include <QGraphicsView>
#include "scene.h"
#include "simpletower.h"

int main(int argc, char *argv[])
{
    QApplication app(argc, argv);
    Scene scene;
    scene.setSceneRect(0,0,640,360);
    QGraphicsView view(&scene);
    QTimer timer;
    QObject::connect(&timer, &QTimer::timeout, &scene,
      &Scene::advance);
    view.show();
    timer.start(10);
    return app.exec();
}
```

The timer kicks over every 10 milliseconds and is connected to the scene's advance slot, responsible for advancing the game's state. The QGraphicsView class is the rendering window for the entire scene; it takes an instance of the Scene object from which it's going to render. The application's main function initializes the view, scene, and timer, starts the timer, and then passes control to Qt's event loop.

The Scene class has two methods: its constructor, which creates some non-moving towers in the scene, and the advance method, which advances the scene's one-time tick, triggered each time that the timer in the main function elapses. Let's look at the constructor first, as follows:

```
#include "scene.h"
#include "mobileunit.h"
#include "simpletower.h"
#include <QDebug>

Scene::Scene(): QGraphicsScene(), ticTacTime(0)
{
    SimpleTower * simpleTower = new SimpleTower();
    simpleTower->setPos(200.0, 100.0);
```

```
    addItem(simpleTower);

    simpleTower = new SimpleTower();
    simpleTower->setPos(200.0, 180.0);
    addItem(simpleTower);

    simpleTower = new SimpleTower();
    simpleTower->setPos(200.0, 260.0);
    addItem(simpleTower);

    simpleTower = new SimpleTower();
    simpleTower->setPos(250.0, 050.0);
    addItem(simpleTower);
```

We continue to create more `SimpleTower` objects, and initialize them using `setPos` and `addItem`, as follows:

```
    simpleTower = new SimpleTower();
    simpleTower->setPos(250.0, 310.0);
    addItem(simpleTower);

    simpleTower = new SimpleTower();
    simpleTower->setPos(300.0, 110.0);
    addItem(simpleTower);

    simpleTower = new SimpleTower();
    simpleTower->setPos(300.0, 250.0);
    addItem(simpleTower);

    simpleTower = new SimpleTower();
    simpleTower->setPos(350.0, 180.0);
    addItem(simpleTower);
}
```

Pretty boring—it just creates instances of the static towers and sets their positions, adding each one to the scene with the `addItem` method. Before we look at the `SimpleTower` class, let's look at the `Scene` class's `advance` method, shown in the following code block:

```
void Scene::advance()
{
    ticTacTime++;

    // delete killed objects
    QGraphicsItem* item = nullptr;
    MobileUnit* unit = nullptr;
    int i = 0;

    while (i < items().count())
```

```
{
    item = items().at(i);
    unit = dynamic_cast<MobileUnit*>(item);
    if ((unit != nullptr) && (unit->getIsFinished() == true))
    {
        removeItem(item);
        delete unit;
    }
    else
        ++i;
}
```

After that, we add a new unit every 20 ticks, like this:

```
// Add new units every 20 tictacs
if (ticTacTime % 20 == 0)
{
    // qDebug() << "add unit";
    MobileUnit* mobileUnit= new MobileUnit();
    qreal h = static_cast<qreal>(qrand() % static_cast<int>
        (height()));
    mobileUnit->setPos(width(), h);
    addItem(mobileUnit);
}

QGraphicsScene::advance();
update();
}
```

From the preceding code, we see that the method has two key sections, described here:

- The first section deletes any mobile units that have expired for some reason (such as their health dropping to 10). This works by looping over all the items in the scene and testing to see whether each is a `MobileUnit` instance. If it is, the code tests its `isFinished` function, and, if it's true, removes the item from the scene and frees it.
- The second section runs once every 20 passes through the `advance` method and creates a new `MobileUnit` object, randomly placing it on the right-hand side of the display. Finally, the method calls the inherited `advance` method, which triggers an advance call to each item in the scene, followed by calling `update`, which triggers a redraw of the scene.

Let's look at the `QGraphicsItem` subclass of `SimpleTower` next. First, let's look at the `SimpleTower` constructor, shown in the following code block:

```
#include <QPainter>
#include <QGraphicsScene>
#include "simpletower.h"
#include "mobileunit.h"

SimpleTower::SimpleTower(): QGraphicsRectItem()
, detectionDistance(100.0), time(0, 0)
, reloadTime(100), shootIsActive(false)
, target(nullptr), towerImage(QImage(":/lightTower.png"))
{
    setRect(-15.0, -15.0, 30.0, 30.0);
    time.start();
}
```

The constructor sets the bounds for the tower and starts a time counter, used to determine the interval between the times that the tower fires at oncoming ships.

`QgraphicsItem` instances do their drawing in their `paint` method; the `paint` method takes the `QPainter` pointer you'll use to render the item, along with a pointer to the rendering options for the item and the owning widget in the hierarchy. Here's the `paint` method of `SimpleTower`:

```
void SimpleTower::paint(QPainter *painter, const QStyleOptionGraphicsItem
*option, QWidget* widget)
{
    painter->drawImage(-15, -15, towerImage);
    if ((target != nullptr) && (shootIsActive))
    { // laser beam
        QPointF towerPoint = mapFromScene(pos());
        QPointF theTarget = mapFromScene(target->pos());
        painter->setPen(QPen(Qt::yellow,8.0,Qt::SolidLine));
        painter->drawLine(towerPoint.x(), towerPoint.y(),
          theTarget.x(), theTarget.y());
        painter->setPen(QPen(Qt::red,5.0,Qt::SolidLine));
        painter->drawLine(towerPoint.x(), towerPoint.y(),
          theTarget.x(), theTarget.y());
        painter->setPen(QPen(Qt::white,2.0,Qt::SolidLine));
        painter->drawLine(towerPoint.x(), towerPoint.y(),
          theTarget.x(), theTarget.y());
        shootIsActive = false;
    }
}
```

The `paint` method has to draw two things: the tower itself, which is a static image loaded at construction time (drawn with `drawImage`), and, if the tower is shooting at a target, it draws colored lines between the tower and the mobile unit targeted by the tower.

Next, we will move on, to learn about the `advance` method, shown in the following code block:

```
void SimpleTower::advance(int phase)
{
    if (phase == 0)
    {
        searchTarget();
        if ((target != nullptr) && (time.elapsed() > reloadTime))
            shoot();
    }
}
```

Each time the scene advances, each tower searches for a target, and if one is selected, it shoots at the target. The scene graph invokes each item's `advance` method twice for each advance, passing an integer, indicating whether the items in the scene are about to advance (indicated when the `phase` argument is 0), or that the items in the scene have advanced (indicated when the `phase` segment is 1).

The `searchTarget` method looks for the closest target within the detection distance, and, if it finds one, sets the tower's target pointer to the closest unit in the range, as follows:

```
void SimpleTower::searchTarget()
{
    target = nullptr;
    QList<QGraphicsItem*> itemList = scene()->items();
    int i = itemList.count() - 1;
    qreal dx, dy, sqrDist;
    qreal sqrDetectionDist = detectionDistance * detectionDistance;
    MobileUnit* unit = nullptr;
    while((i >= 0) && (nullptr == target) )
    {
        QGraphicsItem * item = itemList.at(i);
        unit = dynamic_cast<MobileUnit*>(item);
        if ((unit != nullptr) && (unit->getLifePoints() > 0))
        {
            dx = unit->x() - x();
            dy = unit->y() - y();
            sqrDist = dx * dx + dy * dy;
            if (sqrDist < sqrDetectionDist)
                target=unit;
        }
```

```
            --i;
        }
    }
```

Note that we cache a pointer to the targeted unit and adjust its position because, in subsequent frames, the targeted unit will move. Finally, the `shoot` method, which simply sets the Boolean flag used by `paint` to indicate that the shooting graphic should be drawn, indicates to the target that it's been damaged. The following code shows this:

```
void SimpleTower::shoot()
{
    shootIsActive=true;
    target->touched(3);
    time.restart();
}
```

This restarts the timer used to track the time between subsequent shots taken by the timer. Finally, let's look at the `MobileUnit` class that renders the individual moving spaceships in the scene. Follow these steps:

1. Firstly, we define the `include` directives, and then the constructor, as follows:

```
#include "mobileunit.h"
#include <QPainter>
#include <QGraphicsScene>
#include <math.h>

MobileUnit::MobileUnit(): QGraphicsRectItem()
, lifePoints(10), alpha(0)
, dirX(1.0), dirY(0.0)
, speed(1.0), isFinished(false)
, isExploding(false), explosionDuration(500)
, redExplosion(0.0, 0.0, 20.0, 0.0, 0.0), time(0, 0)
, spacecraftImage(QImage(":/spacecraft00.png") )
{
    alpha = static_cast<qreal>(qrand() % 90 + 60);
    qreal speed = static_cast<qreal>(qrand()% 10 - 5);
    dirY = cos(alpha / 180.0 * M_PI );
    dirX = sin(alpha / 180.0 * M_PI);
    alpha = -alpha * 180.0 ;
    speed = 1.0 + speed * 0.1;
    setRect(-10.0, -10.0, 20.0, 20.0);
    time.start();

    redExplosion.setColorAt(0.0, Qt::white);
    redExplosion.setColorAt(0.2, QColor(255, 255, 100, 255));
    redExplosion.setColorAt(0.4, QColor(255, 80, 0, 200));
```

```
    redExplosion.setColorAt(1.0, QColor(255, 255, 255, 0));
}
```

The constructor's a little more complex than the one for the stationary units. It needs to set an initial heading and speed for the mobile unit. Then, it sets the bounds for the unit and a timer to control its own behavior. If the unit is disabled, it'll explode; we will draw the explosion with concentric circles in a radial gradient, so we need to set the colors at the various points in the gradient.

2. Next is the `paint` method, which paints the unit or its explosion if it's been damaged, shown in the following code block:

```
void MobileUnit::paint(QPainter *painter, const
QStyleOptionGraphicsItem* option, QWidget* widget)
{
    painter->setPen(Qt::NoPen);

    if (!isExploding)
    {
        painter->rotate(alpha);
        painter->drawImage(-15, -14, spacecraftImage);
    }
    else
    {
        painter->setBrush(QBrush(redExplosion));
        qreal explosionRadius = 8.0 + time.elapsed() / 50;
        painter->drawEllipse(-explosionRadius, -explosionRadius,
2.0 * explosionRadius, 2.0 * explosionRadius);
    }
}
```

This is pretty straightforward: if the unit isn't exploding, it just sets the rotation for the image to be drawn and draws the image; otherwise, it draws the circle explosion with the radial gradient brush we configured in the constructor.

3. After that is the `advance` method, which is responsible for moving the ship from one frame to the next, as well as tracking the state of an exploding ship, shown in the following code block:

```
void MobileUnit::advance(int phase)
{
    if (phase==0)
    {
        qreal xx = x(); qreal yy = y();
        if ( (xx < 0.0) || (xx > scene()->width() ) )
        { // rebond
            dirX = -dirX;
```

```
                alpha = -alpha;
            }
            if ( (yy < 0.0) || (yy > scene()->height()))
            { // rebond
                dirY = -dirY;
                alpha = 180 - alpha;
            }
            if (isExploding)
            {
                speed *= 0.98; // decrease speed
                if (time.elapsed() > explosionDuration)
                    isFinished = true; // is dead
            }
            setPos(x() + dirX * speed, y() + dirY * speed);
        }
    }
```

For simplicity's sake, the `advance` method causes items at the edge of the scene to rebound off of the margins by reversing the direction and orientation. If an item is exploding, it slows down, and if the elapsed time in the timer is longer than the explosion duration, the method sets a flag indicating that the item should be removed from the scene during the next scene advance. Finally, this method updates the position of the item by adding the product of the direction and the speed to each coordinate.

4. Finally, the `touched` method decrements the health points of the mobile unit by the indicated amount, as shown in the following code block:

```
void MobileUnit::touched (int hurtPoints)
{
    lifePoints -= hurtPoints; // decrease life
    if (lifePoints < 0)
        lifePoints = 0;
    if (lifePoints == 0)
    {
        time.start();
        isExploding = true;
    }
}
```

If the unit's health points go to zero, it starts the explosion timer and sets the explosion flag.

 For more documentation about the Graphics View framework, see the Qt documentation at `https://doc.qt.io/qt-5/graphicsview.html`.

That's it; we have successfully created a simple game using Qt's Graphics View framework. You may expand the project further and turn it into a full-fledged game, and perhaps release it on the App Store!

Summary

In this chapter, we learned how to draw graphics on screen and off screen, using the `QPainter` class. We also learned how to create our own custom widget in Qt. Then, we explored the Graphics View framework and created a simple game.

Throughout this chapter, we have learned how Qt provides the `QPaintDevice` interface and `QPainter` class to perform graphics operations. Using `QPaintDevice` subclasses such as `QWidget`, `QImage`, and `QPixmap`, you can perform onscreen and offscreen drawing. We also saw how Qt provides a separate viewable object hierarchy for large numbers of lightweight objects through the Graphics View framework, supported by the classes `QGraphicsView` and `QGraphicsScene`, and the `QGraphicsItem` interface.

In the next chapter, we turn from Qt's support for GUIs in C++ to that of Qt Quick. We'll learn about the fundamental Qt Quick constructs, performing animations and other transitions in Qt Quick, and how to integrate Qt Quick with a C++ application.

7
Doing More with Qt Quick

As you saw in `Chapter 3`, *Designing Your Application with Qt Designer*, Qt Quick is Qt's declarative environment for application development. Qt Quick is ideal for fluid, animated user interfaces where you're working more with touch and mouse events, and where the style of your application is based on graphical resources instead of the need to mirror the host platform's widget set.

Qt Quick provides several basic graphical elements and the ability to combine them using a scripting language based on JavaScript, giving you the ability to tap existing skills in web design to create user experiences that are impossible to create entirely in HTML and CSS without a great deal of additional work. However, you can be empowered to do even more with Qt Quick by using some of its other features that we have not explored in the previous chapter. Let's see what else we can achieve using Qt Quick!

In this chapter, we will take a look at Qt Quick in more detail than we did in `Chapter 3`, *Designing Your Application with Qt Designer*.

In this chapter, we will cover the following:

- Understanding the fundamental concepts of Qt Quick
- Using states and transitions in Qt Quick
- Integrating Qt Quick and C++
- Putting it all together – an image gallery application
- Introducing new Qt Quick Controls 2
- Understanding the new graphical editor for SCXML

Technical requirements

The technical requirements for this chapter include Qt 5.13.1 MinGW 64-bit, Qt Creator 4.10.0, and Windows 10.

The GitHub link for this chapter can be found here:

`https://github.com/PacktPublishing/Application-Development-with-Qt-Creator-Third-Edition/tree/master/Chapter07`.

Understanding the fundamental concepts of Qt Quick

As you saw in `Chapter 3`, *Designing Your Application with Qt Designer*, Qt Quick enables you to focus on declaring what's visible on the screen and how it should behave, rather than creating objects. Qt Quick uses the **Qt Modeling Language** (**QML**) to do this, which uses a JavaScript-like syntax and a tree structure to define visible objects and their relationships, as well as script their behavior. Objects have a strict parent-child hierarchy that defines their visual relationship; parent objects contain their children on display.

To create a new Qt Quick project, go to **File** | **New File or Project** | **Qt Quick Application - Empty**.

Objects are placed in Qt Quick's main window using the traditional coordinate system, with **(0, 0)** in the upper left-hand corner of the display. Child objects can be placed in their parents either using coordinates relative to the upper left-hand corner of the parent or through a flexible system of anchors against object boundaries.

Each item has seven invisible anchor lines: `left`, `horizontalCenter`, `right`, `top`, `verticalCenter`, `bottom`, and `baseline`. All of these are self-explanatory, except `baseline`, which corresponds to the line on which text will sit. (For items with no text, Qt defines the baseline to be the same as the `top` anchor line.) Anchors are relative to other objects; each of the anchor lines is a field in the anchor field, and you can set it to the anchor line of another object. For example, let's write the following:

```
import QtQuick 2.12
import QtQuick.Window 2.12

Window {
    visible: true
    width: 360
```

```
height: 360
Rectangle {
    id: rect1
    height: 100
    width: 100
    anchors.centerIn: parent
    color: "gray"
}
Rectangle {
    id: rect2
    height: 100
    width: 100
    anchors.left: rect1.right
    anchors.top: rect1.top
    color: "black"
}
}
```

In the preceding code, we have created two `Rectangle` objects, namely, `rect1` and `rect2`. The `rect1` object is tinted in gray and positioned at the center of its parent, which is the application window. Then, we position the `rect2` object to the right of `rect1` and align its vertical position the same as `rect1`.

This produces the following output:

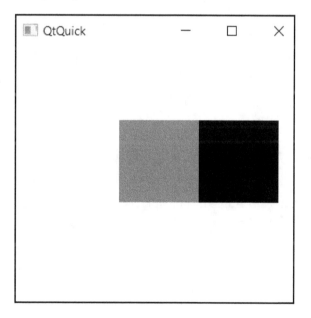

This code creates a window of 360 pixels in height and width, and two rectangles. Qt places the first rectangle centered in the parent window, and it places the second rectangle to the right-hand side of the first one with the same top lines.

Anchoring doesn't just affect placement, but it can affect sizing too. Consider the following QML:

```
import QtQuick 2.12
import QtQuick.Window 2.12

Window {
    visible: true
    width: 360
    height: 360

    Rectangle {
        id: rect1
        height: 100
        width: 100
        anchors.left: parent.left;
        anchors.verticalCenter: parent.verticalCenter
        color: "gray"
    }

    Rectangle {
        id: rect2
        anchors.left: rect1.right
        anchors.top: rect1.top;
        anchors.bottom: rect1.bottom
        anchors.right: rect3.left
        color: "black"
    }

    Rectangle {
        id: rect3
        height: 100
        width: 100
        anchors.right: parent.right;
        anchors.verticalCenter: parent.verticalCenter
        color: "gray"
    }
}
```

This places two squares on either side of the parent window, with a rectangle stretched between the two squares. Note that the `anchor.left` parameter of `rect2` is set to the `rect1.right` value, and `anchor.right` of `rect2` is set to the `rect3.left` value. The following screenshot shows how it looks:

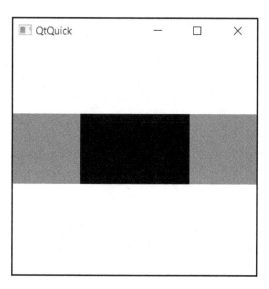

For more complex layouts, Qt Quick defines four positioning elements: `Column`, `Row`, `Grid`, and `Flow`. These behave much as you'd expect:

- `Column`: This lays out its children in a vertical column.
- `Row`: This lays out its children in a horizontal strip.
- `Grid`: This lays out its children in a grid.
- `Flow`: This lays out its children side by side, wrapping the elements if necessary.

The following code uses the `Flow` element to arrange the `Rectangle` objects evenly according to the window size:

```
import QtQuick 2.12
import QtQuick.Window 2.12

Window {
    visible: true
    width: 360
    height: 360

    Flow {
        anchors.fill: parent
```

```
        anchors.margins: 4
        spacing: 10

        Rectangle { height: 40; width: 40; color: "gray" }
        Rectangle { height: 40; width: 40; color: "black" }
        Rectangle { height: 40; width: 40; color: "gray" }
        Rectangle { height: 40; width: 40; color: "black" }
        Rectangle { height: 40; width: 40; color: "gray" }
        Rectangle { height: 40; width: 40; color: "black" }
        Rectangle { height: 40; width: 40; color: "gray" }
        Rectangle { height: 40; width: 40; color: "black" }
        Rectangle { height: 40; width: 40; color: "gray" }
    }
  }
```

This produces a flow of rectangles from the left to the right, spaced by a margin of ten pixels and with a four-pixel margin on the left-hand side, as follows:

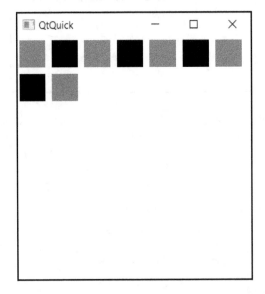

In general, you should use anchoring layouts and the more complex Row, Column, Grid, and Flow elements whenever you don't have total control over the target hardware. Relative-spaced layouts leave Qt making the layout decisions at runtime, so you don't end up with a weird space on big screens or with layouts that overflow the boundaries of small screens. Of course, it takes a little more thought at design time, because you'll need to determine the relative spacing of various items, allocating the maximum space to the items that require it.

Qt Quick defines several visible elements besides `Rectangle`, of course. Visual types include the following:

- `Window`: This is the top-level window for an application.
- `Item`: This is the basic visual object type inherited by all visible objects.
- `Image`: This is used to render bitmaps.
- `AnimatedImage`: This is used to play animated GIF images.
- `AnimatedSprite`: This is used to play animated images stored as a sequence of sprites in a single image.
- `Text`: This is used to draw text in a scene.

All of these require you to import the `QtQuick` module, except `Window`, which requires `QtQuick.Window`. The present version of this module at the time of writing is 2.2, but you can check the documentation for information about specific versions.

Classes such as the `Image` class have a `source` attribute that takes a URL from where it fetches its content. Typically, your images come from either the resource segment of your application or the web; if you need to load them from other sources or create them dynamically, you can provide an image provider. (I'll show you how to do this in the example at the end of this chapter.)

There's also `WebEngineView`, a control built using Qt WebEngine that you can include in your QML and that can render web content. Unlike the other visual elements, you need to import it using `import QtWebEngine` and enable the `webengine` module in the project file to have access to `WebEngineView`. A viewer for a web page in QML is as simple as this:

```
import QtQuick 2.12
import QtQuick.Window 2.12
import QtWebEngine 1.8

Window {
    visible: true
    width: 640
    height: 480

    WebEngineView {
        anchors.top: parent.top;
        anchors.left: parent.left
        anchors.right: parent.right;
        anchors.bottom: parent.bottom;
        id: web
        url: "http://www.zhieng.com"
    }
}
```

The preceding code produces the following result:

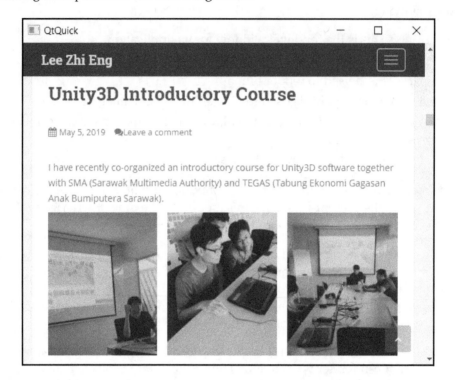

Note that the current version of the Qt WebEngine module only works with MSVC compiler under windows and not any other compilers. This is because the Chromium engine in the Qt WebEngine module has not been ported to other compilers, so we can only use MSVC for now.

Rather than handling user input through event methods, as Qt widgets do, QML defines a collection of objects that accept input. These objects include the following:

- `MouseArea`: This is used for mouse clicks and movement.
- `Keys`: This is used for handling keystrokes.
- `KeyNavigation`: This is used for handling arrow navigation.
- `Flickable`: This is used for handling the flicks of the mouse or touch flicks for scrolling.
- `PinchArea`: This is used for handling pinch-to-zoom or other two-fingered interaction.

- MultiPointTouchArea: This is used for handling generic multi-touch input.
- Drag: This is used for handling drag-and-drop events for visual items.
- DropArea: This is used for accepting items dropped from drag areas.
- TextInput: This is used for capturing free-form text input in a simple input field.
- TextEdit: This is used for multi-line text input.

Each of these defines signals to which you can bind JavaScript, as you saw in Chapter 3, *Designing Your Application with Qt Designer*. For example, MouseArea defines the following signals:

- onClicked: This is emitted when the user clicks on the mouse area.
- onDoubleClicked: This is emitted when the user double-clicks on the mouse area.
- onEntered: This is emitted when the user moves the mouse pointer into the mouse area.
- onExited: This is emitted when the user moves the mouse pointer out of the mouse area.
- onPressed: This is emitted when the user presses down on the mouse in the mouse area.
- onReleased: This is emitted when the user releases the mouse button in the mouse area.
- onWheel: This is emitted when the user manipulates the mouse scroll wheel in the mouse area.

Signals are accompanied by an event containing the specifics of the signal; for example, the MouseArea element sends the MouseEvent events to the signal handlers. These aren't arguments to the bound JavaScript but appear as special variables in the JavaScript.

Qt Quick also defines some other views for user interaction that require data models; these are as follows:

- ListView: As you can imagine, ListView lays out its items in a vertical or horizontal list.
- GridView: This lays out its items in gridPathView. PathView takes an arbitrary path and lays its items out on the path that you provide.

All of these use `ListModel` to contain their data, following the MVC pattern we discussed in the previous chapter. When you do this, you bind the view to the model using the QML binding, and the view relies on model changes to show the changes in the model. You can provide items for your `ListModel` container in Qt Quick or supply a subclass of `QAbstractItemModel` and provide your own data through the Qt Quick C++ bindings. (I will discuss how to bind QML and C++ later in this chapter, in the *Integrating Qt Quick and C++* section.) These views are fully touch-enabled, supporting flicks and inertial scrolling. They use the model and a delegate to perform the drawing; the delegate is just a QML `Item` element that references the field in the model. For example, this QML creates a list with three elements, each with two fields, `name` and `number`:

```
import QtQuick 2.12
import QtQuick.Window 2.12

Window {
    visible: true
    width: 360
    height: 360

    ListModel {
        id: model
        ListElement {
            name: "Bill Smith"
            number: "555 3264"
        }
        ListElement {
            name: "John Brown"
            number: "555 8426"
        }
        ListElement {
            name: "Sam Wise"
            number: "555 0473"
        }
    }

    ListView {
        model: model
        anchors.top: parent.top;
        anchors.bottom: parent.bottom;
        anchors.left: parent.left;
        anchors.right: parent.right;
        delegate: Item {
            width: 180
            height: 100
            Column {
                Text { text: name }
```

```
                    Text { text: number }
                }
            }
        }
    }
}
```

The `ListModel` container is just that: the list of data for `ListView`. The `ListView` delegate is an `Item` element, with `Column` containing two text fields. Note how the text for each field is just the field name in the `ListModel` fields. The preceding code produces the following result:

Of course, we can split this into three files. We can save `ListModel` in a file called `ContactModel.qml` and the delegate item in a file called `ListModelDelegate.qml`, as follows:

```
// ContactModel.qml
import QtQuick 2.12

ListModel {
    id: model
    ListElement {
        name: "Bill Smith"
        number: "555 3264"
    }
    ListElement {
        name: "John Brown"
        number: "555 8426"
    }
    ListElement {
        name: "Sam Wise"
        number: "555 0473"
```

```
        }
    }

// ListModelDelegate.qml
import QtQuick 2.12

Item {
    width: 180
    height: 100
    Column {
        Text { text: name }
        Text { text: number }
    }
}
```

Then, our main application will look similar to the following code:

```
import QtQuick 2.12
import QtQuick.Window 2.12

Window {
    visible: true
    width: 360
    height: 360

    ListView {
        model: ContactModel {}
        anchors.top: parent.top;
        anchors.bottom: parent.bottom;
        anchors.left: parent.left;
        anchors.right: parent.right;
        delegate: ListModelDelegate {}
    }
}
```

Dividing up your QML into separate files is a good idea if you think you'll have a reusable component or when your code gets too long to follow.

That's it—we have learned how to use some of the fundamental features in Qt Quick, such as positioning elements, the web engine, and list view. This will allow you to better understand the differences between the Qt Quick project and Qt Form project while choosing the right one for your project. After this, let's move on to the next section and learn how we can create a state machine for our Qt Quick project.

Using states and transitions in Qt Quick

Traditional GUI programming often involves easy-to-write but boilerplate state machines for controls to track control and application states. For example, a button might have several states: when the mouse hovers over it; when it's pressed; and then once pressed, a separate state for on or off in the case of a checkbox or a push button. While this code isn't hard to write, it does involve some writing, and more sophisticated interfaces require more of it.

Qt Quick provides an abstraction for this through its State construct, which groups a state's name as well as the condition under which it occurs and which properties of an object should take on new values. We first saw this in Chapter 3, *Designing Your Application with Qt Designer*, when we wrote our own button component, reprinted here:

```
import QtQuick 2.12
import QtQuick.Window 2.12

Window {
 visible: true
    width: 256
    height: 256

    Rectangle
    {
        id: button

        anchors.fill: parent

        property alias operation: buttonText.text
        signal clicked

        color: "green"

        Rectangle {
            id: shade
            anchors.fill: button;
            color: "black";
            opacity: 0
        }
}
```

We continue to write the remainder of the code here:

```
Text {
    id: buttonText
    anchors.centerIn: parent;
    color: "white"
    font.pointSize: 16
}

MouseArea {
    id: mouseArea
    anchors.fill: parent
    onClicked: {
        button.clicked();
    }
}

states: State {
    name: "pressed";
    when: mouseArea.pressed === true;
    PropertyChanges {
        target: shade; opacity: .4
    }
}
}
}
```

Here, the button has two states: the default state in which the shade is fully transparent, and when the user is pressing the button—represented by the pressed state—setting the shade's opacity property to 0.4. The preceding code produces the following result—the default state on the left and the pressed state on the right:

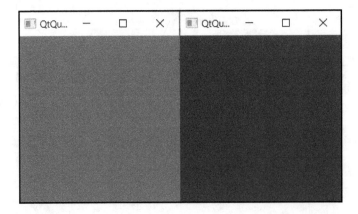

The `states` field of an item can actually be an array; another way to write these states is to declare both explicitly, shown as follows:

```
states: [
    State {
        name: "pressed"; when: mouseArea.pressed === true
        PropertyChanges { target: shade; opacity: .4 }
    },
    State {
        name: "released"; when: mouseArea.pressed !== true
        PropertyChanges { target: shade; opacity: 0.0 }
    }
]
```

Each `State` construct can have more than one `PropertyChanges` element, each with its own target and property, so you can create sophisticated state transitions using simple declarations.

Qt Quick uses transitions to control the animation of a property when a state change occurs. To create a transition, you need to define an animation; you can apply an animation on any property that can be changed, specifying the start and end values of the animation. Consider a simple animation on a mouse press such as the following:

```
import QtQuick 2.12
import QtQuick.Window 2.12

Window
{
    visible: true
  height: 360
    width: 360

    Rectangle {
        id: rect1
        width: 100; height: 100
        color: "red"

        MouseArea {
            id: mouseArea
            anchors.fill: parent
        }

        states: State {
            name: "moved"; when: mouseArea.pressed
            PropertyChanges { target: rect1; x: 100; y: 100 }
        }
```

```
        transitions: Transition {
            NumberAnimation {
                properties: "x,y"
                easing.type: Easing.InOutQuad
            }
        }
    }
}
```

The preceding code produces the following result—the default state is on the left and the pressed state on the right:

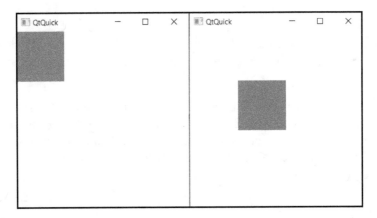

Here, the rectangle starts at the origin of the parent coordinate system, with MouseArea in the rectangle. When you press the mouse in the rectangle, the state of the rectangle changes to moved, and the rectangle's top-left corner moves to (100,100) on the parent's canvas. However, we also specify an animation, NumberAnimation, on the x and y properties, so the property change is animated to this value, with the easing curve we specify (a quadratic curve at both the start and finish of the animation). Following are some of the animation types we can use to animation our Qt Quick objects:

- There are different animations for different kinds of properties. You can use NumberAnimation to animate numeric properties, as you see here.
- There's also ColorAnimation, which animates colors, and RotationAnimation, which animates rotations.

Here's the QML to rotate a red rectangle in a half-circle when it's clicked on:

```qml
import QtQuick 2.12
import QtQuick.Window 2.12

Window
{
    visible: true
    height: 360
    width: 360

    Item {
        width: 300; height: 300

        Rectangle {
            id: rect
            width: 150; height: 100;
            anchors.centerIn: parent
            color: "red"
            antialiasing: true

            states: State {
                name: "rotated"
                PropertyChanges { target: rect; rotation: 180 }
            }

            transitions: Transition {
                RotationAnimation {
                    duration: 1000
                    direction: RotationAnimation.Counterclockwise
                }
            }
        }

        MouseArea {
            anchors.fill: parent;
            onClicked: rect.state = "rotated"
        }
    }
}
```

The preceding code produces the following result—the default state is on the left and the pressed state on the right:

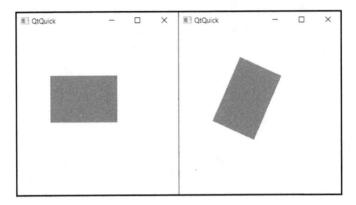

Again, the pattern is the same: we define a state with `PropertyChanges`, indicating the new property value, and then specify a transition over this property using an animation (in this case, `RotationAnimation`). Here, the transition has a duration specified in milliseconds. Note that the rotation only occurs once, and the rotation angles are bound by the values of -360 and 360 degrees.

For more information on the animation and transition framework in Qt Quick, see the Qt Quick documentation at `https://doc.qt.io/qt-5/qtquick-statesanimations-animations.html` and the Qt Quick Animation samples at `https://doc.qt.io/qt-5/qtquick-animation-example.html`.

We have learned how to make use of the state machine provided by Qt to manipulate object properties based on state transitions. Let's move on to the next section and learn how we can integrate our Qt Quick project with the C++ programming language.

Integrating Qt Quick and C++

You can run a simple Qt Quick application using the `qmlviewer` application, an application provided as part of the Qt SDK. However, most of the time, you'll create a Qt Quick application using the Qt Quick application wizard in Qt Creator, which results in a hybrid application consisting of a Qt C++ application container and QML files as resources that the application loads and plays at runtime.

If we take a look at `main.cpp` in a project that we create with this wizard, we will see the following code:

```cpp
#include <QGuiApplication>
#include <QQmlApplicationEngine>

int main(int argc, char *argv[])
{
    QCoreApplication::setAttribute(Qt::AA_EnableHighDpiScaling);

    QGuiApplication app(argc, argv);

    QQmlApplicationEngine engine;
    const QUrl url(QStringLiteral("qrc:/main.qml"));
    QObject::connect(&engine, &QQmlApplicationEngine::objectCreated, &app,
        [url](QObject *obj, const QUrl &objUrl)
        {
            if (!obj && url == objUrl)
                QCoreApplication::exit(-1);
        }, Qt::QueuedConnection);
    engine.load(url);

    return app.exec();
}
```

This is pretty straightforward: it creates an instance of `QQmlApplicationEngine`, a class that inherits from `QGuiApplication`, and instantiates a top-level window containing a single instance of `QQmlEngine`, the Qt Quick playing engine. Among other things, the `QQmlEngine` class keeps an object called the root context that's a list of all named properties in the QML environment. We can access this root context and add any Qt object to it that we wish.

For example, let's create a native C++ object with a property, shown as follows:

```cpp
#ifndef NATIVEOBJECT_H
#define NATIVEOBJECT_H

#include <QObject>

class NativeObject : public QObject
{
    Q_OBJECT

public:
    explicit NativeObject(QObject *parent = nullptr) :
    QObject(parent)
    {
```

```
        m_text = "Hello world!";
    }

    Q_PROPERTY(QString text READ text)
    const QString& text() { return m_text; }
private:
    QString m_text;

};

#endif // NATIVEOBJECT_H
```

We can instantiate and bind one of these to the QML engine's root context when the application starts. To do this, we simply create one and then call the setContextProperty method of rootContext, passing an instance of our object and the name to which the engine should bind it, as follows:

```
#include <QGuiApplication>
#include <QQmlApplicationEngine>
#include <QQmlContext>

#include "nativeobject.h"

int main(int argc, char *argv[])
{
    QCoreApplication::setAttribute(Qt::AA_EnableHighDpiScaling);
    QGuiApplication app(argc, argv);
    QQmlApplicationEngine engine;

    NativeObject object;
    engine.rootContext()->setContextProperty("object",
    dynamic_cast<QObject*>(&object));

    const QUrl url(QStringLiteral("qrc:/main.qml"));
    QObject::connect(&engine, &QQmlApplicationEngine::objectCreated,
      &app, [url](QObject *obj, const QUrl &objUrl)
    {
        if (!obj && url == objUrl)
            QCoreApplication::exit(-1);
    }, Qt::QueuedConnection);
    engine.load(url);

    return app.exec();
}
```

Then, we can access this object using the `object` name anywhere in our QML, as follows:

```
import QtQuick 2.12
import QtQuick.Window 2.12

Window
{
    visible: true
    height: 360
    width: 360

    Text {
        anchors.top: parent.top
        anchors.horizontalCenter: parent.horizontalCenter
        text: object.text
    }
}
```

Here, the `Text` property of our object is dereferenced by the QML engine and used for the text value of the text field in our QML.

This is especially handy for list models; we can create arbitrarily complex models using the filesystem or network resources in C++ and then assign them as the models for the `ListView`, `GridView`, or `PathView` objects, giving us the ability to create a rich user interface in Qt Quick while leveraging Qt's MVC and flexible network architecture. We'll do this in the next section when we create a custom model to store the image data in a hybrid multimedia capture application.

 For more information about how Qt Quick binds with C++, see the documentation for the `QQmlContext` class at `https://doc.qt.io/qt-5/qqmlcontext.html` and `https://doc.qt.io/qt-5/qtquick-modelviewsdata-cppmodels.html`.

Putting it all together – an image gallery application

Let's apply what we've discussed in the last few chapters by putting together a simple image gallery application, like the photo gallery on smartphones. We'll display images from the system's directory in a grid, letting the user flick to scroll the images. Here's how our application will look:

To do this, we need the following components:

- A model containing the paths to the images to be displayed
- A controller responsible for creating the model
- An image provider that can load the images from the system's image directory
- The QML UI

Let's take a look at the application's QML first:

```
import QtQuick 2.12
import QtQuick.Window 2.12

Window {
    visible: true
    width: 1080 / 2
    height: 1920 / 2

    Item {
        anchors.top: parent.top
        anchors.left: parent.left
        anchors.bottom: parent.bottom
        anchors.right: parent.right
        clip: true
```

In the preceding code, we created the application window and an `Item` object, which acts as the parent object for our `GridView` object. After that, we will define `GridView`, which loads the image files from the source location we defined, as follows:

```
GridView {
    id: grid
    anchors.fill: parent;
    cellHeight: 190
    cellWidth: 250
    model: ListModel {}
    delegate: Image {
        width: 240; height: 180
        fillMode: Image.PreserveAspectFit
        source: "image://file/" + path
    }
}
}
```

We then create a `Timer` object to trigger our C++ function after 10 milliseconds:

```
Timer {
    interval: 10
    running: true
    repeat: false
    onTriggered: {
        controller.deferredInit()
        grid.model = model
    }
}
}
```

There's `GridView` with a delegate that uses a single `Image` element to show each element in the gallery. By specifying a URL beginning with `image`, we tell the Qt Quick engine that we want to use a custom image provider; in this case, it is the file image provider that we'll provide at the time of initialization in our `main` function. The images in the grid will be scaled to fit the grid cells, preserving the aspect ratio of the image. The grid begins with an empty list model, which we'll swap for an initialized list model once the timer fires after startup and instructs the controller to initialize the model.

The timer startup is a bit of a hack; the reason for this is that we're going to use a filesystem class that relies on Qt's multithreading to monitor the image directory, and the Qt multithreading system won't be initialized until after we enter the application's main loop. So, we start the main loop, initialize the QML, and then initialize the application controller, which will initialize the model and obtain a list of image files from the directory.

The application's main entry point creates the controller and the model, along with the image provider and binds them to the Qt Quick engine, shown as follows:

```cpp
#include <QGuiApplication>
#include <QQmlApplicationEngine>
#include <QDir>
#include <QQmlContext>

#include "imagegallerycontroller.h"
#include "imagegallerymodel.h"
#include "fileimageprovider.h"

int main(int argc, char *argv[])
{
    QGuiApplication app(argc, argv);
    QQmlApplicationEngine engine;

    ImageGalleryController *controller = new
        ImageGalleryController(&engine);
    ImageGalleryModel *model = controller->model();

    QQmlContext *context = engine.rootContext();
    context->setContextProperty("controller", controller);
    context->setContextProperty("model", model);
    engine.addImageProvider(QLatin1String("file"),
    new FileImageProvider(QQuickImageProvider::Pixmap));
```

After we have initialized the custom C++ classes such as `ImageGalleryController` and `ImageGalleryModel` (which we will check out in a moment), we then initiate `main.qml` and run the application:

```
const QUrl url(QStringLiteral("qrc:/main.qml"));
QObject::connect(&engine, &QQmlApplicationEngine::objectCreated,
&app, [url](QObject *obj, const QUrl &objUrl) {
    if (!obj && url == objUrl)
        QCoreApplication::exit(-1);
}, Qt::QueuedConnection);
engine.load(url);

return app.exec();
}
```

This code creates an instance of the controller, gets a pointer to the model from the controller, and then binds both of them to the Qt Quick engine. Next, we register an instance of our custom image provider with the engine, saying that anything referred to with the base path of the file should invoke our image provider, fetching pixmaps.

An image provider can either return pixmaps or the `QImage` instances; pixmaps are slightly faster to draw. The one you return is a function of your image provider; your image provider just loads images or pixmaps from the disk and scales them to fit the display. The following code is used for this:

```
#ifndef FILEIMAGEPROVIDER_H
#define FILEIMAGEPROVIDER_H

#include <QQuickImageProvider>

class FileImageProvider : public QQuickImageProvider
{
public:
    FileImageProvider(QQuickImageProvider::ImageType type);
    QImage requestImage(const QString& id, QSize* size, const QSize&
      requestedSize);
    QPixmap requestPixmap(const QString& id, QSize* size, const QSize&
      requestedSize);
};

#endif // FILEIMAGEPROVIDER_H
```

After we have declared the functions in the header file, let's define the code in the source file:

```
#include "fileimageprovider.h"

FileImageProvider::FileImageProvider(QQuickImageProvider::ImageType type) :
    QQuickImageProvider(type)
{
}

QImage FileImageProvider::requestImage(const QString& filename, QSize*
size, const QSize& requestedSize)
{
    QImage image(filename);
    QImage result;
    if (requestedSize.isValid()) {
        result = image.scaled(requestedSize, Qt::KeepAspectRatio);
    } else {
        result = image;
    }
    *size = result.size();
    return result;
}
```

The requestPixmap function is identical to the requestImage function but returns the data in a different format:

```
QPixmap FileImageProvider::requestPixmap(const QString& filename, QSize*
size, const QSize& requestedSize)
{
    QPixmap image(filename);
    QPixmap result;

    if (requestedSize.isValid()) {
        result = image.scaled(requestedSize, Qt::KeepAspectRatio);
    } else {
        result = image;
    }
    *size = result.size();
    return result;
}
```

The image provider interface defines two methods, out of which you need to provide an implementation for at least one. The interface specifies an ID for the image, the desired size of the image, and a pointer to the actual size of the image as your method returns it, and you return either a QImage instance or a pixmap.

In this example, I have provided both implementations to give you an idea of how to do this, although you need to provide only one in your image provider.

 For more information on the interface, see the documentation at `https://doc.qt.io/qt-5/qquickimageprovider.html`.

Our implementation loads the desired image from the disk as either a pixmap or `QImage`, and if the caller provides a valid size, it resizes the image without changing the aspect ratio. After scaling, we determine the image's size, assign it to the size parameter, and then return the resulting image or pixmap.

Our application is simple so that the sole purpose of the controller is to initialize the data model; so, the controller is a very simple class:

```
#ifndef IMAGEGALLERYCONTROLLER_H
#define IMAGEGALLERYCONTROLLER_H

#include <QObject>

class ImageGalleryModel;
class QAbstractItemModel;

class ImageGalleryController : public QObject
{
    Q_OBJECT

public:
    explicit ImageGalleryController(QObject *parent = 0);
    ImageGalleryModel* model() const;

signals:

public slots:
    void deferredInit();

private:
    ImageGalleryModel *imageGalleryModel;

};

#endif // IMAGEGALLERYCONTROLLER_H
```

After we have declared the class header, let's define its functions in the source file:

```cpp
#include <QDir>
#include <QDesktopServices>
#include <QStandardPaths>

#include "imagegallerycontroller.h"
#include "imagegallerymodel.h"

ImageGalleryController::ImageGalleryController(QObject *parent) :
    QObject(parent)
{
    imageGalleryModel = new ImageGalleryModel();
}

ImageGalleryModel *ImageGalleryController::model() const
{
    return imageGalleryModel;
}

void ImageGalleryController::deferredInit()
{
    imageGalleryModel->setRootPath(QStandardPaths::standardLocations(
    QStandardPaths::PicturesLocation)[0]);
}
```

There are no surprises here: the controller creates a model on construction, and its deferred initialization sets the root path of the model to the first element in the standard locations for the system's pictures. (This is actually a little risky; some platforms might not have such a directory defined, but it's fine for this example.)

The model is where most of the application's logic resides.

First, let's take a look at the model's interface:

```cpp
#ifndef IMAGEGALLERYMODEL_H
#define IMAGEGALLERYMODEL_H

#include <QStandardItemModel>

class QFileSystemWatcher;

class ImageGalleryModel : public QStandardItemModel
{
    Q_OBJECT
public:
    enum ImageGalleryRoles {
        PathRole = Qt::UserRole + 1
```

```
    };

    explicit ImageGalleryModel(QObject *parent = nullptr);

    QHash<int, QByteArray> roleNames() const;
    void setRootPath(const QString& path);
signals:

public slots:
    void onDirectoryChanged(const QString& path);

private:
    QString path;
    QFileSystemWatcher *watcher;
};


#endif // IMAGEGALLERYMODEL_H
```

Each element in a model can store different pieces of data accessed by different roles; we define a single role, `PathRole`, which will contain the absolute path to a single image. To do this, we need to do two things: define a numeric value for the role (through the `ImageGalleryRoles` enumeration) and then provide a `roleNames` method that returns a hash of the role names indexed by the role values. Qt Quick uses the role names in the returned hash to determine how to access individual roles in a single value of the data model: by looking in the hash to find the role name, then getting the role value, and finally calling the data on the model entry with the desired role.

The model class is the largest class in the application, although even here, we use `QStandardItemModel` to actually do most of the work of the model. Here's the implementation:

```
#include "imagegallerymodel.h"
#include <QDir>
#include <QFile>
#include <QFileSystemWatcher>

ImageGalleryModel::ImageGalleryModel(QObject *parent) :
  QStandardItemModel(parent)
{
    watcher = new QFileSystemWatcher(this);
    connect(watcher, SIGNAL(directoryChanged(QString)),
        this, SLOT(onDirectoryChanged(QString)));
}

QHash<int, QByteArray> ImageGalleryModel::roleNames() const
{
    QHash<int, QByteArray> roles;
```

```
    roles[PathRole] = "path";
    return roles;
}
```

We then declare the `setRootPath` function, which allows us to set the directory of the image gallery:

```
void ImageGalleryModel::setRootPath(const QString &p)
{
    this->clear();

    if (path != "") {
        watcher->removePath(path);
    }

    path = p;
    watcher->addPath(path);

    // Sync the model
    onDirectoryChanged(path);
}
```

We then implement the `onDirectoryChanged` slot function, which is a bit long:

```
void ImageGalleryModel::onDirectoryChanged(
    const QString &path)
{
    QStringList nameFilters;
    nameFilters << "*.png" << "*.jpg";
    QDir directory(path);
    directory.setNameFilters(nameFilters);
    QStringList files = directory.entryList();

    QHash<QString, int> fileIndexes;

    // Sync the model with the list.

    // Now delete anything in the model not on the filesystem
    for(int i = 0; i < rowCount(); i++) {
        QString absolutePath = data(index(i, 0), PathRole).toString();
        QString name = directory.relativeFilePath(absolutePath);
        if (!files.contains(name)) {
            removeRow(i);
            i--;
            continue;
        }
        fileIndexes[absolutePath] = i;
    }
```

We continue to implement the `onDirectoryChanged` function. We loop through all of the files located in the source directory and obtain its absolute file path:

```
// Add anything to the model that's on disk
// and not in the model
foreach(const QString &file, files) {
    QString absolutePath = directory.absoluteFilePath(file);
    if (!fileIndexes.contains(absolutePath)) {
        QStandardItem *item = new QStandardItem();
        item->setData(absolutePath, PathRole);
        appendRow(item);
    }
  }
}
```

Let's take this method by method:

- The constructor creates an instance of `QFileSystemWatcher`, which monitors the paths you give for changes to files or directories in the background, emitting the `directoryChanged` and `fileChanged` signals for the directories or files that change, respectively. We'll initialize this watcher with the desired path in the `setPath` method.

- The `roleNames` method establishes the relationship between the name of our data role, path, and the enumeration value we use to fetch this data from the model. As noted before, Qt expects this relationship in a hash table of role enumerations and their textual names. Qt Quick will use the values in the hash to determine the appropriate roles to fetch data, so I can simply refer to the field path in my QML, and under the hood, the Qt Quick engine fetches the value from the corresponding role value.

- The `setRootPath` method must first reset the model's contents, and then if the watcher was watching a directory, stop watching the old directory before watching the directory you pass. Once the code initializes the watcher, it forces a model update by invoking the same slot that the watcher invokes (remember the `connect` instance in the constructor?) whenever the directory changes.

- The `onDirectoryChanged` slot gets a list of PNG and JPEG files in the directory it's passed; then, it synchronizes the model by first deleting anything in the model that's not on the disk and then adding anything that's on the disk to the model. As we walk through the model for the first time to process any deletes, we build a hash table of the files in the model; later, when we go to add items to the model, we can just check the hash table for entries. This is a little faster than a sequential search of the model or a list of the model's contents because a hash table search is usually faster than a sequential search.

We have successfully created an image gallery using Qt Quick. Let's move on to the next section and learn what the new features are that come with Qt Quick Control 2.

Introducing the new Qt Quick Controls 2

Ever since Qt 5.6, Qt Quick Controls 2 has been released to replace version 1, which is known to have performance issues and technical problems, which led to its deprecation. With Qt Quick Controls 2, everything has been rebuilt from scratch with performance in mind. Qt Quick Controls 2 not only run smoothly on PC, but also mobile and embedded devices.

To use Qt Quick Controls 2 in your project, perform the following steps:

1. Add the following module to your QML file:

   ```
   import QtQuick.Controls 2.12
   ```

2. If you somehow need to use Qt Quick Control 2 in your C++ code, you must first add the `quickcontrols2` module to your `qmake` project file:

   ```
   QT += quickcontrols2
   ```

3. After that, you may include the `QtQuickControls2` header in your C++ source code:

   ```
   #include <QtQuickControls2>
   ```

Following are some of the QML Types available under Qt Quick Control 2:

- **Button** – A push button allows the user to click or press on it and trigger an event.
- **CheckBox** – A checkbox can be toggled on or off to represent enabling or disabling an option.
- **ComboBox** – A combobox is a selection box that lists down options for the user to pick from.
- **TextField** – A text field is the simplest text input that allows the user to key in a single line of text.
- **TextArea** – Unlike the text field, the text area is a multi-line text input field that also supports text decoration.
- **MenuBar** – A menu bar is an array of drop-down menus located along the edge of the application window.

- **RoundButton** – The round button is identical to the button, except it supports rounded corners.
- **Slider** – Sliders allow user to manipulate a value by moving a handle along a track.
- **SpinBox** – A spin box is an integer selection box with up and down indicator buttons for manipulating the integer value.

There are many more than the ones listed here. For the full list of QML types, visit https://doc.qt.io/archives/qt-5.11/qtquick-controls2-qmlmodule.html.

Let's look at some example code applying Qt Quick Control 2 in our application:

```
import QtQuick 2.13
import QtQuick.Window 2.13
import QtQuick.Controls 2.12

ApplicationWindow {
    visible: true
    width: 200
    height: 200
    title: qsTr("Hello World")

    Button {
        text: "Push Me"
        anchors.centerIn: parent
    }
}
```

In the preceding code, we imported the QtQuick.Controls module to our QML file then created a Button object with the label **Push Me**. The result looks like the following:

Qt Quick Control 2 comes with `Default Style`, which mainly consists of gray and black colors, as shown in the preceding screenshot.

There are several other styles that you can choose for making your application match the operating system you're running. Some other options are as follows:

- **Fusion style**: `Fusion Style` is a style that looks very similar to the native widgets of a desktop operating system and is suitable to use for a desktop application.
- **Imagine style:** `Imagine Style` relies on image assets to display the widgets, which are suitable for applications that required a more customized look and feel.
- **Material style**: `Material Style` is specifically designed to make your application look like a native android application as it follows the official **Google Material Design Guidelines** entirely.
- **Universal style**: `Universal Style` makes your application look like a native Universal Windows Platform application as it follows the **Microsoft Universal Design Guidelines**.

For more information regarding all of the styles listed here, check out `https://doc.qt.io/archives/qt-5.11/qtquickcontrols2-styles.html`.

To apply the style to your application, you need to perform a few steps:

1. You need to create a file called `qtquickcontrols2.conf` and add it to your project resource. Then, add the following code to the file:

   ```
   [Controls]
   Style=Material

   [Material]
   Theme=Light
   Accent=Teal
   Primary=BlueGrey
   ```

2. Under `[Controls]`, we set our Qt Quick Control 2 style as `Material`.
3. After that, under `[Material]`, we set the colors of our material style. If we run our program again, you should see the button has changed:

Our application now looks like it's running on the Android operating system! Each style has its own distinctive configuration so you'll have to check out respective documentation to learn more it.

> To get information about various styles, please visit the following:
>
> - For Fusion Style, check out https://doc.qt.io/archives/ qt-5.11/qtquickcontrols2-fusion.html.
> - For Imagine Style, check out https://doc.qt.io/archives/ qt-5.11/qtquickcontrols2-imagine.html.
> - For Material Style, check out https://doc.qt.io/ archives/qt-5.11/qtquickcontrols2-material.html.
> - Finally, check out https://doc.qt.io/archives/qt-5.11/ qtquickcontrols2-universal.html for Universal Style.

Other than setting the colors in the qtquickcontrols2.conf file, you can also override it in the QML file. This is really helpful if you want a particular QML file to carry a different style than others. The following code shows this:

```
ApplicationWindow {
    visible: true
    width: 200
    height: 200
    title: qsTr("Hello World")

    Material.theme: Material.Dark
    Material.accent: Material.Green
```

```
    Button {
        text: "Push Me"
        anchors.centerIn: parent
    }
}
```

The preceding code produces the following result:

You can also override the style of each individual QML object, shown as follows:

```
ApplicationWindow {
    visible: true
    width: 200
    height: 200
    title: qsTr("Hello World")

    Material.theme: Material.Dark
    Material.accent: Material.Green

    Button {
        text: "Push Me"
        anchors.centerIn: parent
        highlighted: true
        Material.accent: Material.Blue
        Material.background: Material.Orange
        Material.foreground: Material.Pink
    }
}
```

Since the button now has its own `Material.accent` property, it will override the one we set at the top. The code produces the following result:

Lastly, Qt also provides you with a C++ method to change the Qt Quick Control 2 style through the `QQuickStyle` class. You can call the `setStyle` function under `QQuickStyle` to change the style:

```
QQuickStyle::setStyle("Material");
```

We have gone through some of the features of Qt Quick Control 2 and how to change its appearance. In the next section, we will look into the new graphical editor for SCXML and how we can create a simple state machine using it.

Understanding the new graphical editor for SCXML

Qt introduced SCXML as a new feature in 5.7, which serves as a notation format for building a sophisticated state machine for your application. A state machine is a mechanism for which a program or a widget of a program changes its properties based on the current state you defined for it. We have seen how a `Push Button` changes its appearance when the mouse hovers on it or when pressed by the user. These are different states of `Push Button` and its behavior is determined and executed by the state machine.

With SCXML, you can define a more sophisticated state machine for your program and save it in the human-readable SCXML file format for Qt to parse and process. Qt will then generate C++ classes according to the content of the SCXML file to drive the state machine you defined earlier. Qt also provides a graphical editor for you to easily define your state machine without manually writing the content of the SCXML file. The editor looks something like this:

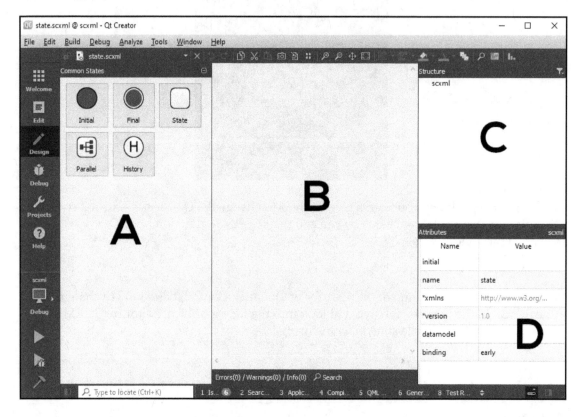

The editor consists of four different parts:

- **Common States Panel (A):** This is where you pick and choose the type of state you want to add to the state editor.
- **State Editor (B):** This is where you define the state machine. You can drag and drop different types of states from the **Common States** panel here and link them together to form state transitions.
- **Structure Panel (C):** The panel here shows the structure of your state machine in the form of a tree list. All of the states that you placed in the state editor will be shown here along with its hierarchical relationship.

- **Attributes Panel(D):** This window shows the attributes of the selected state, which you can view and edit to suit your needs.

To create an SCXML file, do the following:

1. Go to **File I New File or Project**.
2. Then, pick the **State Chart** option under **Files and Classes I Modeling** and press the **Choose...** button.
3. Once you've created the file, Qt Creator will open it up automatically with the SCXML editor. You will see an empty SCXML file just like that in the preceding screenshot.
4. You can start creating your first state machine by dragging the Initial node to the state editor to kick-start the state machine.
5. After that, you can drag some State nodes to the state editor and link them together by first selecting one of the nodes and click on the arrow icon. Then, a dashed-line arrow will follow your cursor whenever you go.
6. Left-click on the state editor to create a breakpoint to change the direction of the arrow, or right-click on one of the other nodes to establish a transition from the previous node that you have selected. When a State node links with multiple other nodes, it creates an option for the state machine to pick and choose. The state machine will choose an appropriate path by following the condition that you set later in your code. For now, you just define what are the states available for the state machine. The following diagram shows an example of what a state machine looks like inside the SCXML editor:

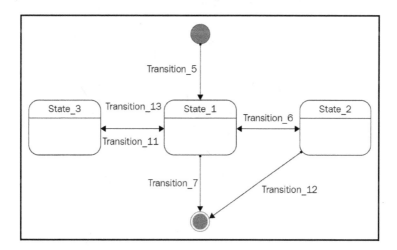

The preceding diagram shows the new graphical editor for the SCXML section, we see that, starting from the top, there is an `Initial` node, which represents the initial state of the program, then it will travel down to a `State` node called **State_1**. From there onward, it might go to a different state depending on the condition that you set in your code. The arrows indicate the direction in which the state can travel. Lastly, the state will eventually end up at the `Final` node, at which point the state machine will cease its operation.

7. Finally, place a `Final` node to define the final state the state machine can reach. Once it reaches this state, the state machine has accomplished its task and ceases to operate anymore.

Other than that, there is a `Parallel` node that you can use if it fits your needs. Unlike the `State` node, which only goes to one other node at once, the `Parallel` node can travel to multiple other states simultaneously, hence its name.

The `History` node is much more complicated than the other nodes. It represents a history state that has been saved previously. You can use this node to travel back to a previous state from a distant state that is not linked directly. To save a state to the history stack, create a `History` node as a child of a `State` node. When the state machine detects the existence of the `History` node at runtime, it will automatically record the current state. The state machine will travel back to this state whenever it reaches the `History` node during transition. The following diagram shows an example of how to use the `History` node:

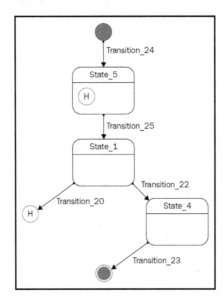

From the preceding diagram, we see that when traveling from **State_1** to the History state through **Transition_20**, your program's state will go return to **State_5**, which is where the other History node is located before **State_1**. If you have multiple History states in your state machine, then it will pick the last one that it stumbled upon.

Other than adding a History node into a State node, you can also add State nodes into another State node to establish a parent-children relationship. Recursive states like these increase the complexity of your state machine and you should be extra careful when going for such an approach.

For each State node, you can apply additional elements to it, called Executable Content. Following are the list of Executable Content elements you can add to your states:

- raise: raise events.
- send: communicate with external entities.
- script: run scripts and do something with the values in the data model.
- assign: add or modify a value in the data model.
- cancel: cancel an action execution.
- log: record information into a log.
- if: execute actions based on a condition.
- foreach: loop through a set of values and execute an action for each of them.

You can add these elements to a state by right-clicking on its node and select one of the preceding from the onentry or onexit option on the pop-up menu. Most of these Executable Content elements are methods used to manipulate your state's data model when entering or exiting the state. Therefore, you can only add these elements to State or Parallel nodes that have datamodel assigned to it. If you have not done so, right-click on the State node you want to apply and select datamodel.

To add data to datamodel, right-click on it at the **Structure Panel** and select data on the pop-up menu. You can now assign data to datamodel and manipulate it through the Executable Content element we talked about earlier.

Let's try it out ourselves:

1. First, create a new Qt Quick project and add the scxml module to our project:

```
QT += quick scxml
```

2. Then, set up our GUI like this:

```
import QtQuick 2.12
import QtQuick.Window 2.12

Window {
    id: window
    visible: true
    width: 640
    height: 480
    title: qsTr("State Machine")

    Rectangle {
        id: rectangle
        width: 200
        height: 200
        color: "red"
        anchors.verticalCenter: parent.verticalCenter
        anchors.horizontalCenter: parent.horizontalCenter
    }
}
```

3. There's nothing fancy here, just a simple rectangle that stays in the middle of the window:

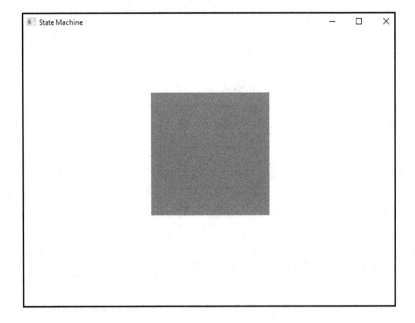

4. After that, create an SCXML file and name it `statemachine.scxml`.

5. Once you have created the file, please make sure you also add this file into the project resource as we're going to use it later in our QML code.

6. After that, open up the file with Qt Creator and create a simple state machine that looks like this:

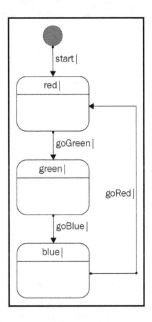

As can be seen from the preceding diagram, the preceding state machine consists of three different states: **red**, **green**, and **blue**. We will use these states to change the color of the rectangle we defined in our QML code earlier. Other names that you can see from the state machine such as `start`, `goGreen`, `goBlue`, and `goRed` are the names of the transitions.

7. Once you're done, right-click on each of the `State` nodes (**red**, **green**, and **blue**) and select **onentry | send** from the pop-up menu.

8. Set the `event` attribute of the `send` executable content of `red` as `goGreen` and set its delay as `2s`. This will allow the state machine to automatically trigger the `goGreen` transition two seconds after entering the `red` state. The following screenshot shows you where to set the values on the **Attributes** window:

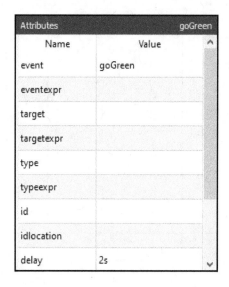

Repeat the preceding steps for the `green` and `blue` states, except change the `event` attributes to `goBlue` and `goRed` respectively. This means that the state machine will keep running in a circle until we stop the program.

9. Next, open up our `main.qml` file and import the `QtScxml` module to our QML code:

```
import QtScxml 5.8
```

10. After that, add the following code under our window object:

```
StateMachineLoader {
    source: "qrc:///statemachine.scxml"
    stateMachine.onReachedStableState: {
        if (stateMachine.red)
            rectangle.color = "red"
        else if (stateMachine.green)
            rectangle.color = "green"
        else if (stateMachine.blue)
            rectangle.color = "blue"
    }
}
```

We created a `StateMachineLoader` object, which is used to load the SCXML file we created earlier and automatically generate the state machine code for us. However, we must write the logic ourselves, which can be seen under the `onReachedStableState` slot function. This function will be triggered when our state machine has successfully changed its state. Then, we check whether each of the states is the current state (it will return true if it is the current state) and change the color of the rectangle shape accordingly.

If we run the code now, we will see the rectangle changes its color every two seconds. That's it—we have learned how we can make use of the new SCXML editor provided by Qt and create a simple state machine for our application.

Summary

In this chapter, you took a whirlwind tour of Qt Quick, Qt's declarative framework for application development. You learned about the basic visible items that Qt Quick provides as a foundation for application development and how to position items using Qt Quick's layout system, create a simple web browser using a web engine component, and create a simple list using Qt Quick's list view.

Other than that, you also understood about Qt Quick's support for animations and transitions. We saw how to make use of the state construct to change the property of an object based on its current state, but also learned how to make use of the latest SCXML editor to create a much more sophisticated state machine.

Finally, we saw how to link Qt Quick and C++, giving you the best of both worlds in Qt development. By following the example shown in this chapter, we learned how to create an image gallery from scratch!

In the next chapter, we will take a look at Qt Quick's support for multimedia recording and playback. Stay tuned!

Implementing Multimedia with Qt Quick

8

Today's applications increasingly use multimedia to enhance their appeal to users. Sound effects are a key part of most user interfaces, and many applications include video tutorials or other video content. Some applications even use the camera provided on many devices; this is especially true of mobile applications, where most mobile devices have at least one, if not two or more cameras.

In this chapter, we will take a look at Qt Quick's support for multimedia. We'll begin with an overview of what's possible so that you understand what you can and can't build using the platform-agnostic support for multimedia that Qt provides. Next, we will look at the Qt Quick components that provide access for audio and video playback in detail, as well as how to use the camera, if it is supported.

In this chapter, we will cover the following topics:

- Implementing multimedia in Qt
- Playing audio clips and sound effects
- Playing video clips
- Accessing the camera

Technical requirements

The technical requirements for this chapter include Qt 5.13.1 MinGW 64-bit, Qt Creator 4.10.0, and Windows 10.

The GitHub link for the chapter can be found here:

```
https://github.com/PacktPublishing/Application-Development-with-Qt-Creator-
Third-Edition/tree/master/Chapter08.
```

Implementing multimedia in Qt

Qt has long provided some support for multimedia on the platforms it supports in C++ through the inclusion of its Phonon library. In Qt 5.0 and beyond, Qt Quick provides several objects to interact with the native support provided by Qt and the underlying platform that Qt provides. Using these QML components, you can do the following:

- Play sound clips and short sound effects in the background
- Play video content
- Display the camera viewfinder
- Capture camera content from the camera

What's actually supported by Qt depends on the target platform; for example, if the hardware doesn't have a camera, you can't display a camera viewfinder or take pictures. In practice, the level of support varies further; for example, as I write this, multimedia support on Windows is very poor. Moreover, the actual format of the audio and video that Qt can play depends on the libraries installed with Qt, which themselves depend on the target platform. Platforms such as Linux might require additional libraries to fully support the audiovisual coder/decoders (codecs) used by many audio and video files.

To use any of the multimedia types we will discuss in this chapter, your QML instance must import the `QtMultimedia` module, as follows:

```
import QtMultimedia 5.12
```

 In this chapter, we'll focus on the Qt Quick multimedia interfaces. If you're interested in using the lower-level C++ APIs, see the Qt Multimedia documentation at `https://doc.qt.io/qt-5/multimediaoverview.html`.

We have been introduced to the functionality and uses of the multimedia module in Qt. Let's proceed to the next section to learn how we can empower this module and play audio clips with it.

Playing audio clips and sound effects

Qt Quick provides the `SoundEffect` type to play short sound effects with minimum latency. This is especially good for things such as button click sounds, virtual keyboard sounds, and alert tones as part of a rich and engaging multimedia experience. Using it is straightforward; you provide the type with a `source` field and call its `play` method to start the playback, as follows:

```
import QtQuick 2.12
import QtQuick.Window 2.12
import QtMultimedia 5.12

Window {
    visible: true
    width: 320
    height: 240
    title: qsTr("Play Sound")

    Text {
        text: "Click Me!";
        font.pointSize: 24;
        width: 150; height: 50;

        SoundEffect {
            id: playSound
            source: "soundeffect.wav"
        }
        MouseArea {
            id: playArea
            anchors.fill: parent
            onPressed: { playSound.play() }
        }
    }
}
```

The preceding code produces the following result:

Here, SoundEffect will play the contents of the soundeffect.wav file stored in the application's resource when you click on the mouse area. You can stop a sound effect by calling its stop method, or else it simply plays until it gets completed.

The SoundEffect type has some additional fields that change how the sound effect is played:

- The loops field indicates the number of times the sound should be looped in the playback once you invoke play.
- The loopsRemaining field indicates how many loops of playback remain while the sound is playing.
- The playing field is true while the sound is playing.
- The volume field indicates the volume, which spans from 0.0 (no audio) to 1.0 (the loudest possible volume).
- The status field is an enumeration that indicates the state of playback. It can have one of the following values:
  - SoundEffect.Null: No sound has been set.
  - SoundEffect.Loading: The sound is being loaded.
  - SoundEffect.Ready: The sound is ready to be played.
  - SoundEffect.Error: An error occurred during loading or playback.

For longer bits of audio, it's best to use the Audio type. The Audio type's use is similar; you give it a source indicating where the audio should come from and then invoke its play method to start the playback. You can pause the playback by invoking its pause method, stop the playback by invoking its stop method, or seek a time offset in the audio by invoking seek and passing an offset in the time to seek (assuming that the audio source supports seeking; some sources, such as web streams, do not). You can use it as follows:

```
import QtQuick 2.12
import QtQuick.Window 2.12
import QtMultimedia 5.12

Window {
    visible: true
    width: 320
    height: 240
    title: qsTr("Play Sound")

    Text {
        text: "Click Me!";
        font.pointSize: 24;
```

```
        width: 150; height: 50;

        Audio {
            id: playMusic
            source: "music.wav"
        }
        MouseArea {
            id: playArea
            anchors.fill: parent
            onPressed: { playMusic.play() }
        }
    }
}
```

The `Audio` type includes the following properties that affect the playback:

- `autoLoad`: This defaults to `true` and forces the element to start loading the media on initialization.
- `autoPlay`: This defaults to `false`, but when it is `true`, it starts the playback once the element has loaded on initialization.
- `bufferProgress`: This is a real number in the range of `0.0` to `1.0`, indicating how full the playback buffer is.
- `duration`: This indicates the duration of the audio clip.
- `error` and `errorString`: These contain error information in the event of a playback failure.
- `hasAudio` and `hasVideo`: These indicate whether or not the clip has audio and video, respectively.
- `loops`: This indicates the number of times that the audio should be played.
- `muted`: This is `true` if the audio has been muted by the user.
- `position`: This indicates the position in the playback of the audio.
- `seekable`: This property is `true` if the audio stream supports seeking.
- `volume`: This indicates the playback volume as a real number from `0.0` (no audio) to `1.0` (full volume).

The `Audio` type also has a `metaData` property that includes information about the audio being played, if it is encoded in the stream. It includes fields such as `albumArtist`, `albumTitle`, `audioBitRate`, `category`, `comment`, and so on.

Similar to the `Audio` type is the `MediaPlayer` type, which supports the playback of both audio and (as we'll see in the next section) video playback. For audio playback, its use is identical to the `Audio` type.

We have learned how to play audio clips and sound effects using the `SoundEffect` object. Let's move on to the next section and learn how to play video clips!

Playing video clips

Playing video is as easy as playing audio; there's a `Video` type that supports playing the video and displaying the video on the display. Here's a video player that plays video when you click on it, and pauses and restarts the playback when you press the spacebar:

```
import QtQuick 2.12
import QtQuick.Window 2.12
import QtMultimedia 5.12

Window {
    visible: true
    width: 800
    height: 600
    title: qsTr("Play Video")

    Video {
        id: video
        width : 800
        height : 600
        source: "video.avi"

        MouseArea {
            anchors.fill: parent
            onClicked: {
                video.play()
            }
        }

        focus: true
        Keys.onSpacePressed:
            video.playbackState == MediaPlayer.PlayingState ?
                video.pause() :
                video.play()
    }
}
```

The preceding code produces the following result:

The Keys type emits signals for the various keys that are pressed; here, we're tying the spacePressed signal to a script that pauses and plays a video.

Most of the properties of Video are the same as of Audio, except that there's no metaData property. It's a subclass of Item, so the usual positioning properties such as anchors, x, y, width, and height are available to place the item in its parent. Note that all the transforms might not be available on the Video instances for performance reasons; for example, you usually can't freely rotate one.

You can also play the video content with a MediaPlayer instance and a VideoOutput instance. The VideoOutput type is also a subclass of Item, like Video, and is essentially a rendering canvas for the video codec associated with a MediaPlayer instance to render the video. You use it by specifying a MediaPlayer instance in its source property, as follows:

```
import QtQuick 2.12
import QtQuick.Window 2.12
import QtMultimedia 5.12

Window {
```

```
        visible: true
        width: 800
        height: 600
        title: qsTr("Play Video")

        Rectangle {
    width: 800
    height: 600
    color: "black"

    MediaPlayer {
    id: player
    source: "video.avi"
    autoPlay: true
    }

    VideoOutput {
    id: videoOutput
    source: player
    anchors.fill: parent
    }
    }
    }
```

The preceding code produces the following result:

Here, the `MediaPlayer` instance will play `video.avi` as soon as it's loaded, and the video will appear in the `VideoOutput` item, which is sized to fill the parent rectangle. Generally, you'll want to just use the `Video` instance, unless you need to have multiple playback windows, or else display a camera viewfinder, which we'll discuss next.

Due to the nature of the video codecs, although `VideoOutput` is a subclass of `Item`, not all transformations are supported; for example, you can't rotate the video player, nor can you place items on top of it and expect it to draw the child objects. This makes sense when you think of the many codecs today that run directly on the graphics hardware of the host system.

`VideoOutput` has only a few properties. These are as follows:

- `autoOrientation`: This, when `true`, uses the screen orientation to orient the video.
- `contentRect`: This indicates the content rectangle in the `VideoOutput` item where the video should be rendered.
- `fillMode`: This can be one of `Stretch` (indicating whether the video should be stretched), `PreserveToFit` (have its aspect ratio preserved), or `PreserveAspectCrop` (preserve the aspect ratio by cropping the image) when rendering to the content rectangle. (The default is to preserve the aspect ratio and to fit the video in the rectangle.)
- `orientation`: This lets you set the orientation of the video at increments of 90 degrees. This is most useful when using the `VideoOutput` class as a camera viewfinder, which we'll discuss in the next section.
- `sourceRect`: This specifies the source rectangle from which the video should be considered for rendering.

We have learned how to easily play video clips in Qt using Qt Quick and its multimedia module. To learn how to access your webcam, let's proceed to the next section.

Accessing the camera

To access the camera when it is supported by the hardware and Qt Multimedia, use the `Camera` type and its associated types to control the camera's capture behavior, exposure, flash, focus, and image processing settings. A simple use of the camera to show a viewfinder is done with the following code:

```
import QtQuick 2.12
import QtQuick.Window 2.12
```

```
import QtMultimedia 5.12

Window {
    visible: true
    width: 640
    height: 480
    title: qsTr("Webcam")

    Item {
        width: 640
        height: 480

        Camera {
            id: camera
        }

        VideoOutput {
            source: camera
            anchors.fill: parent
        }
    }
}
```

The preceding code produces the following result:

In short, the `Camera` type acts like a source for the video just as a `MediaPlayer` instance does.

The `Camera` type provides a few properties to control its behavior. They are as follows:

- `imageCapture`: This is an instance of `CameraCapture`, which defines how the camera should capture an image.
- `videoRecording`: This is an instance of `CameraRecorder`, which defines how the camera should capture a video.
- `exposure`: This is an instance of `CameraExposure`, which controls the various options for the exposure mode of the camera.
- `focus`: This is an instance of `CameraFocus`, which controls the auto- and manual-focusing behaviors.
- `flash`: This is an instance of `CameraFlash`, which controls the camera flash.
- `imageProcessing`: This is an instance of `CameraImageProcessing`, which controls the real-time image processing pipeline options such as white balance, saturation, and sharpening.

The types associated with these fields can't be instantiated directly.

To have the camera take a picture, specify the `imageCapture` property and invoke its `capture` method, as follows:

```
import QtQuick 2.12
import QtQuick.Window 2.12
import QtMultimedia 5.12

Window {
    visible: true
    width: 640
    height: 480
    title: qsTr("Webcam")

    Item {
        width: 640
        height: 360

        Camera {
            id: camera

            imageCapture {
                onImageCaptured: {
                    // Show the preview in an Image
                    photoPreview.source = preview
```

```
                }
            }
        }

        VideoOutput {
            source: camera
            focus : visible // to receive focus and capture key events
            width: 320
            height: 180
            anchors.top: parent.top
            anchors.horizontalCenter: parent.horizontalCenter

            MouseArea {
                anchors.fill: parent;
                onClicked: camera.imageCapture.capture();
            }
        }

        Image {
            id: photoPreview
            width: 320
            height: 180
            anchors.bottom: parent.bottom
            anchors.horizontalCenter: parent.horizontalCenter
        }
    }
}
```

The preceding code produces the following result:

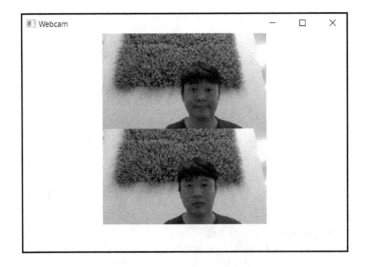

Here, the camera displays its viewfinder in the top `VideoOutput` item and has an `Image` item at the bottom to display the captured image. When you touch the viewfinder, the QML invokes the `capture` method of `imageCapture`, which is part of `Camera`, capturing the image and updating the bottom image.

The `imageCapture` property of the `Camera` item also has a `capturedImagePath` property, which is a string to the path where the last captured image is stored.

Recording works in a similar manner; you specify the attributes of the recording, such as the desired codec in the `videoRecording` property, and then invoke its `record` and `stop` methods to start and stop recording. The resulting video will be stored at the location indicated by the property's `actualLocation` field.

 For more information on the actual attributes available to applications using the `Camera` type, see the Qt Multimedia documentation for the `Camera` type at `https://doc.qt.io/qt-5/cameraoverview.html`.

That's it, we have successfully connected our application to the webcam and can retrieve images from it.

Summary

In this chapter, you saw the types that Qt Quick provides for managing audio and video media, as well as how to control the camera (if one exists). Using these types, you can add sound effects and ambient audio to your applications, which will make your videos more pleasing and help viewers to understand better what is being put across. You can also play videos from resources, the filesystem, or the web. In addition, as well as controlling the camera, if one exists, you can also capture still and moving images with it.

In the next chapter, we will look at the support that Qt has for accessing hardware sensors, such as those pertaining to the device location, orientation, and power state.

Sensors and Qt Quick

9

any of today's devices come with a myriad of sensors, including a means to determine the device's position and orientation, as well as to measure the characteristics of its surroundings through thermometers, luminescence sensors, accelerometers, gyroscopes, and other sensors. This is especially true of cell phones and other portable devices. To learn more about all the sensors that are available in our mobile devices, please read the article at: `https://gizmodo.com/all-the-sensors-in-your-smartphone-and-how-they-work-1797121002`.

In this chapter, we will take a look at Qt's sensor and positioning frameworks since they're supported in QML. You'll learn how to determine a device's position on the surface of the Earth and how to measure the other characteristics of its environment, as reported by its onboard sensors.

In this chapter, we will cover the following topics:

- Accessing sensors in Qt
- Determining device location
- Obtaining a device's position
- Placing a position marker on a Map View
- Accessing sensors in C++

Technical requirements

The technical requirements for this chapter are as follows:

- Qt 5.12.3 arm64-v8a
- Qt Creator 4.9.0
- Windows 10

Accessing sensors in Qt

Qt has had a robust porting layer for device sensors for several years, starting with the Qt Mobility libraries, which were meant to facilitate software development for cell phones. As Qt continued to evolve, support for sensors was added to Qt Quick and the list of supported sensors grew. Today, Qt supports the following sensors:

- An accelerometer is supported through the `Accelerometer` type.
- An altimeter is supported through the `Altimeter` type.
- An ambient light sensor is supported through the `AmbientLightSensor` and `LightSensor` types.
- An ambient temperature sensor is supported through the `AmbientTemperatureSensor` type.
- A compass is supported through the `Compass` type.
- A gyroscope is supported through the `Gyroscope` type.
- Whether or not the device is in a holster is determined through the `Holster` type.
- Proximity to the device's screen is determined through the `IRProximitySensor` and `ProximitySensor` types.
- An ambient magnetic field is supported through the `Magnetometer` type.
- The device's orientation is supported through the `OrientationSensor` type.
- The rotation of the device is supported through the `RotationSensor` type.
- How the device case is tapped on its *x*, *y*, and *z* axes is supported through the `TapSensor` type.
- How the device is tilted is reported through the `TiltSensor` type.

Each of these types has corresponding types that contain the reading; for example, the `Accelerometer` type reports its current value through the `AccelerometerReading` type.

To access the sensor library, you must add the `sensors` keyword to your `.pro` file, as follows:

```
QT += quick sensors
```

The pattern you'd follow to use all of these types is essentially the same: you import the `QtSensors` module, instantiate a sensor, activate it or deactivate it, and connect a script to its `readingChanged` slot. For example, to read from the accelerometer, you'd write the following code:

```
import QtQuick 2.12
import QtQuick.Window 2.12
import QtSensors 5.12
Window {
    visible: true
    width: 360
    height: 360

    Accelerometer {
        id: accel
        dataRate: 100
        active: true

        onReadingChanged: {
            // print out the x, y, and z values from accelerometer
            console.log(x + "," + y + "," + z);
        }
    }
}
```

Sensors have three key properties that you need to know about:

- `dataRate`: This indicates the rate at which the sensor should be sampled in milliseconds.
- `active`: This indicates whether the application should sample the sensor (indicated by the value of `true`) or not.
- `onReadingChanged`: This contains the script that processes the sensor reading, which is obtained by accessing the `reading` variable in the script you provide.

Each and every sensor returns different types of readings, depending on its purpose; for this accelerometer sensor, it provides us with a set of three-dimensional readings, namely x, y, and z.

It's important to realize that although Qt has interfaces for all of these sensors, not every platform supports all of these sensors, and even on a particular platform (say, Android), different devices might have different sensors. For example, in Qt 5.3, Qt supports the accelerometer, ambient temperature sensor, gyroscope, light sensor, magnetometer, proximity sensor, and rotation sensor, but not any other sensors. Moreover, not every Android device has these sensors; my Android tablet does not have a magnetometer. When designing your application, you need to take both of these facts into account: which sensors are supported by the Qt porting layer for your target and the kinds of sensors on the hardware that your target audience actually has. A matrix showing which platforms supported by Qt provide which sensors are available at `http://qt-project.org/doc/qt-5/compatmap.html`.

As we will learn in `Chapter 12`, *Developing Mobile Applications with Qt Creator*, sensors consume battery power, so your application should use them judiciously. Turn them on when you need to make a measurement by setting the active property, and turn them off when you're done.

In this section, we learned how to read data from an accelerometer on our mobile phones. Next, we will check out how we can determine our device's location by reading data from the GPS sensor.

Determining device location

Many devices support position determination, either through hardware such as a **Global Positioning System** (**GPS**) receiver or through network resources such as **Internet Protocol** (**IP**) geolocation. Similar to the other sensor support, this facility was introduced to Qt in Qt 4.x through the Qt Mobility module and is now supported through the Qt Positioning module. It's supported on many mobile devices, including Android.

To use the Qt Positioning module, you need to include the `positioning` keyword in your `.pro` file, as follows:

```
QT += quick network positioning
```

The Qt Positioning module provides three types of positioning; you can access these by importing the `QtPositioning` module:

- `PositionSource`: This provides position updates at a specified rate, emitting the `positionChanged` signal when position updates are available.
- `Position`: In the slot that you assign to the `positionChanged` signal, you'll receive a `Position` instance.

- `Coordinate`: The `Position` instance has a `Coordinate` property that specifies the location of the device.

The `PositionSource` type has the following properties:

- `active`: This, when true, indicates to the system that the positioning system should be activated and returns device positioning readings to your application.
- `name`: This indicates the unique name of the positioning plugin that is currently reporting the device's position.
- `preferredPositioningMethods`: This indicates your application's preferences for positioning. The preferred positioning methods can be one of the following:
    - `PositionSource.NoPositioningMethods`: This indicates that no positioning method is preferred.
    - `PositionSource.SatellitePositioningMethods`: This indicates that satellite-based methods such as GPS should be preferred.
    - `PositionSource.NonSatellitePositioningMethods`: This indicates that non-satellite-based methods such as IP geolocation should be preferred.
    - `PositionSource.AllPositioningMethods`: This indicates that any positioning method is acceptable:
        - `sourceError`: This holds the error that last occurred with the `PositionSource` method.
        - `supportedPositioningMethods`: This indicates the supported positioning methods that are available.
        - `updateInterval`: This specifies the desired update interval in milliseconds.
        - `valid`: This specifies whether or not the positioning system has obtained a valid backend plugin to provide data.

Here's a simple use of `PositionSource`:

```
PositionSource {
    id: src
    updateInterval: 1000
    active: true

    onPositionChanged: {
        var coord = src.position.coordinate;
```

```
            position.text =
                    Math.abs(coord.latitude) + (coord.latitude < 0 ? " S "
                        : " N " ) + Math.abs(coord.longitude) +
                        (coord.longitude < 0 ? " W " : " E " );
        }
    }
```

You can start positioning on `PositionSource` by calling its `start` method, and you can stop updating by calling its `stop` method. In addition to doing this, you can request for a one-shot positioning report by invoking its `update` method.

The `Position` type has a number of properties that can be used to encapsulate the device's position. These are as follows:

- `altitudeValid`: This indicates whether the altitude reading is valid.
- `coordinate`: This contains a coordinate containing the latitude, longitude, and altitude.
- `directionValid`: This indicates whether the direction is valid.
- `horizontalAccuracy`: This indicates the degree of horizontal accuracy in the position reported.
- `horizontalAccuracyValid`: This indicates whether the horizontal accuracy is valid.
- `latitudeValid` and `longitudeValid`: These indicate whether the latitude and longitude are valid.
- `speed`: This indicates the device's speed.
- `speedValid`: This indicates whether the device's speed is valid.
- `timestamp`: This indicates when the measurement was taken.
- `verticalAccuracy`: This indicates the vertical accuracy of the measurement.
- `verticalAccuracyValid`: This indicates whether the vertical accuracy is valid.
- `verticalSpeed`: This indicates the vertical speed of the device.
- `verticalSpeedValid`: This indicates whether the vertical speed is valid.

All distances and speeds are in metrics, while the latitude and longitude are in decimal degrees. This is done through the WGS-84 datum.

In addition to providing the latitude, longitude, and altitude of the device, the `Coordinate` type offers the `distanceTo` and `azimuthTo` methods, letting you compute the distance between two `Coordinate` instances or the bearing from one `Coordinate` instance to another. It also provides the `atDistanceAndAzimuth` method for computing the destination point when you travel a particular distance at a specific azimuth from the coordinate's latitude and longitude. These methods are the solutions to the so-called **forward geodetic problem** and the **reverse geodetic problem**, both of which are used in cartography. Go to `http://www.ngs.noaa.gov/TOOLS/Inv_Fwd/Inv_Fwd.html` for details on how these are computed.

The following code shows an example use of the `PositionSource` type. But first, let's create a window and some text objects:

```
import QtQuick 2.12
import QtQuick.Window 2.12
import QtPositioning 5.12

Window {
    visible: true
    width: 360
    height: 360

    Text {
        id: positionLabel
        text: qsTr("Position:")
        anchors.top: parent.top
        anchors.left: parent.left
    }

    Text {
        id: position
        text: qsTr("Hello World")
        anchors.horizontalCenter: parent.horizontalCenter
        anchors.top: parent.top
    }
```

After that, we implement the `PositionSource` object, which gives us the data from the GPS sensor:

```
PositionSource {
    id: src
    updateInterval: 1000
    active: true

    onPositionChanged: {
        var coord = src.position.coordinate;
```

```
position.text =
        Math.abs(coord.latitude) + (coord.latitude < 0 ? "
           S " : " N " ) +
        Math.abs(coord.longitude) + (coord.longitude < 0 ?
           " W " : " E " );
      }
    }
  }
```

Here, the `PositionSource` type is active on application start and updates once per second. When it receives a position report, it emits a `positionChanged` signal, which triggers the `onPositionChanged` script. This obtains the coordinate from the position and formats it for presentation in the `position` text field.

Like other device sensors, obtaining position reports uses additional battery power over normal program execution. Generally, your application should only determine the device's position when it actually needs it, such as before submitting the position to a service in order to determine nearby points of interest or to tag the user's location in some way. In general, you should not run the positioning system all the time (unless you're building an application that needs it, such as a turn-by-turn navigation application), because doing so can greatly diminish battery life.

In the preceding example, we learned how we can obtain the GPS position of our device. Next, we will dive into the other miscellaneous sensors available to us on our device and how to obtain the respective data from them.

Obtaining a device's position

Let's move on to a simple example that returns the device's position, accelerometer, gyroscope, ambient light, and magnetometer readings. Here's what our application looks like when running on a Huawei phone:

Position:	3.1995291 N 113.0491118 E	
Accel X: -4.52	Accel Y: 1.93	Accel Z: 8.15
Gyro X: 4.23	Gyro Y: -15.62	Gyro Z: -4.33
	Light Sensor:20.40	
Mag X: N/A	Mag Y: N/A	Mag Z: N/A
	Mag Cal: N/A	

Note that my Huawei phone does not have a magnetometer, so these readings aren't being updated. Let's see how this works:

1. First, we need to ensure that we include the positioning and sensor modules in our `.pro` file (if we don't, the application will compile but fail to launch):

```
QT += quick positioning sensors
```

2. Next, we'll move on to the QML itself. This is long but straightforward. First, we add the necessary modules to our project; then, we define the `Window` object for our program:

```
import QtQuick 2.12
import QtQuick.Window 2.12
import QtPositioning 5.12
import QtSensors 5.12

Window {
    visible: true
    width: 360
    height: 360
```

3. After that, we create some `Text` objects to display static text:

```
Text {
    id: positionLabel
    text: qsTr("Position:")
    anchors.top: parent.top
    anchors.left: parent.left
    color: position.valid ? "red" : "black"
}

Text {
    id: position
    text: qsTr("Hello World")
    anchors.horizontalCenter: parent.horizontalCenter
    anchors.top: parent.top
}
```

4. Then, we create a `PositionSource` object and an `Accelerometer` object to acquire data from the positioning sensor and accelerometer sensor, as follows:

```
PositionSource {
    id: src
    updateInterval: 1000
    active: true

    onPositionChanged: {
        var coord = src.position.coordinate;
        position.text =
                Math.abs(coord.latitude) + (coord.latitude < 0
? " S " : " N " ) +
                Math.abs(coord.longitude) + (coord.longitude <
0 ? " W " : " E " );
    }
}

LabelThreePart {
    id: accelerometerReading
    label: "Accel"
    anchors.top: position.bottom
    anchors.horizontalCenter: parent.horizontalCenter
}

Accelerometer {
    id: accel
    dataRate: 100
    active:true

    onReadingChanged: {
        accelerometerReading.xValue = (reading.x).toFixed(2);
        accelerometerReading.yValue = (reading.y).toFixed(2);
        accelerometerReading.zValue = (reading.z).toFixed(2);
    }
}

LabelThreePart {
    id: gyroscopeReading
    label: "Gyro"
    anchors.top: accelerometerReading.bottom
    anchors.horizontalCenter: parent.horizontalCenter
}
```

5. Right after that, we create a `Gyroscope` object, a `LightSensor` object, and a `Magnetometer` object to obtain the rotation movement, light sensitivity, and direction data from the respective sensors. Consider the following code:

```
Gyroscope {
    id: gyroscope
    dataRate: 100
    active: true

    onReadingChanged: {
        gyroscopeReading.xValue = (reading.x).toFixed(2);
        gyroscopeReading.yValue = (reading.y).toFixed(2);
        gyroscopeReading.zValue = (reading.z).toFixed(2);
    }
}

Text {
    id: lightSensorLabel
    anchors.top: gyroscopeReading.bottom
    anchors.right: lightSensorValue.left
    text: qsTr("Light Sensor:")
}

Text {
    id: lightSensorValue
    anchors.top: lightSensorLabel.top
    anchors.horizontalCenter: parent.horizontalCenter
    text: "N/A"
}

// Light Sensor
LightSensor {
    id: lightSensor
    dataRate: 100
    active: true

    onReadingChanged: {
        lightSensorValue.text = (reading.illuminance).
            toFixed(2);
    }
}

// Magnetometer
LabelThreePart {
    id: magnetometerReading
    label: "Mag"
    anchors.top: lightSensorValue.bottom
    anchors.horizontalCenter: parent.horizontalCenter
```

```
        }

        Text {
            id: magcLabel
            anchors.right: magcValue.left
            anchors.top: magnetometerReading.bottom
            text: "Mag Cal: "
        }
        Text {
            id: magcValue
            anchors.horizontalCenter: parent.horizontalCenter
            anchors.top: magcLabel.top
            text: "N/A"
        }

        Magnetometer {
            onReadingChanged: {
                magnetometerReading.xValue = (reading.x).toFixed(2);
                magnetometerReading.yValue = (reading.y).toFixed(2);
                magnetometerReading.zValue = (reading.z).toFixed(2);
                magcValue.text = (reading.calibrationLevel).toFixed(2);
            }
        }
    }
```

First up is the position label and position field, which we color red if
`PositionSource` is unable to get a fix; otherwise, it will display as black. The
code that produces this result is as follows:

```
color: position.valid ? "red" : "black"
```

The remainder of the sensors come next. Here, I'm using a little `LabelThreePart`
control that I wrote, which looks as follows:

```
import QtQuick 2.12

Rectangle {
    property string label: "Something"
    property alias xValue: xValue.text
    property alias yValue: yValue.text
    property alias zValue: zValue.text
    width: parent.width
    height: 32

    Text {
        id: xLabel
        anchors.left: parent.left
        anchors.top: parent.top
```

```
        text: label + " X: "
    }
    Text {
        id: xValue
        anchors.left: xLabel.right
        anchors.top: parent.top
        text: "N/A"
    }
```

We continue to add the rest of the `text` objects to our QML code:

```
Text {
    id: yLabel
    anchors.right: yValue.left
    anchors.top: parent.top
    text: label + " Y: "
}
Text {
    id: yValue
    anchors.horizontalCenter: parent.horizontalCenter
    anchors.top: parent.top
    text: "N/A"
}
Text {
    id: zLabel
    anchors.right: zValue.left
    anchors.top: parent.top
    text: label + " Z: "
}
Text {
    id: zValue
    anchors.right: parent.right
    anchors.top: parent.top
    text: "N/A"
}
}
```

From the preceding code, we can see that this is just a rectangle containing six fields; it uses its `label` property to create meaningful labels for the X, Y, and Z values to be shown, along with the property aliases to the text fields, which actually show those values.

Make sure that you included the **LabelThreePart.qml** file in your project; otherwise, you won't be able to compile:

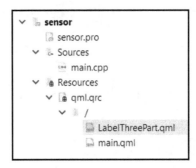

6. After that, you must also make sure that you have enabled location permission if you are building for mobile platforms. For the Android platform, go to **Projects** | **Build Steps** | **Build Android APK** and click on the **Create Templates** button to create the `AndroidManifest.xml` file, which you can then add the **android.permission.ACCESS_FINE_LOCATION** permission to before being able to access your phone's location data. The following screenshot shows the permission that is required for our application. You can add more permissions by selecting the desired permission from the selection box located at the bottom. Then, click the **Add** button to proceed:

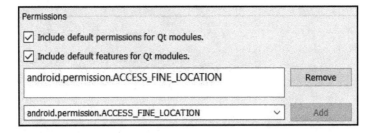

For Android 6.0 and above, you must also enable the location permission on your phone in order for it to work. Every phone is different; for mine, it's located at **Settings** | **Apps & notifications** | **Permissions**, as shown here:

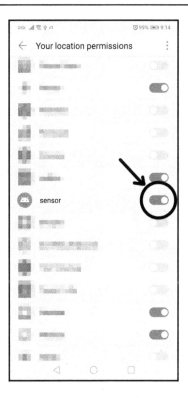

So far, we have learned how to obtain the location data from our device as well as from the sensors. Let's proceed and learn how to visualize the positioning data by placing a position marker on a Map View.

Placing a position marker on a Map View

Since version 5.0, Qt provides us with a Map View component that displays a map or image of the Earth, similar to Google Maps. Due to licensing issues, Qt Map View doesn't support Google Maps. The default tiled map service provider for Qt Map View is the community mapping project **OpenStreetMap (OSM)** since it is free of charge. Other than OSM, you can use other commercial service providers such as Mapbox, ArcGIS, and HERE.

Unlike other third-party mapping solutions, Qt Map View renders the tiled map using a native rendering engine (powered by Qt Quick) instead of embedding a web view onto the app. Native rendering speeds up performance and keeps your app size small since it doesn't include all the unnecessary resources needed by the web view. However, you can't interact with the Map View using C++ at the moment, only QML. I'm sure the developers will make it possible in the coming versions.

Let's get started by writing a very simple Map View application in QML:

```qml
import QtQuick 2.12
import QtQuick.Window 2.12

import QtLocation 5.12
import QtPositioning 5.12

Window {
    id: window
    visible: true
    width: 640
    height: 480
    title: qsTr("Map View")

    Plugin {
        id: mapPlugin
        name: "osm"
    }

    Map {
        id: map
        anchors.fill: parent
        plugin: mapPlugin
        zoomLevel: 14
        minimumZoomLevel: 6
        maximumZoomLevel: 18
        copyrightsVisible: false
        gesture.enabled: true
        gesture.acceptedGestures: MapGestureArea.PinchGesture |
            MapGestureArea.PanGesture
    }
}
```

What we added here was the `Map` object, which displays the tiled map, alongside a `Plugin` object, which determines the service provider for our Map View. We can also define the zoom levels, maximum and minimum zoom level, display of copyright text, and gesture settings. Gesture settings only apply to touchscreen applications, so we won't be able to test this on a desktop.

Other than that, we also must include the `location` module for our Qt project:

```
QT += quick location positioning
```

The preceding code produces the following output:

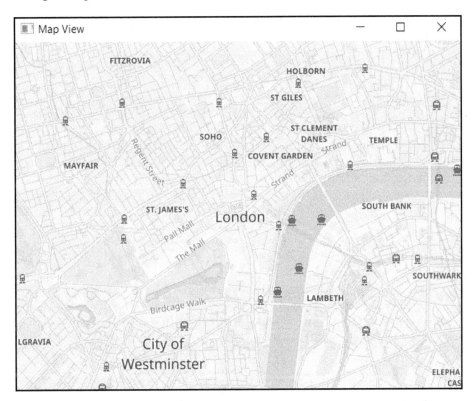

Very simple and easy, isn't it? If you see an empty map, please make sure that you have downloaded the OpenSSL library files to your computer as OSM no longer accept HTTP requests, and only accept HTTPS requests. You can download the latest OpenSSL builds at `https://indy.fulgan.com/SSL`. For Windows users, please also make sure both the `libcrypto` and `libssl` DLL files are placed alongside your executable.

If you're developing an app for Android, you must include the `.so` libraries in your application APK by using the following settings in your project file:

```
contains(ANDROID_TARGET_ARCH,armeabi-v7a) {
    ANDROID_EXTRA_LIBS = \
        $$PWD/android/32bit/libcrypto.so \
        $$PWD/android/32bit/libssl.so
}
```

```
contains(ANDROID_TARGET_ARCH,arm64-v8a) {
    ANDROID_EXTRA_LIBS = \
        $$PWD/android/64bit/libcrypto.so \
        $$PWD/android/64bit/libssl.so
}
```

 Please make sure that you only include the 32-bit library if you are building a 32-bit application, and only include a 64-bit library if you're building a 64-bit application.

Let's have a look at the following steps:

1. After that, let's create another empty QML file and call it marker.qml. We will create a separate QML file so that it can be reused in our main QML file or any other QML files we want. Now that we have created the file, we can add the following code to implement our map marker:

```
import QtQuick 2.12
import QtQuick.Controls 2.12
import QtLocation 5.12

MapQuickItem
{
    id: marker
    anchorPoint.x: 0
    anchorPoint.y: icon.height / 2

    sourceItem: Item
    {
        Image
        {
            id: icon
            source: "img/mapmarker.png"
            sourceSize.width: 120
            sourceSize.height: 120
            width: 120
            height: 120
            anchors.centerIn: parent
        }
    }
}
```

2. Next, we need to add the following code within the `Map` object:

```
Component.onCompleted: {
    map.center = QtPositioning.coordinate(-37.8163521,144.9275631);
    map.zoomLevel = 12;

    var component = Qt.createComponent("marker.qml");
    var item = component.createObject(window, { coordinate:
    QtPositioning.coordinate(-37.8163521,144.9275631) });
                                                    //Melbourne
    map.addMapItem(item);
}
```

In the preceding code, the `onCompleted` slot function gets called when the `Map` object has been successfully initiated. We then reposition the map's center point to somewhere in Melbourne and set its zoom level to `12`. After that, we create a new component based on the `marker.qml` file we created in the previous step and place it at the same coordinates that the center point of our map is at.

3. Run the program again. Now, you should see something like this:

Do note that you need to add the marker image file to your project resource; otherwise, it will not appear on the map when launching the program. If you haven't created one, go to **File** | **New File or Project** and select the **Qt Resource File** option under **Files and Classes** | **Qt**.

4. After that, open up the resource file and add a prefix, which works similarly to a folder, to categorize different groups of files. Once you have created a prefix, add the marker image file to the prefix and save it:

5. Finally, we need to add the following code to obtain the device's position and display its position using the map marker we used in the previous step:

```
property MapQuickItem item

PositionSource {
    id: src
    updateInterval: 1000
    active: false

    onPositionChanged: {
        var coord = src.position.coordinate;

        map.center = coord;
        item.coordinate = coord;
    }
}
```

Do note that we have moved the `item` object variable away from the `onComplete` function because we are going to use it in the `onPositionChanged` function as well. We also set the `active` property to `false` by default since we only want it to be active once the map has been successfully initialized:

```
Component.onCompleted: {
    map.center = QtPositioning.coordinate(-37.8163521,144.9275631);
    map.zoomLevel = 12;

    var component = Qt.createComponent("marker.qml");
    item = component.createObject(window, { coordinate: QtPositioning.
       coordinate(-37.8163521,144.9275631) });
```

```
    map.addMapItem(item);

    src.active = true
}
```

If we run the application again, on mobile, we should see that the marker has been moved from the initial position (Melbourne) to our device's position. The marker will also change its position every second if we start moving around with our device. Other than that, we can also zoom into the map by pinching our fingers:

That's it – in this section, we have learned how to display an OSM map using the Map View provided by Qt, display a marker on the Map View, and obtain our device's position!

Next, we will discuss how we can access the same sensors on our mobile device using Qt's C++ classes.

Accessing sensors with C++

So far, we have learned how we can access the sensors' data through QML scripting. However, the sensors can also be accessed through Qt's various C++ classes. We will walk through some examples of this and demonstrate how we can achieve that.

First, create an empty Qt project (you can continue from the previous example if you wish, though). Instead of writing the code in the `.qml` file, we will open up `main.cpp` instead. After that, we will include some headers so that we can access these classes. Remember to add the `sensors` module to your project file (`.pro`) if you are creating a new Qt project:

```
#include <QDebug>
#include <QTimer>

#include <QAccelerometer>
#include <QAmbientLightSensor>
#include <QProximitySensor>

#include <QAccelerometerReading>
#include <QAmbientLightReading>
#include <QProximityReading>
```

Then, in the `main` function, add the following code:

```
QAccelerometer *accSensor = new QAccelerometer;
accSensor->start();
QSensorReading *accReading = accSensor->reading();

QTimer* timer = new QTimer;
QObject::connect(timer, &QTimer::timeout, [=]{
    qreal x = accReading->property("x").value<qreal>();
    qreal y = accReading->value(1).value<qreal>();
    qDebug() << "Accelerometer:" << x << y;
});
timer->start(1000);
```

In the preceding code, we created a `QAccelerometer` object called `accSensor`, which activates the accelerometer sensor in our mobile device. Then, we created a `QSensorReading` object called `accReading`, which helps retrieve data from `accSensor`.

After that, we created a timer that triggers the lambda function every 1,000 milliseconds (or 1 second). Within the lambda function, which gets called every time our timer triggers its `timeout` signal, we obtained the x and y properties from the `accReading` object, which is the latest data from the accelerometer sensor. Finally, we printed out the x and y values by using the `qDebug` function. Do note that I used property and value functions to obtain the x and y data, respectively, just to show you two different methods that you can use to achieve the same result – the first by mentioning the property name (x, in this case) and the second by referring to its position within the property array (1, in this case, for obtaining the y value).

If you build and run the app on your mobile device now, you should see some values being printed on the **Application Output** window on your Qt Creator. Try and swing your device around to see a more drastic change in the x and y values:

```
D libSensorCPP.so: Accelerometer: 0.699519 0.850353
D libSensorCPP.so: Accelerometer: -0.332152 1.04697
D libSensorCPP.so: Accelerometer: -3.32985 2.8791
D libSensorCPP.so: Accelerometer: 0.562877 9.5493
D libSensorCPP.so: Accelerometer: 0.110468 9.82264
D libSensorCPP.so: Accelerometer: 1.65357 -1.63815
D libSensorCPP.so: Accelerometer: 0.759278 0.8346
```

Once we get this working, we can easily use the same method to access the other sensors on our device. Let's add the following to our code:

```
QAmbientLightSensor *ambSensor = new QAmbientLightSensor;
ambSensor->start();
QAmbientLightReading * ambReading = ambSensor->reading();

QProximitySensor *proxSensor = new QProximitySensor;
proxSensor->start();
QProximityReading *proxReading = proxSensor->reading();
```

Then, add the following code to the lambda function we created previously:

```
qDebug() << "Ambient Light:" << ambReading->lightLevel();
qDebug() << "Proximity:" << proxReading->close();
```

If you build and run the project now, you should see all the different data being displayed on your Qt Creator:

```
D libSensorCPP.so: Accelerometer: 2.46714 0.646176
D libSensorCPP.so: Ambient Light: 3
D libSensorCPP.so: Proximity: false
D libSensorCPP.so: Accelerometer: 2.47853 3.31007
D libSensorCPP.so: Ambient Light: 3
D libSensorCPP.so: Proximity: false
D libSensorCPP.so: Accelerometer: 1.08533 3.96756
D libSensorCPP.so: Ambient Light: 2
D libSensorCPP.so: Proximity: false
```

The data that's provided by different sensors is varied, so please read the documentation to find out what data is provided by each sensor, available at https://doc.qt.io/qt-5/ qtsensors-cpp.html#reading-classes. Besides the classes that we used in the preceding example, there are many other Qt classes that allow you to access its respective sensor, which you can find on the same page of the documentation.

In this section, we learned how we can access the device's sensors through Qt's C++ classes, which gives you more choices when developing your application. You are not limited to just QML scripting, but are also able to achieve the same with C++.

Summary

In this chapter, you learned how to determine measurements from device sensors, including the device's positioning system, accelerometer, and other sensors. You also learned how to display the device's location on a map so that the user can see the location, along with its context, instead of just coordinating numbers, since positioning helps us trace exact locations.

In the next chapter, we will take a look at how we can use Qt's localization framework and tools to localize our application.

Section 3: Practical Matters

3

In the third section of this book, we will apply the information presented throughout the book and understand the development and implementation of applications in Qt. Additionally, we will also learn a few tips and tricks of Qt.

This section comprises the following chapters:

- Chapter 10, *Localizing Your Application with Qt Linguist*
- Chapter 11, *Optimizing Performance with Qt Creator*
- Chapter 12, *Developing Mobile Applications with Qt Creator*
- Chapter 13, *Embedded and IoT Development with Qt Creator*
- Chapter 14, *Qt Tips and Tricks*

10
Localizing Your Application with Qt Linguist

Localization is an important yet commonly neglected part of software development today. Most authors of applications, irrespective of whether those applications are commercial or open source, hope to capture a large number of users for their applications. Increasingly, this means supporting multiple languages in multiple locales, and often needing support for multiple languages in one locale (think of it as French and English coexisting in Canada).

For a long time, Qt has had a framework for making applications easy to localize with tools that help you to avoid hardcoding strings in your application and a GUI named **Qt Linguist** to help manage translation. In this chapter, we will take a look at Qt's strategy for localization, discussing the three tools (`lupdate`, `lrelease`, and Qt Linguist) that Qt provides and how to use them, along with what you need to do as you write your application to take advantage of Qt's localization framework.

In this chapter, we will take a look at the following topics:

- Understanding the task of localization
- Marking strings for localization
- Localizing your application with QLinguist
- Localizing special parameters – currencies and dates with QLocale

Technical requirements

The technical requirements for this chapter include Qt 5.12.3, MinGW 64-bit, Qt Creator 4.9.0, and Windows 10.

Understanding the task of localization

Localization is an important feature for your product if you want to sell it worldwide. When a user sees that their native language is being displayed and used in a piece of software, they will more likely stay attached to it and become one of your loyal customers. However, localization wasn't always an easy feature to implement, at least not until Qt introduced an easier way to do it.

Localizing your application has several phases that typically overlap throughout a project's life cycle.

The following diagram shows how these phases interact:

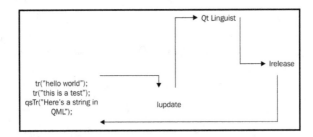

These phases are as follows:

1. As you write your application, you place strings that need to be localized into a specific function (see *step 5*) so that Qt can identify the strings as needing localization.
2. Periodically, you extract all the strings in your application and give them to translators in order to translate.
3. Translators provide translations for the strings in your application.
4. You compile translation files with the translated strings for each language you want to support.
5. The `tr` and `qsTr` functions for C++ and QML let you identify the strings in your application that require localization. Qt provides four tools to facilitate these phases.
6. The `lupdate` command generates a list of the strings that need localization in your application.
7. Translators use Qt Linguist to provide translations of the strings in your application.
8. The `lrelease` command takes the translated strings from Qt Creator and packages them in a format for your application to consume.

Software development is iterative, and localization is no exception. Small projects might prefer to do the localization just once, or perhaps twice, waiting until the application is nearly done before submitting the application strings for localization. Larger applications, or larger companies with a dedicated staff of translators, might prefer a more iterative approach, going through the localization cycle several times throughout application development. Qt supports both models.

We have learned the importance of localization and how it is implemented in Qt. In the following section, we will learn how to do it with the C++ method.

Marking strings for localization

All the way back in Chapter 1, *Getting Started with Qt Creator*, I told you to always mark your strings for localization using the tr and qsTr functions: tr for C++ and qsTr for QML strings. Doing so has two key advantages:

- It enables Qt to find every string that needs localization.
- If you install a Qt translator object in your application and provide a translation file, the strings you wrap with these functions are automatically replaced by their localized equivalent.

Let's examine the use of tr in more detail. All Qt objects that include the Q_OBJECT macro in their declaration include the tr function. You've seen it with one argument, as follows:

```
button = new QPushButton(tr("&Quit"), this);
```

The leading & in the string isn't for the tr function, but it is for the keyboard accelerators; you can prefix a letter with & to assign a keyboard accelerator and it gets the default system (a key combination with *Alt* for Windows, *cmd* for Apple, and *Alt* for Linux). If no translated version of the string appears in the application's current translation table, the tr function uses the string you pass as the string in the user interface, or it uses the string in the current translation table if one does exist.

The tr function can take a second argument, a disambiguation context that tr uses for the same string that might require different translations. This is shown as follows:

```
tr("&Copy", "Menu");
```

This function can also handle strings with plurals, as follows:

```
tr("%n item(s) replaced", "", count);
```

Depending on the value of `count` and the locale, a different string is returned. So, a native English translation could return "`0 items replaced`", "`1 item replaced`", "`2 items replaced`", and so on, while a French translation could return "`0 item remplacé`", "`1 item remplacé`", "`2 items remplacés`", and so on.

In QML, you simply use the `qsTr` function, which works exactly the same as the `tr` method in C++.

In this section, we have learned how we can mark our strings to let Qt know which string needs to be localized. Next, we will learn how to run the localization process in Qt and display the correct language according to the user's language preference.

Localizing your application with QLinguist

Once you've marked your strings using `tr` or `qsTr`, you need to generate a table of those strings for Qt Linguist to localize. You can do this using the `lupdate` command, which takes your `.pro` file and walks your sources to look for strings to localize and creates an XML file of the strings you need to translate for Qt Linguist. You need to do this once for each language you want to support. When doing this, it's best to name the resulting files systematically; one way to do this is to use the name of the project file, followed by a dash, followed by the ISO-639-2 language code for the language.

A concrete example is in order. This chapter makes use of `QtLinguistExample`; we can run `lupdate` using a command such as this to create a list of strings that we'll translate to Esperanto (ISO-639-2 language code, EPO):

```
% lupdate -pro .\QtLinguistExample.pro -ts .\QtLinguistExample-epo.ts
```

 Don't forget that the `%` character is the Command Prompt, which might differ from system to system.

Here, the `-pro` file indicates that the `.pro` file contains the list of sources to scan for strings to translate, and the `-ts` argument indicates the name of the translation file to be written. You'll need `lupdate` in your path, of course. How you set your path will depend on whether you're working on Windows, macOS X, or Linux, and where you've installed Qt. Some installations of Qt might update your path automatically, while others might not do so. On my Windows machine, for example, I can find `lupdate` at `C:\Qt\5.13.0\msvc2017_64\bin\lupdate.exe`.

The .ts file is an XML file with tags to indicate the strings to be translated, their context in your application's source code, and so forth. Qt Linguist will save the translations to its output file, which is named with a QM suffix as well, but don't worry: lupdate is smart enough to not overwrite the existing translations if you run it again after providing some translations.

You can also easily run the Command Prompt from Qt Creator by right-clicking on the .pro file from the project panel and selecting the **Build Environment** option to automatically configure the Command Prompt's path relative to your project directory, shown as follows:

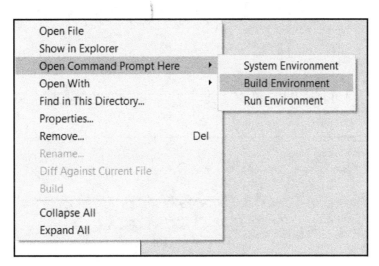

Besides using the commands, you can also use lupdate and lrelease directly from Qt Creator by going to **Tools | External | Linguist | Update Translations (lupdate)** or **Release Translations (lrelease)**. Do note that this will update or release all the translation files. If you want to just update or release a specific file/language, a command is still your best friend.

The following screenshot shows you where the `lupdate` tool is located on the application menu:

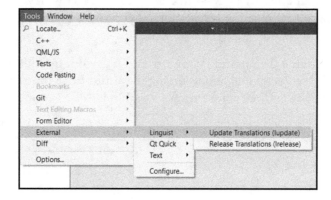

Qt Linguist is a GUI application; on starting this application, you'll see a screen very similar to the next screenshot:

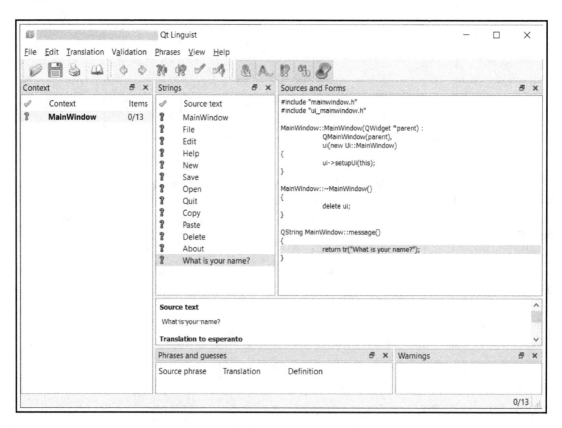

To begin, you need to open a `.ts` file you generated by navigating to **File** | **Open** and choosing a translation file. You'll be prompted for the destination language, and then you're given a list of the strings found:

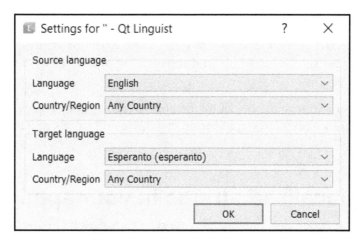

You or your translators only need to walk through each string and enter the corresponding string in the translated language. As you do so, you can see the context of the string in the source code in the rightmost pane; the line of the source from which the string was captured is highlighted.

Qt Linguist lets you track which strings you've translated and also those that still need translation. The icon to the left-hand side of each of the strings can be one of the following:

- A black question mark, indicating that a string is yet to be translated
- A yellow question mark, indicating that the string doesn't pass all of Qt Linguist's validation tests, but you're ignoring the failures
- An exclamation point, indicating that the string you've provided doesn't pass Qt Linguist's validation tests
- A yellow checkbox, indicating that you've provided a translation, but Qt Creator might have found a problem with it
- A green checkbox, indicating that the string has been translated and is ready to go

Qt Linguist provides some simple validation tests, such as ensuring that strings with `printf`-style arguments have the same number of arguments in each translation.

Qt Linguist also supports phrasebooks; you might be able to download a phrasebook with common strings already localized to the language you're targeting.

At any point, you can generate a translation file for inclusion in your application by running `lrelease`. For example, to create one for our Esperanto strings, we'd use `lrelease` as follows:

```
% lrelease .\QtLinguistExample-epo.ts .\QtLinguistExample-epo.qm
```

This takes the incoming `.ts` file and generates a `.qm` file with the strings. The `.qm` files are highly compressed binary files used by Qt directly in the process of rendering the application.

We have learned how we can export all the text into a list using Qt Linguist and allow you and your translator to work on the translation. Next, we will proceed to include the localized text in our application.

Including localized strings in your application

In order to supply translated strings to the `tr` and `qsTr` functions in your application, your application needs to include a `QTranslator` object to read the `.qm` files and replace the strings provided to `tr` and `qsTr` with their translated counterparts.

We can do this in your main entry point function, as follows:

```
QApplication a(argc, argv);
QTranslator translator;
bool result = translator.load("QtLinguistExample-epo.qm");
a.installTranslator(&translator);

    // Other window setup stuff goes here
return a.exec();
```

This code allocates a `QTranslator` object and loads the indicated translation file into the translator before installing it into the `QApplication` object. In this example, we're hardcoding the language in order to localize to Esperanto.

Note that if you want to support the locale as picked by the system, you might choose to do it this way:

```
QString locale = QLocale::system().name();
QTranslator translator;
translator.load(QString("QtLinguistExample-") + locale);
```

The `QLocale` class here is a class for managing the system's locale. Here, we use it to determine the system's locale, and then we attempt to load the localized string file for the system's current locale.

For this to work, the .qm files for the application need to be locatable by the application. They should be in the output directory; one way to do this during development is to turn off shadow builds in Qt Creator, under **Build Settings** in the **Project** pane. Building your application installer is a platform-specific task outside the scope of this book for which you need to include .qm files with the application binary.

> For more information on Qt Linguist, refer to its manual at https://doc.qt.io/qt-5/qtlinguist-index.html.

Next, we will see how to localize a few special parameters to suit our requirements.

Localizing special parameters – currencies and dates with QLocale

A common thing you might need to do is localize currencies and dates. Qt makes this easy, although the solution isn't obvious until you've thought about it a bit. Let's try it out.

1. You need to know about the QString arg method. This replaces an escaped number with the formatted version of its argument. For example, if we write the following:

    ```
    QString s = QString("%1 %2").arg("a").arg("b");
    ```

    Then, s will contain the string "a b".

2. You need to know about the toString method of QLocale, which formats its argument in a locale-specific way. So, we could write the following:

    ```
    QString currencyValue = QString("%1 %2")
        .arg(tr("$")).arg(QLocale::toString(value, 'g', 2)
    ```

    This uses tr to localize the currency symbol and the QLocale class's static method, toString, to convert the value of the currency to a string with the locale-specific decimal separator (a period in the US and Canada, and a comma in Europe).

Date formatting is similar; the `toString` method of `QLocale` has overloads for the `QDateTime`, `QDate`, and `QTime` arguments, so you can simply write the following:

```
QDateTime whenDateTime = QDateTime::currentDateTime();
QString when = QLocale::toString(whenDate);
```

This gets the current date and time and stores it in `whenDateTime` and then makes a string out of it using the locale's default formatting. The `toString` method can take a second argument that determines the output format; it's one of the following:

- `QLocale::LongFormat`: This uses the long version of month and day names.
- `QLocale::ShortFormat`: This uses the short version of month and day names.
- `QLocale::NarrowFormat`: This provides the narrowest form of formatting for the date and time.

That's it. We have learned not only how to localize text with Qt, but also how to localize special characters such as currencies and dates.

Summary

Localizing applications with Qt is easy with Qt Linguist and the localization framework in Qt. To use the framework, though, you must mark your strings to localize with `tr` or `qsTr` in your source code wherever they appear. Once you do this, you can create a source file of strings to translate with QLinguist using Qt's `lupdate` command and then provide translations for each string. Once you've provided the translations, you compile them using `lrelease` and then include them in your application by installing a `QTranslator` object in your application's main function and by loading the translation table generated by `lrelease`.

In this chapter, we have learned how to mark translatable texts so that Qt knows which text needs to be localized. Next, we also learned how to export these texts using Qt Linguist into a list that can be easily edited by you and your translator for each language. Then, we learned how we can load the translated texts back into Qt applications and display them according to a user's preferences. Lastly, we also learned how to localize special characters such as currency and dates.

In the next chapter, we will take a look at another important aspect of software development that Qt Creator supports: performance analysis with the QML Profiler and Valgrind.

Optimizing Performance with Qt Creator

11

We don't use performance analysis tools every day, but we're glad that they're there when we need them. Commercial tools, such as the ones that come with Microsoft Visual Studio, or standalone tools, such as IBM's Rational Rose Purify, can set you back due to their complexity and beginner-unfriendly design. Fortunately, Qt Creator has most of what you need in terms of built-in support for working with open source tools to help you profile the runtime and the memory performance of your application.

In this chapter, we will see how to perform the runtime profiling of QML applications using the QML performance analyzer and learn how to read the reports it generates to identify performance issues. We will then turn our attention to memory performance analysis with Valgrind using Qt Creator, which is a free option that helps you look for memory leaks and heap corruption on the Linux platform.

In this chapter, we will take a look at the following topics:

- Introducing QML performance analysis
- Introducing QML Profiler
- Doing more with QML Profiler
- Implementing test integration
- Adding better support for test integration

Technical requirements

The technical requirements for this chapter include Qt 5.12.3, MinGW 64-bit, Qt Creator 4.9.0, and Windows 10.

Introducing QML performance analysis

Qt Quick applications are supposed to be fast, with smooth and fluid user interfaces. In many cases, this is easy to accomplish with QML; the contributors to QML and the Qt Quick runtime have put a great deal of effort into creating an environment that performs well in a wide variety of circumstances. Sometimes, however, try as you might, you will find that you just can't squeeze the performance out of your application that you'd like. Some mistakes are obvious, such as the following:

- Doing a lot of compute-intensive tasks between state changes or actions that trigger drawing operations
- Excessively complex view hierarchies with thousands of elements on display at once
- Running on very limited hardware (often in combination with the first two problems)

Knuth famously said, "*Premature optimization is the root of all evil*," and he's definitely right. However, there might come a time when you will need to measure the performance of your application, and Qt Creator includes a special performance analyzer for just this purpose. With this, you can see how much time your application spends in each QML method and measure the critical aspects of your application that are at the edge of your control, such as how long it takes to create your application's view hierarchy.

Let's take a closer look.

QtSlowButton – a Qt Quick application in need of performance tuning

Let's analyze the performance of QtSlowButton, a poorly performing example program that I have put together. The QtSlowButton program has two QML components: a button based on the calculator button from Chapter 3, *Designing Your Application with Qt Designer* (under the *Creating the Qt application* section), and a view with buttons that you can press. Here's the button implementation:

```
import QtQuick 2.12

Rectangle {
    id: button

    width: 128
    height: 64
```

```
    property alias label: buttonText.text
    property int delay: 0

    color: "green"

    Rectangle {
        id: shade
        anchors.fill: button;
        color: "black"; opacity: 0
    }

    Text {
        id: buttonText
        anchors.centerIn: parent;
        color: "white"
        font.pointSize: 16
    }

    MouseArea {
        id: mouseArea
        anchors.fill: parent
        onClicked: {
            for(var i = 0; i < button.delay; i++);
        }
    }

    states: [
        State {
            name: "pressed"; when: mouseArea.pressed === true
            PropertyChanges { target: shade; opacity: .4 }
        }
    ]
}
```

Each button simply runs a `for` loop when you press it; its `delay` property controls the number of cycles through the loop. In addition, each button has an instance of `label`, named `buttonText`, which the button draws in the center of the clickable area.

The main user interface of the program consists of three buttons in `Column`, labeled `fast`, `medium`, and `slow`, with progressively longer delays:

```
import QtQuick 2.12
import QtQuick.Window 2.12

Window {
    visible: true
    width: 180
```

```
height: 360
title: qsTr("Slow Button")

Column
{
    spacing: 20
    Button    // custom Button from button.qml
    {
        delay: 10000;
        label: "fast";
    }
    Button    // custom Button from button.qml
    {
        delay: 100000;
        label: "medium";
    }
    Button    // custom Button from button.qml
    {
        delay: 300000;
        label: "slow";
    }
}
}
```

You can either load the source project that comes with this book for this example, or you can create a new Qt Quick project and build a button and a main view with this code. Build and run the program now. You should see something like this; a window with three buttons labeled **fast**, **medium**, and **slow**:

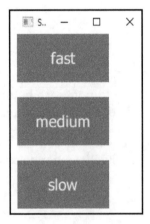

Perform the following steps to analyze the application's performance:

1. Build the application by clicking the build button on the left panel.
2. Select **QML Profiler** from the **Analyze** window. The application will start, and Qt Creator will switch to the **Analyze** view.
3. Click on each button a few times. Expect to wait after you click on a button.
4. Quit the application and check out the QML Profiler window.

 QML Profiler uses TCP/IP to make a connection between the running application and the profiler, by default, on port `3768`. You might have to tinker with your host's firewall settings in order to get things to work correctly. On Windows, be sure to permit the connection in the Windows Firewall dialog that appears.

The following screenshot shows the **Analyze** view after the application is run:

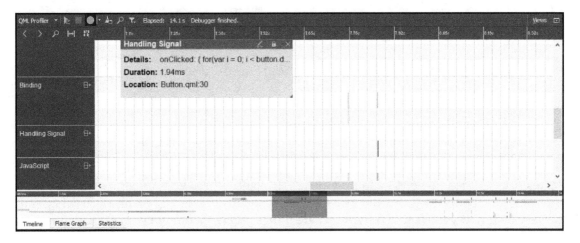

QML Profiler has the following three tabs and shows the first tab by default:

- The first tab is **Timeline**, indicating what happened at which point in time through the application and how long it took.
- The second tab, **Flame Graph**, lists the events that the QML application processed and how much time was spent on each event.
- The third tab, **Statistics**, lists the JavaScript functions that the program encountered while running and the time that the application spent in the total running of each function.

I have clicked on the **Handling Signal** row to expand the signals that the application handled.

You can see that it handled one signal, the `onClicked` signal, a total of three times and the amount of time spent each time is shown as varying bars on the graph. Clearly, if this were doing real work, there'd be an opportunity for performance improvement here.

The next screenshot shows a different view of this information, the JavaScript runtime for your application. This indicates that up to the limit of numerical accuracy, the application spent all of its measured time on the `onClicked` handler for the button—clearly, a performance *hotspot* in this case:

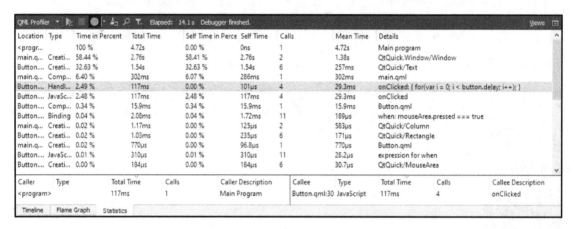

From the preceding screenshot, we can see that, interestingly, every incident of my JavaScript is measured here, including the $when clause (three lines under the selected line) that puts the opaque filter in front of the button when it's pressed. Looking at this view can be very helpful if you need to observe where things are happening in your application in a broad sense.

The next screenshot is likely to be most interesting to performance geeks because it shows the amount of time QML spent for each and every event it handled while running the application:

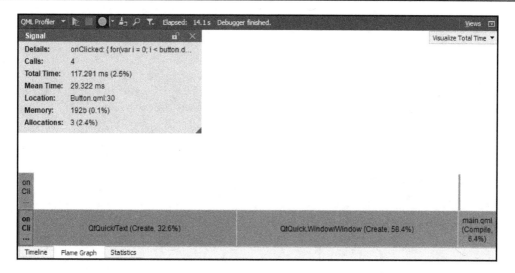

We can see that the `onClicked` handler consumes the lion's share of the processor resources, but other things, such as the creation of the rectangles for the view and the variable binding for the state of a push button, are shown as well. Typically, we'll use the **Statistics** view to get a broad picture of where the problems in your application are located, while we'll use the **Flame Graph** view to zero in on specific problems.

In this section, we have learned how we can identify problems in our Qt Quick project by looking at the details in QML Profiler. Let's move on to the next section and look at how we can easily detect problems in our Qt form project with the help of Valgrind. Do note that Valgrind only supports Linux, so after this, we will also look at how we can detect problems on other operating systems.

QtLeakyButton – a Qt C++ application in need of memory help

QtLeakyButton is an application that does one thing: presents a button that, when clicked, allocates 512 KB of RAM. Here's the code (you can either run the sample code that accompanies this book or create a Qt GUI application with a single button and a label and use this code for your `MainWindow` class).

First, let's look at the changes in `mainwindow.h`:

```
public slots:
    void leakPressed();
```

```
private:
    Ui::MainWindow *ui;
    int m_count;
```

After that, let's check out the changes in `mainwindow.cpp`:

```
MainWindow::MainWindow(QWidget *parent) : QMainWindow(parent),
    ui(new Ui::MainWindow), m_count(0)
{
    ui->setupUi(this);
    connect(ui->leakButton, &QPushButton::clicked, this,
&MainWindow::leakPressed);
}

void MainWindow::leakPressed()
{
    void *p = new char[512 * 1024];
    m_count++;
    ui->leakCount->setText(QString::number(m_count));
}
```

From the code, we can observe the following:

- The `MainWindow` class has an integer counter and a `ui` slot for the instantiated form.
- The `MainWindow` constructor instantiates this form and then connects the `leakButton` clicked signal to `MainWindow::leakPressed`.
- The `leakPressed` method just allocates memory and bumps the counter, updating the counter with the number of times you've pressed the button.

Detecting a memory leak on Linux using Valgrind

To use Valgrind, we need to add a new run target to your application. To accomplish this, perform the following steps:

1. Click on **Projects** in the left-hand panel and then click on **Run**.
2. You will see the **Valgrind Settings** interface when you reach the **Run Settings** page. The default settings should work. If you want to set other settings, be sure that you know what you are doing and what you're trying to look for from the debug information.
3. Under **Memory Analysis Options**, enable **Show reachable and indirectly lost blocks** if you want to look for pointers that might have been freed before the program exited.

4. You can also ask Valgrind to display different amounts of leaks that occurred during the application runtime by selecting different options for the **Checks for leaks on finish** drop-down box, namely, **Summary Only** or **Full**. This is shown in the following screenshot:

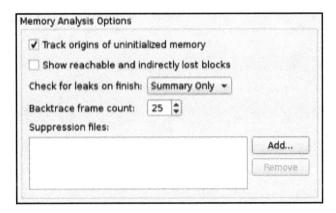

Now, you can select the Valgrind run target for your application. You need to do this with the debug build because Valgrind requires the debug symbols in your application to produce a meaningful report. To use Valgrind, start the application and click on the button a few times. The Valgrind process outputs information continually, but most of the output comes after we quit the application.

Valgrind produces a lot of output, which can take you some time to sort through. We're looking for the leak summary, which indicates the number of bytes that are definitely lost and indirectly lost. Definitely lost blocks are the memory you've allocated and not freed; indirectly lost memory is the memory that has leaked because it's referred to by another pointer and the referring pointer wasn't freed.

The output will look something similar to the following code:

```
X bytes in 1 blocks are definitely lost in loss record n of m at
0x........: function_name (filename:line number)
```

The X indicates the number of bytes that leaked, and the address of the leaked block is shown in the second line. The record numbers indicate the internal record numbers used by the application's memory allocator and probably won't help you much. The following screenshot shows what it looks like in action:

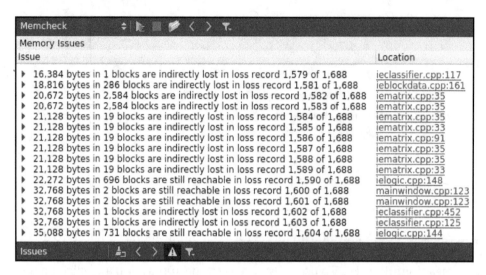

We should focus on leaks in our application because it's possible that Qt might have leaks of its own. Valgrind supports suppression files, which indicate the leaks that should be ignored; if you can find and download one for the version of Qt you're building against, you can include a reference to the suppression file by modifying the argument line to read as follows:

```
-q --tool=memcheck --leak-check=full --leak-resolution=low --
suppressions=suppresion.txt ./[your-app-target-name]
```

Detecting a memory leak on Windows using Visual Leak Detector

Since Valgrind only supports Linux, let's take a look at how we can detect memory leaks on Windows. For the Windows platform, the best tool you can use is Visual Studio itself, which can be downloaded for free. You must also compile your project using the Visual C++ compiler instead of MinGW in order for the Visual Studio leak detector to work. Then, you need to download Visual Leak Detector, which is a library that adds features on top of the existing Visual C++ detector. You can download Visual Leak Detector from https://kinddragon.github.io/vld.

Once you have installed Visual Leak Detector, open up the Leaky Button example again. This time, switch over to one of the kits that supports the Visual Studio compiler, and then open up your project file (.pro) and add the following code to it:

```
INCLUDEPATH += "C:/Program Files (x86)/Visual Leak Detector/include/"
LIBS += -L"C:/Program Files (x86)/Visual Leak Detector/lib/Win64" -lvld
```

The preceding code will link the folders containing Visual Leak Detector's header and library files with your project. Next, open up main.cpp and include the following header:

```
#include <vld.h>
```

Then, copy the following files from the Visual Leak Detector installation folder to your application's build folder:

- dbghelp.dll
- Microsoft.DTfW.DHL.manifest
- vld_x64.dll

Now, build and run the program and you should see the following line in the **Application Output** window when starting up your application in debug mode:

```
Visual Leak Detector read settings from: C:\Program Files (x86)\Visual Leak
Detector\vld.ini
Visual Leak Detector Version 2.5.1 installed.
```

If you see the preceding message, congratulations! Visual Leak Detector has been successfully implemented for your project. After that, press the leak push button. You will see the number only increase by 1 every time you press the button because Visual Leak Detector has detected a leak and has stopped the operation. You can now close your program and check out the long messages telling you the issues you might face. If you look closely line by line, you may notice something like this from the messages:

```
f:\dd\vctools\crt\vcstartup\src\startup\exe_winmain.cpp (17):
QtLeakyButton.exe!WinMainCRTStartup()
KERNEL32.DLL!BaseThreadInitThunk() + 0x14 bytes
ntdll.dll!RtlUserThread ucrtbased.dll!malloc()
f:\dd\vctools\crt\vcstartup\src\heap\new_array.cpp (29):
QtLeakyButton.exe!operator new[]()
c:\users\leezh\desktop\qtleakybutton\mainwindow.cpp (19):
QtLeakyButton.exe!MainWindow::leakPressed() + 0xA bytes
```

The first line indicates the program has been started. Then, there are the `malloc` and `new` keywords, which means the problem has something to do with memory allocation. After that, we also see `leakPressed`, which is exactly the function that causes the memory leak. From here, we know that something is going wrong in the `leakPressed` function that has something to do with an unused pointer not being cleared, and therefore we can go and fix the problem in our code. The debug messages may look different depending on the issue you face, so look closely at the messages and make sure you don't miss any important details.

Finding memory leaks in your application is partly art and partly science. It's a good exercise to go through periodically during application development in order to ensure that the leaks you might introduce are found quickly while you're most familiar with the new code you're running. Next, we will proceed to learn how we can do more with QML Profiler and optimize our existing application.

Introducing QML Profiler

In the previous section, *Introducing QML performance analysis*, you were introduced to QML Profiler and its basic functionality. In this section, we will explore what other features QML Profiler can offer us to make our debugging process faster and more effective. We will also learn how to examine the data displayed in QML Profiler and what the data indicates, so that we can determine the cause of slowdowns or crashes happening to our application.

To demonstrate this, let's perform the following steps:

1. Let's create a new Qt Quick project and change the code of `main.qml` to the following:

```
import QtQuick 2.12
import QtQuick.Window 2.12

Window {
    id: window
    visible: true
    width: 640
    height: 480
    title: qsTr("Hello World")

    Component.onCompleted: {
        for (var i = 0; i < 200; i++)
        {
            var x = Math.floor((Math.random() * window.width) + 1);
            var y = Math.floor((Math.random() * window.height) +
```

```
    1);
                    Qt.createQmlObject('import QtQuick 2.12; Rectangle
                        {color: "red"; width: 20; height: 20; x: ' + x + ';
                        y: ' + y + ';}', window, 'rect');
            }
        }
    }
```

In the preceding code, we set an `id` instance for the `Window` object, called `window`. When `window` gets created, the `onCompleted` function will be called, and we tell the program to start spawning 200 rectangular shapes at random positions across the screen. We used `Math.random` to generate the x and y values for each rectangle, and the range for the random generator goes from 1 to the `width` or `height` value of `window`.

2. If we run the program now, we should see something like this:

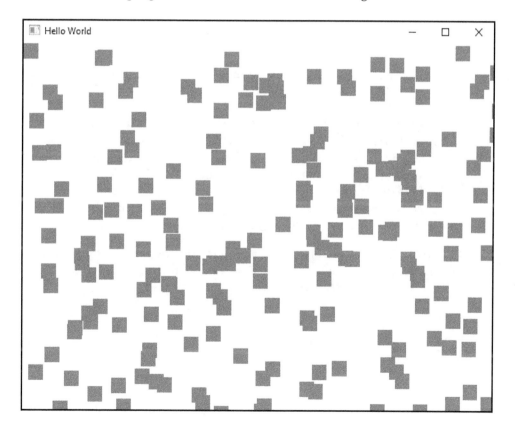

3. After that, go to **Analyze | QML Profiler** to open up QML Profiler and start analyzing the application. Once the program has been started and the rectangles have been spawned, you can now close it and head over to the QML Profiler interface.

4. Before going to **Timeline** or **Flame Graph**, it's better to first check out **Statistics** as this is the quickest way to get an overview of the overall performance of your application in a linear fashion:

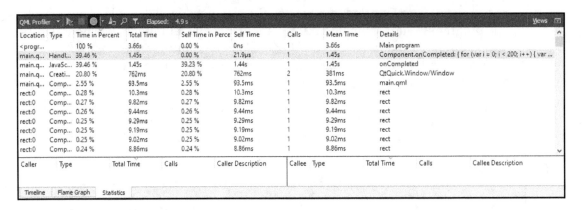

As you can see, the **Total Time** it takes for the onCompleted function to complete its task is **1.45** seconds on my computer, which is expected as we spawned 200 rectangles on the screen. You can try and increase the number of i to 300 or 400 and see how many seconds it takes to spawn all those rectangles in QML Profiler. You can double-click on an individual item on the list to look at the breakdown details of the operation to further your investigation. Through the **Statistics** window, we can easily examine the performance of our application and spot the operation that slows down our program.

5. Other than that, you can also look at the left side of your script to look at the **Self Time in Percent** data, which is also available in the **Statistics** window:

```
~2.9%    1    import QtQuick 2.12
         2    import QtQuick.Window 2.12
         3
~22.9%   4  ▼ Window {
         5        id: window
         6        visible: true
         7        width: 640
         8        height: 480
         9        title: qsTr("Hello World")
         10
≥38.1%   11 ▼    Component.onCompleted: {
         12           for (var i = 0; i < 200; i++)
         13 ▼         {
         14               var x = Math.floor((Math.random() * window.width) + 1);
         15               var y = Math.floor((Math.random() * window.height) + 1);
         16               Qt.createQmlObject('import QtQuick 2.12; Rectangle {color:
         17           }
         18        }
         19   }
         20
```

6. Next, we look at the **Flame Graph** window:

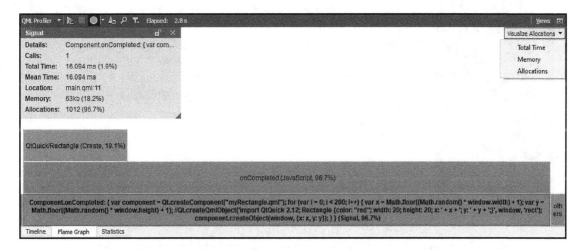

The **Flame Graph** window is mainly used to visualize the overall performance of the application in the form of a bar graph, including the total time spent compiling and creating each component, its memory usage, and the number of memory allocations performed by the functions.

7. Now, let's proceed to the **Timeline** window. The **Timeline** window basically shows you similar data to what's in the **Statistics** window. However, it also lays out all the operations along a timeline that tells you which operation occurred at what time (from the start of the program execution) and how long it took to run any particular operation. Other than that, it also displays the memory usage of each operation and the rendering duration of the scene graph.

8. Let's take a look at our example program's timeline and see whether or not we can spot performance issues. If you scroll through the **Timeline** window, you will see a ton of colorful bars along the **Compiling** and **Creating** sections. Each of these bars indicates the creation of an individual rectangle shape in our application's window:

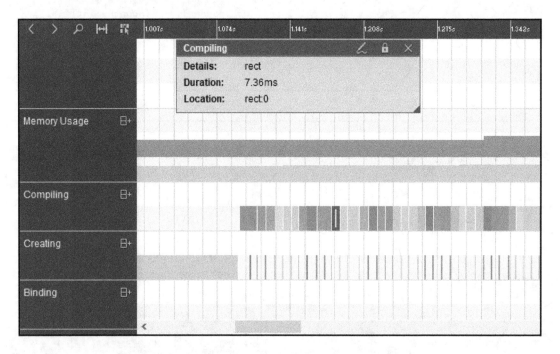

Very quickly, we notice that the compiling time is much longer than the creating time. Each rectangle only took a few nanoseconds to create, but took several milliseconds to compile. This is because we asked our program to load fresh QML code every time we tried to create a rectangle, so it needed to compile repeatedly even though each rectangle essentially carries the same properties (except the x and y values). From the **Timeline** window, we found a performance issue that we can improve further.

9. To solve this issue, let's move the rectangle's QML code into a separate QML file, by going to **File | New File or Project**. Then, select **QML File (Qt Quick 2)** under the **Files and Classes | Qt** category. After that, open up the newly created file (here I call it `myRectangle.qml`) and change the code to the following:

```
import QtQuick 2.12;

Rectangle{
    color: "red";
    width: 20;
    height: 20;
    x: 0;
    y: 0;
}
```

The preceding code is basically the same as the rectangle code we used in `main.qml`, except the x and y values are now set to 0 by default. We will set the x and y values later after we have spawned the individual rectangle.

Then, in `main.qml`, we change the code in the `onCompleted` function:

```
Component.onCompleted: {
    var component = Qt.createComponent("myRectangle.qml");

    for (var i = 0; i < 200; i++)
    {
        var x = Math.floor((Math.random() * window.width) + 1);
        var y = Math.floor((Math.random() * window.height) + 1);

        component.createObject(window, {x: x, y: y});
    }
}
```

Instead of having to compile new QML code every time we spawn a rectangle shape, we now only need to do it once before the `for` loop. We did so by calling `Qt.createComponent` and loading `myRectangle.qml`, which stores the rectangle's QML code. Then, we called `component.createObject` to spawn the rectangles and changed its x and y values to a random number. `createObject` duplicates the compiled rectangle component from the memory and, thus, no additional compilation is required.

If we run QML Profiler again, we should see something completely different in the **Timeline** window:

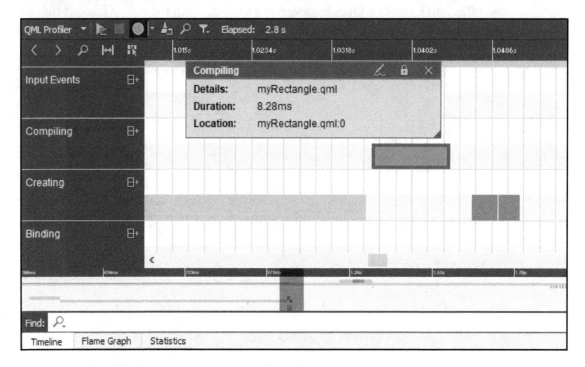

Instead of spending around 1.6 seconds to compile all the 200 rectangle shapes, now we only need 8 milliseconds because we only need to compile it once instead of 200 times. As a result, our program has been optimized and is performing much better! Even though a 1 second improvement doesn't seem significant here, as your program grows, there would otherwise have been more and more performance hiccups here and there that would have snowballed into a performance nightmare.

Doing more with QML Profiler

Let's now learn how we can use QML profiler for something other than just normal GUI applications. In the following example, we will try and create a simple 3D renderer using Qt Quick and make use of QML Profiler to examine its performance.

First, let's create an empty Qt Quick project. Then, open up `main.qml` and add the following modules to it:

```
import QtQuick 2.12 as QtQuick2
import QtQuick.Scene3D 2.0
import Qt3D.Core 2.0
import Qt3D.Render 2.0
import Qt3D.Extras 2.0
```

We added the modules for 3D rendering that are required for later use. We also set an alias for the `QtQuick` module, which is `QtQuick2`, as we will be using it later in our code. After that, let's remove the default `Window` item and add `Entity` instead. We call this `Entity` instance `sceneRoot`, and it will act as the parent item for all objects in the 3D scene. We also add a `Camera` instance to set the point of view of the rendering:

```
Entity {
    id: sceneRoot

    Camera {
        id: camera
        projectionType: CameraLens.PerspectiveProjection
        fieldOfView: 45
        aspectRatio: 16/9
        nearPlane : 0.1
        farPlane : 1000.0
        position: Qt.vector3d(0, 0, -30)
        upVector: Qt.vector3d(0, 1, 0)
        viewCenter: Qt.vector3d(0, 0, 0)
    }
```

We position the camera at `x:0 y:0 z:-30`, then set its view target at the origin. After that, add `ForwardRenderer`, which renders the scene from the camera view into our Qt window. We set the background color to light blue by setting the `clearColor` property:

```
    components: [
        RenderSettings {
            activeFrameGraph: ForwardRenderer {
                clearColor: Qt.rgba(0, 0.5, 1, 1)
                camera: camera
            }
        }
    ]
```

The next step is more complicated. We create another `Entity` instance, which this time will carry a 3D cube model. To achieve that, we need three different components: mesh, material, and transform:

```
PhongMaterial {
    id: material
}

CuboidMesh {
    id: mesh
    xExtent: 10
    yExtent: 10
    zExtent: 10
}

Transform {
    id: transform
    property real userAngle: 0.0
    matrix: {
        var m = Qt.matrix4x4();
        m.rotate(userAngle, Qt.vector3d(0, 1, 0));
        m.translate(Qt.vector3d(0, 0, 0));
        return m;
    }
}

Entity {
    id: entity
    components: [mesh, material, transform]
}
```

The mesh is essentially the 3D data that contains all the position information of the vertices. In this example, we only need a simple cube model, so we used the `CuboidMesh` component, which is a built-in shape that resembles a cube. The material is the definition of the surface property of the 3D mesh, such as its color, roughness, and reflectivity. In this case, we simply apply the standard Phong material to the 3D mesh. The transform component is the position, rotation, and scale of the mesh, which is represented by a matrix value. We then supply these components to the `Entity` item to form a 3D object.

Lastly, we use the `NumberAnimation` animation type to rotate the cube infinitely so that we can see some motion in our 3D scene. We use the `QtQuick2` alias, which we created at the beginning, to call `NumberAnimation` since it belongs to the `QtQuick` module:

```
QtQuick2.NumberAnimation
{
    target: transform
    property: "userAngle"
    duration: 10000
    from: 0
    to: 360

    loops: QtQuick2.Animation.Infinite
    running: true
}
}
```

Before we build our project, let's open up `main.cpp` and change the whole `main` function to this:

```
#include <QGuiApplication>
#include <Qt3DQuickExtras/qt3dquickwindow.h>

int main(int argc, char *argv[])
{
    QGuiApplication app(argc, argv);
    Qt3DExtras::Quick::Qt3DQuickWindow view;
    view.setSource(QUrl("qrc:/main.qml"));
    view.show();

    return app.exec();
}
```

We changed the window class to `Qt3DQuickWindow` because we no longer need a normal GUI window. Let's build and run the program now. You should see something like this:

To analyze the program, go to **Analyze** | **QML Profiler**. From the QML Profiler window, we will be able to see how long it takes to set up the 3D model, how long it takes to render each frame, and so on. This example scene is quite simple so everything seems lightning-fast, but if you have a complex scene with many high-polygon models and complex material, then you will notice a bottleneck here:

```
~99.2%   1   import QtQuick 2.12 as QtQuick2
         2   import QtQuick.Scene3D 2.0
         3
         4   import Qt3D.Core 2.0
         5   import Qt3D.Render 2.0
         6   import Qt3D.Extras 2.0
         7
         8
~0.6%    9 ▾ Entity {
        10       id: sceneRoot
        11
<0.1%   12 ▾     Camera {
```

QML Profiler ▾ ▶ ▮ ◯ ▾ ▲ 𝒫 ▼   Elapsed: 6.0 s

Location	Type	Time in Percer	Total Time	Self Time in P	Self Time	Calls	Mean Time	Details
<progr...		100 %	169ms	0.00 %	0ns	1	169ms	Main program
main.q...	Compiling	99.16 %	168ms	99.16 %	168ms	1	168ms	main.qml
main.q...	Creating	0.55 %	937µs	0.05 %	90.2µs	1	937µs	Qt3D.Core/Entity
main.q...	Creating	0.22 %	370µs	0.22 %	370µs	1	370µs	Qt3D.Extras/PhongMaterial
main.q...	Binding	0.21 %	349µs	0.00 %	6.8µs	1	349µs	matrix: { var m = Qt.matrix4x4(); m.rotate(userAngle,
main.q...	JavaScript	0.20 %	343µs	0.20 %	343µs	1	343µs	expression for matrix
main.q...	Creating	0.09 %	153µs	0.09 %	153µs	1	153µs	Qt3D.Extras/OrbitCameraController
main.q...	Creating	0.08 %	144µs	0.03 %	44µs	1	144µs	Qt3D.Render/RenderSettings
main.q...	Creating	0.06 %	99.7µs	0.06 %	99.7µs	1	99.7µs	Qt3D.Extras/ForwardRenderer
main.q...	Binding	0.06 %	99.7µs	0.04 %	73.5µs	1	99.7µs	components: [mesh, material, transform]
main.q...	Creating	0.05 %	84.3µs	0.05 %	84.3µs	1	84.3µs	Qt3D.Render/Camera
main.q...	Creating	0.04 %	73.6µs	0.04 %	73.6µs	1	73.6µs	Qt3D.Extras/SphereMesh
main.q...	JavaScript	0.02 %	26.2µs	0.02 %	26.2µs	1	26.2µs	expression for components
main.q...	Binding	0.01 %	22.6µs	0.00 %	2µs	1	22.6µs	clearColor: Qt.rgba(0, 0.5, 1, 1)
main.q...	JavaScript	0.01 %	20.6µs	0.01 %	20.6µs	1	20.6µs	expression for clearColor

That's it—we have not only used QML Profiler to analyze the performance of a normal GUI program, but this time we also learned how we can analyze a 3D renderer using QML Profiler.

Next, we will learn how to implement test integration in our Qt application.

Implementing test integration

Unit testing is a very important stage during application development but is oftentimes ignored by developers, especially beginners. Unit testing ensures that the quality of your application is up to scratch and improves the user experience. One of the methods for unit testing is to integrate auto tests into your project. In this section, we will learn how we can implement different types of auto tests in Qt Creator.

The Qt Test framework consists of two parts—**Qt Test** and **Qt Quick Test**, which test C++, QML, and GUI features, whereas the other two frameworks only test C++ features. Pick the one that suits your project the most. We will look into each of them here.

Creating Qt and Qt Quick tests

Qt and Qt Quick tests are built into Qt Creator, so you don't need to install any third-party components into your project. Learn how to create a Qt or Qt Quick test by following the steps given here:

1. Create a new project by going to **File | New File or Project**.
2. Select **Auto Test Project** under the **Other Project** category.
3. In the **Project and Test Information** dialog, pick either **Qt Test** or **Qt Quick Test** for the **Test framework** option.
4. There are two additional options under **Qt Test**, which are **GUI Application** and **Requires QApplication**. You can check these two options if you're building a GUI application.
5. After that, fill in the **Test case name**—anything will do.
6. Select your **Build system**. Leave it as **qmake** if you are not sure of what to do. You only need to change this option if you are using some other build systems such as **CMake** or **Qbs**.
7. Press **Next** and complete the rest of the process. This is shown in the following screenshot:

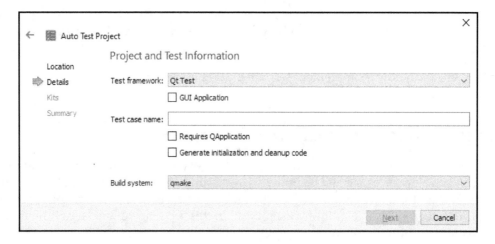

Once we have created the project, open up the `.pro` file. You will see something quite different from the ordinary project files we have used in all previous example projects:

```
QT += testlib
QT += gui
CONFIG += qt warn_on depend_includepath testcase
```

As you can see, this project comes with the `testlib` module by default. This module contains all the functionalities we need to conduct our tests later in this section. In the config section, we also included `warn_on`, `depend_includepath`, and `testcase`, which are all new to us at this point:

- `warn_on`: This option tells the compiler to output as many warnings as possible. We need this feature to show us whatever issues occur during the auto test.
- `depend_includepath`: This option tells Qt to append the values of `INCLUDEPATH` and `DEPENDPATH` so that all dependencies are loaded correctly.
- `testcase`: We must include this option in our project to indicate that it is an auto test. A check target will be added to the Makefile before running the test. Without this, Qt Creator will not execute the application as an auto test.

After that, open up the CPP file in your project directory. The class in the CPP file is named after the **Test case name** you have inserted during the creation of the project. There are three slot functions created for you under the class—`initTestCase`, `cleanupTestCase`, and `test_case1`.

- `initTestCase`: This is a built-in slot that won't be treated as a test function. This function will be called before the test begins. You can use this to initialize variables or pointers that are needed for the tests.
- `cleanupTestCase`: As the name implies, this function is used to clean up variables or pointers after all the tests have been executed.
- `test_case1`: This is an example test function that is created for you by default. You can create more slot functions yourself and all of them will be treated as test functions. There is no limit to how many test functions you can create, and you can use any names for your test functions, as long as they do not clash with `initTestCase`, `cleanupTestCase`, `init`, and `cleanup`.

Besides `initTestCase` and `cleanupTestCase`, there are another two slot functions that are not treated as test functions, `init` and `cleanup`; they were shown briefly previously:

- `init`: Unlike `initTestCase`, this slot function gets called between every test function. The following test function will be skipped if this function fails, and the test will proceed to the next test function.
- `cleanup`: This is similar to `cleanupTestCase`, but runs after every test function.

Let's take a look at some simple code and how we can create our own auto test:

```
void Testing::test_case1()
{
    QString str = "Testing";
```

```
        QVERIFY(str.toUpper() == "TESTING");
    }
```

If we run the application now, we should see something similar to this:

```
********* Start testing of Testing *********
Config: Using QtTest library 5.13.1, Qt 5.13.1 (x86_64-little_endian-llp64
shared (dynamic) debug build; by GCC 7.3.0)
PASS   : Testing::initTestCase()
PASS   : Testing::test_case1()
PASS   : Testing::cleanupTestCase()
Totals: 3 passed, 0 failed, 0 skipped, 0 blacklisted, 1ms
********* Finished testing of Testing *********
```

We used QVERIFY to make the test. If the result is true, then the test will pass. Otherwise, the test will fail. Now, let's change something in the code so that it fails:

```
void Testing::test_case1()
{
    QString str = "Testing1234";
    QVERIFY(str.toUpper() == "TESTING");
}
```

Now, let's run the program again. You should now see a failed status being displayed:

```
********* Start testing of Testing *********
Config: Using QtTest library 5.13.1, Qt 5.13.1 (x86_64-little_endian-llp64
shared (dynamic) debug build; by GCC 7.3.0)
PASS   : Testing::initTestCase()
FAIL!  : Testing::test_case1() 'str.toUpper() == "TESTING"' returned FALSE.
()
..\autotest\tst_testing.cpp(44) : failure location
PASS   : Testing::cleanupTestCase()
Totals: 2 passed, 1 failed, 0 skipped, 0 blacklisted, 2ms
********* Finished testing of Testing *********
```

You can use QVERIFY to check for a specific function or variable. As long as the result returns true, the test will pass and continue on. Besides QVERIFY, you can also use QCOMPARE to compare two values. Let's create a second test function and use QCOMPARE in it:

```
class Testing : public QObject
{
    Q_OBJECT
public:
    Testing();
    ~Testing();
private slots:
```

```
        void initTestCase();
        void cleanupTestCase();
        void test_case1();
        void test_case2();
};

void Testing::test_case2()
{
    int a = 10;
    QCOMPARE(a, 10);
}
```

QCOMPARE works very similarly to QVERIFY. The only difference is that it only accepts two inputs instead of one.

 To learn more about the functions and macros provided by the QTest namespace, please check out the documentation at https://doc.qt.io/qt-5/qtest.html.

Testing signals and slots using QSignalSpy

We can also test the signals and slots in our program by using the QSignalSpy class. QSignalSpy is a class provided by Qt to enable connecting to the signal of any object and recording its emission. QSignalSpy will then append the signal's arguments into a QVariant list for unit testing.

Let's continue our previous code and add a new slot function called test_signalslot:

```
    private slots:
        void initTestCase();
        void cleanupTestCase();
        void test_case1();
        void test_case2();
        void test_signalslot();
```

Next, in the constructor of the `Testing` class, we create a new `QObject` and connect its `objectNameChanged` signal to the `test_signalslot` slot function. We also connected the `objectNameChanged` signal to a `QSignalSpy` object so that it can record the emission. After that, we trigger the signal by changing the name of the object, as follows:

```
Testing::Testing()
{
    QObject* object = new QObject(this);
    connect(object, &QObject::objectNameChanged, this,
      &Testing::test_signalslot);
    spy = new QSignalSpy(object, &QObject::objectNameChanged);
    object->setObjectName("New Name");
}
```

Then, we implement the `test_signalslot` function. First, we check whether the signal has been emitted. We also considered all the arguments recorded by `QSignalSpy` and check whether the first argument is "New Name", so that we can verify that the signal is the one we emitted just now:

```
void Testing::test_signalslot()
{
    QCOMPARE(spy->count(), 1);
    QList<QVariant> arguments = spy->takeFirst();
    QVERIFY(arguments.at(0).toString() == "New Name");
}
```

Build and run the program now and you should see something like this:

```
********* Start testing of Testing *********
Config: Using QtTest library 5.13.0, Qt 5.13.0 (x86_64-little_endian-llp64
shared (dynamic) debug build; by GCC 7.3.0)
PASS   : Testing::initTestCase()
PASS   : Testing::test_case1()
PASS   : Testing::test_case2()
PASS   : Testing::test_signalslot()
PASS   : Testing::cleanupTestCase()
Totals: 5 passed, 0 failed, 0 skipped, 0 blacklisted, 1ms
********* Finished testing of Testing *********
```

You can change the value in QCOMPARE and QVERIFY to see what will happen if the unit test failed. If you are testing the signal of a timer that doesn't emit immediately, you can use the wait function to ask Qt to wait for a few milliseconds before verifying it:

```
QVERIFY(spy->wait(1000));
```

That's it. We have learned how we can make use of Qt and Qt Quick tests to automatically check our code and ensure that quality is maintained properly. We also learned how we can unit test the signals and slots within our Qt application through QSignalSpy.

 To learn more about the QSignalSpy class, please visit https://doc.qt. io/qt-5/qsignalspy.html.

Next, we will move on to third-party auto test suites and make our test integration even more diverse and better.

Adding better support for test integration

Even though Qt and Qt Quick tests are both really good auto-testing frameworks, we can also integrate some other third-party unit testing frameworks to test for different issues. You can also compare the results from different frameworks to make sure there are no false positives and ensure that the quality of your product is at its best. Besides their own Qt Test framework, Qt Creator also integrates several other different auto test suites into the editor, such as **Google C++ Testing Framework** and **Boost.Test**, for automated unit testing.

First, we will learn how we can integrate Google Test into our project.

Creating Google tests

Before we start setting up Google Test, let's download Google C++ Testing Framework from the GitHub link here: `https://github.com/google/googletest`. Click on the **Clone or download** button and then **Download ZIP**:

Once you have all the required files, unzip the files to a directory on your PC and follow these steps to create a test project:

1. Create a new project by going to **File | New File or Project**.
2. Select **Auto Test Project** under the **Other Project** category.
3. In the **Project and Test Information** dialog, pick `Google Test` for the **Test framework** option.
4. After that, fill in the **Test suite name** and **Test case name** fields.
5. Check the **Enable C++ 11** checkbox if you want to support C++ 11 features in the test.
6. As for the Google test repository field, select the directory where you unzipped the file you just downloaded from GitHub—for example, `C:\googletest-master`.
7. Select your **Build system**. Leave it as **qmake** if you are not sure of what to do. You only need to change this option if you are using certain other build systems such as **CMake** or **Qbs**.
8. Press **Next** and complete the rest of the process.

Once the project has been created, you will see that several things have been set up for you by the project wizard we just walked through. If you open up `gtest_dependency.pri`, you can see that the settings for `INCLUDEPATH`, `SOURCES`, and so on have all been set for you. The actual source file that contains the test functions is located at `tst_testscene.h`, which looks something like this:

```
#ifndef TST_TESTCASE_H
#define TST_TESTCASE_H

#include <gtest/gtest.h>
#include <gmock/gmock-matchers.h>

using namespace testing;

TEST(TestSuite, TestCase)
{
    EXPECT_EQ(1, 1);
    ASSERT_THAT(0, Eq(0));
}

#endif // TST_TESTCASE_H
```

Similar to Qt Test, Google Test also uses macros such as `EXPECT_EQ` and `ASSERT_THAT` to do the test. This is what they do:

- `EXPECT_EQ`: A non-fatal assertion that does simple true/false condition testing, similar to `QCOMPARE`. Any macros that start with `EXPECT_` will not terminate the auto test when detecting a failure. The test will carry on after displaying the failure on the terminal.
- `ASSERT_THAT`: This macro allows a much more complicated test to be done. The first input is the value you want to test with this assertion, while the second input is the condition of the test. In the preceding example, the assertion tests for value 0 and the condition is equal to 0, which can be represented by `Eq(0)`. You can use this to compare much more complicated variables, such as maps or vectors—for example, `ASSERT_THAT(v, ElementsAre(5, 10, 15));`. The `ASSERT_` keyword tells us that this is a fatal assertion, which means that the test will be stopped immediately when detecting a failure.

If you build and run the project now, you should see a similar result to this:

```
 C:\Qt\Tools\QtCreator\bin\qtcreator_process_stub.exe
[==========] Running 1 test from 1 test suite.
[----------] Global test environment set-up.
[----------] 1 test from TestSuite
[ RUN      ] TestSuite.TestCase
[       OK ] TestSuite.TestCase (0 ms)
[----------] 1 test from TestSuite (5 ms total)

[----------] Global test environment tear-down
[==========] 1 test from 1 test suite ran. (58 ms total)
[  PASSED  ] 1 test.
Press <RETURN> to close this window...
▄
```

 To learn more about the other macros available in Google C++ Testing Framework, visit https://github.com/google/googletest/blob/master/googletest/docs/primer.md.

Now, let's see how Boost tests work.

Creating Boost tests

Finally, we will learn how to create Boost tests. As the name implies, Boost tests require a set of third-party C++ libraries called Boost. You can download it from Boost's official website at https://www.boost.org. Once you have downloaded the ZIP file, extract it somewhere on your PC as we will need it later. When you're done, check out these steps to create a test project:

1. Create a new project by going to **File | New File or Project**.
2. Select **Auto Test Project** under the **Other Project** category.
3. In the **Project and Test Information** dialog, pick **Boost Test** for the **Test framework** option.
4. After that, fill in the **Test suite name** and **Test case name** fields.
5. Then, go to the directory of Boost where you unzipped the download and copy the directory path to the **Boost include dir (optional)** field—for example, C:\boost_1_71_0.
6. Select your **Build system**. Leave it as **qmake** if you are not sure of what to do. You only need to change this option if you are using certain other build systems such as **CMake** or **Qbs**.
7. Press **Next** and complete the rest of the process.

When the project has been created, open up `main.cpp`:

```
#define BOOST_TEST_MODULE TestSuite
#include <boost/test/included/unit_test.hpp>

BOOST_AUTO_TEST_CASE( testCase )
{
    BOOST_TEST( true /* test assertion */ );
}
```

We can see the resemblance between the different unit test suites. Boost also uses macros, though they start with BOOST_, and it works pretty similar to Qt Test and Google Test too. The most common macro that you will use is BOOST_TEST, which works for most of the test cases. For instance, we can change the BOOST_AUTO_TEST_CASE function as follows:

```
BOOST_AUTO_TEST_CASE( testCase )
{
    int a = 5;
    int b = 6;
    BOOST_TEST(a != b - 1);
}
```

As you can see from the preceding code, we've intentionally made it a fail test, just to see what the outcome from the application is. Let's build and run the program now. You should see something similar to the following screenshot:

Other than that, Boost also supports assertions with different severity levels:

- BOOST_TEST_WARN: Lowest severity level. This would not even raise the error count if the test failed to perform. The auto test will continue to proceed to the next test function if the current test has failed.
- BOOST_TEST_CHECK: Medium severity level. This is actually the same as BOOST_TEST, which we used in the previous example. If this test failed to perform, it would increase the error count but would not stop the auto test from continuing.

- `BOOST_TEST_REQUIRE`: Highest severity level. This assertion would both increase the error count and stop the auto test when the test returns a failed result.

 There are plenty of other macros that you can use to test various types of test cases. To learn more about this, please visit the Boost documentation at `https://www.boost.org/doc/libs/1_71_0/libs/test/doc/html`.

In this section, we have learned how we can set up effective auto tests using various types of unit test suites.

Summary

Qt Creator provides the QML analyzer, which lets you perform runtime analysis of your Qt applications. You can see a graph (in time) of how your application is running, as well as dive into the details about how your application spends its time drawing, binding to variables, and executing JavaScript.

Qt Creator also integrates well with Valgrind on Linux, letting you look for memory leaks in your application. Using Valgrind on Linux, you can see the blocks that were allocated but not freed, and, more importantly, see how big they were and where they were allocated in the code, giving you a head start in determining why they were not freed. Since Valgrind only works on Linux, we also discussed another memory leak detector called Visual Leak Detector, which works great on Windows.

Other than that, we have also learned how to implement automated unit testing using Qt Test, Google Test, and Boost tests to help improve the quality of our application. Speaking of quality, we also learned how to use QML Profiler to improve the performance of our application by examining memory usage and code efficiency.

In the next chapter, we will turn our attention from specific parts of Qt Creator to one of its most exciting aspects in general: the ability to use Qt Creator to compile and test applications for mobile platforms such as Android.

12
Developing Mobile Applications with Qt Creator

Qt and mobile development have a long history. Qt's beginnings included early releases on Linux personal digital assistants in the late nineties and at the turn of this century. Since then, it's been ported to a number of mobile environments, including the mobile variants of Linux that Nokia shipped, such as MeeGo and Symbian. While Symbian and MeeGo came and went, Qt's acceptance of mobile platforms lives on, most recently with support for Android.

In this chapter, we will talk a little about writing mobile applications and then learn how to set up Qt Creator to write applications for Android. It's worth noting that while we will leverage everything you have learned about Qt development when developing a mobile application, we also need to understand how the environments that the mobile software runs on are different from traditional desktop and laptop environments, as well as how to design those constraints. Once we understand these differences, writing software for mobile platforms such as Android with Qt is a matter of snapping your fingers!

We will cover the following topics in this chapter:

- Understanding mobile software development
- Setting up Qt Creator for Android
- Deploying applications to Android devices
- Setting up Qt Creator for iOS
- Improving support for iOS and Android applications

Technical requirements

The technical requirements for this chapter include Qt 5.12.3 `arm64-v8a`, Qt Creator 4.9.0, and Windows 10.

Understanding mobile software development

The key point to remember when developing software for any mobile platform, such as a cell phone or tablet, is that every resource is premium. The device is smaller, meaning the following:

- Your user will pay less attention to your application and use it for shorter periods of time.
- The screen is smaller, so you can display less information on the display (don't be fooled by the high dot pitch of today's displays; reading a six-point font on a four-inch display is no fun, high pixel densities or not.)
- The processor and graphics processing unit are slower.
- There's less RAM and less graphics memory.
- There's less persistent storage for your application's data.
- The network is slower, by as much as three orders of magnitude.

Let's take a look at each of these in more detail.

User attention is at a premium

Can you walk and chew gum at the same time? I can't, but many people walk, chew gum, and use their mobile devices at the same time (worse, some even drive while using their devices). It's very rare for an application on a cell phone or tablet to have 100 percent of the user's attention for more than a few minutes at a time. A good rule of thumb is the smaller the device, the more likely the user is bound to treat it as something to pick up and glance at, or use while they're doing something else.

The limited attention that your user gives to your application has three key consequences:

- **Your application must be fast**: Mobile devices are no place for extra progress bars, spinning cursors, or lengthy splash screens.
- **Your application must be succinct**: The best mobile applications show data on only a page or two, having very flat navigation hierarchies. A common structure is to have a single screen with information and a single screen with preferences that lets you configure what information should be shown (such as the location from which you're getting the information). Favor clear iconography over verbose text – if you can't draw, find someone who can, or buy icons from a site such as The Noun Project (http://thenounproject.com/).

- **Your application must be accessible**: Buttons should be big (a good guideline is that no hit target in your application should be smaller than the pad of your finger, which is about a square centimeter), and text should be bigger, if possible.

For these reasons, Qt Quick is a better choice for most mobile applications that you'll write. You can create smooth, responsive applications that are visually pleasing and don't overwhelm your users.

Computational resources are at a premium

Mobile devices must carry their power source with them: batteries. While batteries have improved over the last 20 years, they haven't kept up with Moore's Law; most of the improvements have been made on the processor side, as processors have become smaller and dissipate less heat in the course of a normal operation.

Nonetheless, mobile devices aren't as fast as desktops or laptops. A good way to think of this is that the last generation's processor design probably scales well for mobile devices today. That's not to say that mobile devices are slow, but just that they're slower. An equally important point to consider is that you can't run the processor or graphics processor at full tilt without seriously affecting the battery life.

Qt, especially Qt Quick, is optimized for low power consumption, but there are still things that you can do to help squeeze the best performance out of your mobile application:

- **Don't poll**: This is probably the single most important point. Use Qt's asynchronous signal-slot mechanism wherever possible, and consider multithreading using `QThread` and the rest of Qt's multithreading environment if you need to do something in the background. The more your application sleeps, the more it prolongs the battery life.
- **Avoid gratuitous animations**: Some amount of animation is both customary and important in today's applications; well-thought-out animations can help orient the user as to where they've come from in an application's user interface and where they're going. However, don't flash, blink, or otherwise animate just to see pixels move; under the hood, a lot has to take place to move those pixels, and this consumes battery.
- **Use the network judiciously**: Most mobile devices have at least two radios (cellular and Wi-Fi); some have more. Accessing the network should be seen as a necessary evil, because radios consume power when transmitting and receiving data. Also, don't forget data parsing: if you're parsing a lot of data, it's likely that you're running the CPU at full tilt to do the heavy lifting and that means a lower battery life.

Next up, let's check out how network resources affect devices.

Network resources are at a premium

You've already been warned about the high cost to the battery of using the network. To add insult to injury, most mobile devices run on networks that can be up to three orders of magnitude slower than a desktop; your office desktop might have gigabit Ethernet, but in many parts of the world, a megabit a second is considered fast. This situation is rapidly improving as network operators deploy cellular wireless networks such as **Long-Term Evolution** (**LTE**) and Wi-Fi hotspots everywhere, but these are by no means uniformly available. On a recent trip to California, in the course of eight hours, my cellular network connectivity throughput ran a gamut faster than my cable modem (running at 25 megabits a second) down to the dreaded megabit per second, which can make a large web page crawl.

For most applications, you should be fine with the **Hypertext Transfer Protocol** (**HTTP**); Qt's QNetworkAccessManager class implements HTTP and HTTPS, and using HTTP means that you can build web services to support your backend in a standard way.

If you're developing a game or a custom application, you might need to build a custom protocol. Consider using QTcpSocket or QUdpSocket for your network protocol, keeping in mind of course that TCP is a reliable protocol. However, with UDP, there's no guarantee of your data reaching its destination; reliability is up to you.

Something to make a special note of is error handling in networked applications. Unlike a desktop, where network failures are likely to be rare because your computer is tethered to the network, wireless networks can suffer all sorts of transitory problems. These don't necessarily lead to logical failures; a short drop in network connectivity can result in **Domain Name Service** (**DNS**) problems, **Transport Layer Security** (**TLS**) timeouts, or retry timeouts.

Handle errors in your application, and ensure that there are mechanisms to retry important network operations, such as data synchronization and content uploads. Be prepared for duplicate requests and uploads too, in cases where your device uploads something to a server, but doesn't get an acknowledgment from the server because of a network problem, and so tries again.

Next, let's see how storage resources work.

Storage resources are at a premium

Mobile devices typically all use solid-state memory. Although solid-state memory has come down in price significantly in the last several years, it's still not as cheap as the rotating magnetic memory that makes up the disk drives in most desktops and many laptops. As a result, mobile devices might have as little as 8 GB of flash memory for persistent storage, or if you're lucky, 16 or 32 GB. This is shared across the system and all the applications; your application shouldn't use more than a few gigabytes at most, and that's only if your user is expecting it, say for a podcast application. That should be the sum total of the size of your application: its static resources such as audio and video, and anything it might download and cache from the network.

An equally important point is that the runtime size of your application needs to be smaller. Most mobile devices have between a half-gigabyte and 2 GB of dynamic RAM available; the system shares this across all running applications, so it's important to allocate only what you need and free it when you're done.

Finally, don't forget that your graphics textures and things can eat valuable GPU memory as well. While Qt manages the GPU for you, whether you're using Qt or Qt Quick, you can write an application that consumes all of the device's texture memory, making it difficult or impossible for the native OS to render what it needs should it need to interrupt your application with another application or system message.

Next up, let's discuss whether we should port our application to different platforms.

To port or not to port?

To paraphrase the immortal bard, that's the question. With Qt's incredible flexibility across numerous platforms, the temptation to grab an existing application and port it can be overwhelming, especially in the vertical markets where you have a piece of custom software written in Qt for the desktop and you have a customer who wants *the same thing* for the latest mobile device for their mobile workers. In general, the best advice I can offer you is to avoid porting the UI and to only port the business logic in an application if it seems well behaved for mobile devices.

A UI ported from the desktop or a laptop environment seldom works well on mobile devices. The user's operating patterns are just too different: what a person wants to do while seated at a desktop or laptop is just not the same as what they want to – or can – do when they are standing up, walking around, or in brief spurts in a conference room, canteen, or café. If you're porting from one mobile device to another, it might not be so bad; for example, a developer with a Qt application for Android shouldn't have too much trouble bringing their application to iOS.

Porting business logic might be a safer bet, assuming that it doesn't make heavy use of the CPU, network, or dynamic or static storage. Qt offers a wrapper for SQLite through `QtSql`, and many enterprise applications use that for local storage. This is a reasonable alternative for data storage, and most HTTP-based networking applications shouldn't be too hard on the network layer, as long as they have reasonable caching policies and don't make too many requests for data too often. However, if the application uses a lot of storage or has a persistent network connection, it's time to rearchitect and rewrite.

A word on testing

Testing any application is important, but mobile applications require an additional effort in testing, especially Android applications. There's a wide variety of devices available on the market, and users expect your application to perform well on any device they might have.

The most important thing you can do is test your application on real devices – as many of them as you can get your hands on – if you're interested in releasing your application commercially. While the Android SDK used by Qt Creator comes with an emulator that can run your Android application on your desktop or laptop, running on an emulator is no substitute for running on the device. A lot of things are different, from the size of the hardware itself to having a touchscreen, and of course, the network connection and raw processing power.

Fortunately, Android devices aren't terribly expensive, and there are an awful lot of them around. If you're just starting out, eBay or the Google Play Store can be a good place to shop for an inexpensive used or new device. If you're a student or a budding entrepreneur, don't forget that many family members might have an Android device that you can borrow; or, you can use the Android cell phone that you already have.

When and what should you test? Often, and everything! In a multi-week project, you should never be more than a few days away from a build running on a device. The longer you spend on writing the code that you haven't tested on a device, the more assumptions you will make about how the device will perform, and many of those assumptions will turn out wrong.

Be sure to not just test your application in good circumstances, but in bad ones as well. Network connectivity is a prime example; you should test the error handling in cases with no network coverage. If you have good network coverage where you're working, one trick you can use is to put the device in a metal cookie tin or paint can; the metal attenuates the signal and has the same effect as the signal being lost in the real world (say, in a tunnel or in the subway).

In the following section, we will learn how we can set up our Qt Creator for creating Android applications.

Setting up Qt Creator for Android

Android's functionality is delimited in API levels; Qt for Android supports Android level 16 and above: that's Android 4.1, a variant of Gingerbread. Fortunately, most devices in the market today are at least Marshmallow (Android 6.0), making Qt for Android a viable development platform for millions of devices.

Qt doesn't require the Java programming language to develop Android applications because it uses the Android NDK toolset, which supports C++ out of the box. You can just write your C++ or QML code as usual and don't have to worry about anything else, as Qt will handle it for you.

Without further ado, let's start downloading all the pieces required for our project.

Downloading all the pieces

To get started with Qt Creator for Android, you're going to need to download a lot of stuff. Let's get started:

1. Begin with a release of Qt for Android. If it was not part of the Qt installation you downloaded in `Chapter 1`, *Getting Started with Qt Creator*, you need to go back and download it from `https://www.qt.io/download`.

2. The Android developer tools require the current version of the **Java Development Kit (JDK)** (not just the runtime, the Java Runtime Environment, but the whole kit and caboodle); you can download it from `http://www.oracle.com/technetwork/java/javase/downloads/jdk7-downloads -1880260.html`.

3. You need the latest Android **Software Development Kit** (**SDK**), which comes together with the Android Studio installation package. You can download Android Studio for macOS X, Linux, or Windows at `https://developer. android.com/studio`.

4. You need the latest Android **Native Development Kit (NDK)**, which you can download at `https://developer.android.com/ndk/downloads`.

5. Unlike the older versions, you no longer need to install Ant to build your Android application. Instead, Qt uses the Gradle build system that comes together with the Android SDK.

Download, unzip, and install each of these in the given order. On Windows, I installed the Android SDK by installing Android Studio, and then installed NDK by unzipping it to the root of my hard drive. Lastly, I installed the JDK at the default location I was offered.

Setting environment variables

Once you install the JDK, you need to be sure that you've set your `JAVA_HOME` environment variable to point to the directory where it was installed so that Qt Creator can automatically detect your JDK directory. Otherwise, you must manually set the directory path in Qt Creator, which I will also explain in a moment.

How you will do this differs from platform to platform; on a macOS X or Linux box, you'd edit `.bashrc`, `.tcshrc`, or the likes; on Windows, go to **System Properties**, click on **Environment Variables**, and add the `JAVA_HOME` variable. The path should point to the base of the JDK directory; for me, it was `C:\Program Files\Java\jdk1.8.0_221\`, although the path for you will depend on where you installed the JDK and which version you installed.

Make sure you set the path with the trailing directory separator; the Android SDK is pretty fussy about that sort of thing.

Next, you need to update your PATH to point to all the stuff you just installed. Again, this is an environment variable and you'll need to add the following:

- The `bin` directory of your JDK
- The `Android\Sdk\tools` directory
- The `Android\Sdk\platform-tools` directory

For me, on my Windows 10 computer, my PATH now includes the following:

```
...C:\Program
Files\Java\jdk1.8.0_221\bin;C:\Users\YourName\AppData\Local\Android\Sdk\too
ls;;C:\Users\YourName\AppData\Local\Android\Sdk\platform-tools;...
```

Don't forget the separators: on Windows, it's a semicolon (`;`), while on macOS X and Linux, it's a colon (`:`). Also, do note that the Android SDK path in Windows is hidden away in the `AppData` directory, which is not immediately visible to you unless you turn on the **Hidden items** option under the **View** properties of your user folder.

An environment variable is a variable maintained by your operating system that affects its configuration; see `http://en.wikipedia.org/wiki/Environment_variable` for more details.

At this point, it's a good idea to restart your computer (if you're running Windows) or log out and log in again (on Linux or macOS X) to make sure that all these settings take effect. If you're on a macOS X or Linux box, you might be able to start a new Terminal and have the same effect (or reload your shell configuration file) instead, but I like the idea of restarting at this point to ensure that the next time I start everything up, it'll work correctly.

Finishing the Android SDK installation

Now, we need to use the Android SDK tools to ensure that you have a full version of the SDK for at least one Android API level installed. We'll need to start Android Studio and run the Android SDK manager. To do this, follow these steps:

1. Once Android Studio has started, look for the **Configure** button (circled in the next screenshot):

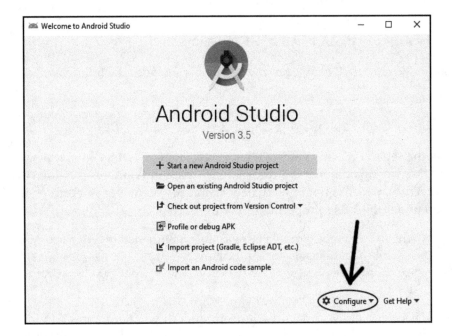

2. Click on the **SDK Manager** button in the pop-up menu to open up the Android SDK Manager.
3. Make sure that you have at least one Android API level above API level 16 installed, along with the Google USB Driver (you'll need this to debug on the hardware).
4. Quit Android Studio.

Next, let's see whether the **Android Debug Bridge** (**ADP**) – the software component that transfers your executables to your Android device and supports on-device debugging – is working as it should. Fire up a shell prompt and type adb. If you see a lot of output and no errors, the bridge is correctly installed. If not, go back and check your PATH variable to be sure it's correct.

While you're at it, you should developer-enable your Android device too so that it'll work with ADB. Follow the steps provided at `http://bit.ly/1a29sal`.

Let's move on to the next section to start configuring our Qt Creator.

Configuring Qt Creator

Now, it's time to tell Qt Creator about all the stuff you just installed. Perform the following steps:

1. Start Qt Creator but don't create a new project.
2. Under the **Tools** menu, select **Options** and then click on **Devices** and **Android**.
3. Fill in the blanks, as shown in the next screenshot. They should be set as follows:
   - The path to the SDK directory, in the directory where you installed the Android SDK
   - The path to where you installed the Android NDK
   - Check **Automatically create kits for Android tool chains**
   - The directory where you installed the JDK (this might be automatically picked up from your `JAVA_HOME` directory), as shown in the following screenshot:

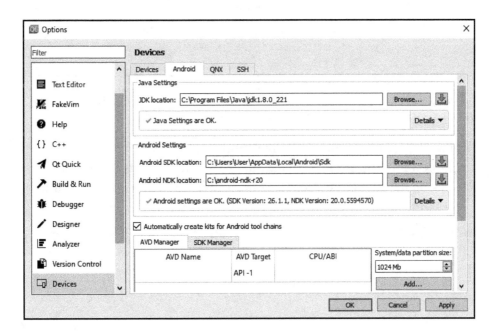

4. Click on **OK** to close the **Options** window.

You should now be able to create a new Qt GUI or Qt Quick application for Android! Do so, and ensure that Android is a target option in the wizard, as the next screenshot shows; be sure to choose at least one ARM target, one x86 target, and one target for your desktop environment:

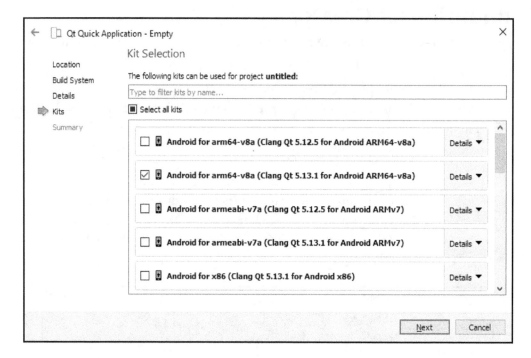

If you want to add Android build configurations to an existing project, the process is slightly different. Perform the following steps:

1. Load the project as you normally would.
2. Click on **Projects** in the left-hand side pane. The **Projects** pane will open.
3. Click on the desired Android (or other) device build kit under **Build & Run** options and it will get enabled for your project.

The following screenshot shows you where the **Projects** button and **Build & Run** options are in Qt Creator:

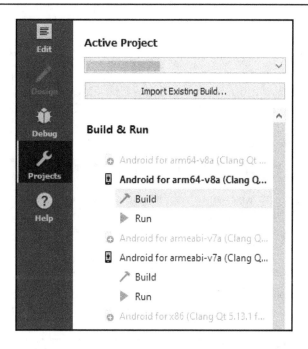

Next, we will move on to learn how we can build and run our Android application.

Building and running your application

Write and build your application normally. A good idea is to build the Qt Quick Hello World application for Android first before you go to town and make a lot of changes, and test the environment by compiling for the device. When you're ready to run on the device, perform the following steps:

1. Navigate to **Projects** (on the left-hand side) and then select the **Android for arm** kit's **Run Settings**.
2. Under **Package Configurations**, ensure that the Android SDK level is set to the SDK level of the SDK you installed.
3. Ensure that the **Package name** reads something similar to org.qtproject.example, followed by your project name.
4. Connect your Android device to your computer using the USB cable.
5. Select the **Android for arm** run target and then click on either **Debug** or **Run** to debug or run your application on the device.

That's it! We have now set up Qt Creator for Android and saw how to build and run our application on it. Next, we will see how to deploy these applications.

In addition to supporting Android, Qt also supports iOS; other platforms might be supported in the future. For more information on Qt's support for mobile platforms, refer to the Qt documentation at `https://doc.qt.io/qt-5/mobiledevelopment.html`.

Deploying applications to Android devices

In this section, we will learn how we can build and deploy our Qt application specifically for Android devices. Deploying to Android devices is quite different from desktop or iOS. There are some setups that we need to do before we're able to deploy the app to an Android device:

1. Let's open up the **Build Settings** interface by clicking on the wrench icon that says **Projects** located on the left panel. Please make sure that you have selected one of the Android kits (for example, **Android for arm64-v8a**) before doing so:

2. After that, you will see some additional settings available on the **Build Settings** interface, called **Build Android APK**, which is specifically for the Android platform only. You will not see these settings on other build platforms:

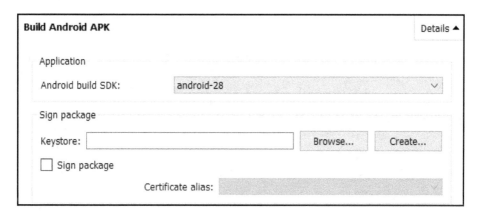

Let's take a look at the settings one by one:

1. First, you will see the **Android build SDK** option, which allows you to select the version of the Android SDK you're using to build your app. You must install the Android SDK through Android SDK Manager before you will see it appear on the combo box. Please refer to the previous *Finishing the Android SDK installation* section to learn how to do this.

2. Then, underneath this is another setting for package signing. You need to sign your app before you are able to upload it to the app store. Signing an app means generating a public key certificate that is unique for your app, with encrypted information such as password and developer details. Before you upload your app to an app store, you must sign your app so that the app store can identify it and can make sure it is built by the actual developer, and not any other person pretending to be the developer.

If you have not generated your certificate, click on the **Create...** button to start the process. A window called **Create a keystore and a certificate** will pop out and you must fill in all the information before pressing the **Save** button:

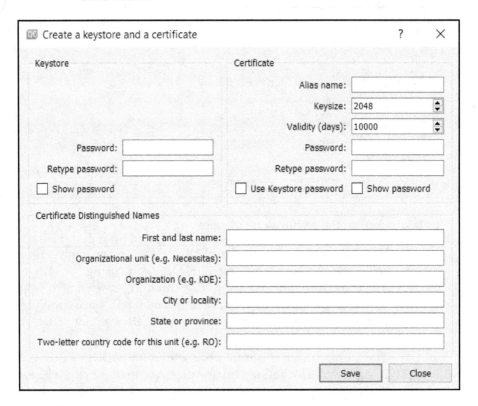

Once you press the **Save** button, a `.keystore` file will be generated. Please make sure that this file is kept safely and never lose it. If you lose the certificate, you will not be able to upload your app to the app store anymore, unless you change your app's identifier, which is considered a new app on the app store.

You don't have to sign your app if you are just testing it during the development phase. However, if you want to publish the app to the app store, you must sign it before you build your app.

To sign your app, do the following:

1. Go to the **Build Settings** interface.
2. Click on the **Browse...** button located under the **Sign package** section.
3. Select the `.keystore` file that you have generated previously.
4. After that, check on the **Sign package** checkbox. A window will appear and ask you to key in the password. After you have inserted the correct password, you can now proceed to build your project.

3. Let's continue to the next section on the **Build Android APK** interface. The options under the **Advanced Actions** section are mostly optional:

   - **Open package location after build**: Opens up the folder automatically after a successful build.
   - **Verbose output**: Outputs the list of missing dependencies for each included plugin.
   - **Use Ministro service to install Qt**: Ministro acts as the central repository for Qt libraries, which allows Qt applications to share the libraries and thus minimizes your app size. However, the user will be asked to install Ministro before they can run your app.

4. After that, you will see a **Create Templates** button underneath the **Advanced Actions** settings. If you have not generated the template before, please do so now by clicking on the button:

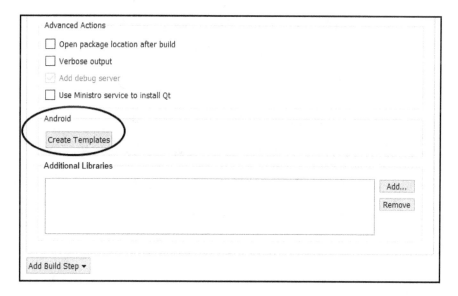

5. By clicking on **Create Templates**, a window will pop out. Keep the default settings and click on the **Finish** button:

A bunch of files will then be created for you under the android folder in your project directory, which looks like this:

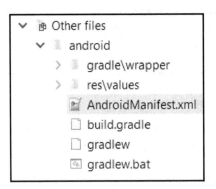

The files with the word **gradle** in them are part of the Gradle build toolkit for Android that manages dependencies and build logic. It is similar to CMake on the desktop that customizes, configures, and extends the build process. We don't have to touch these files for now.

The more important file is `AndroidManifest.xml`, which we need to open and configure:

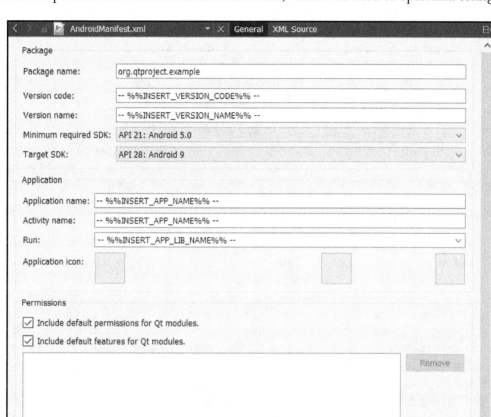

First, under the **Package** section, we have the following options:

- **Package name**: This is our app's identifier. Set it to something like
  `com.companyname.appname` as you desire. This can't be changed after you have
  uploaded your app to the app store, as the app store uses the package name to
  identify your app.
- **Version code**: This is the version of your app in numerical format. The version
  code will not be shown to the user but is used by the app store to identify the
  actual build version of your app. This number must be incremented every time
  you upload an update to the app store.

- **Version name**: This is the version label seen by the users on the app store. You can set anything you want as the app store does not depend on it for version identification.
- **Minimum required SDK**: This is the minimum Android SDK version that the user device must support. Users will not be able to install the app if their devices do not meet the minimum requirement. Please note that you can't simply set it to the lowest version available if your app depends on a specific feature that is only supported on a higher version.
- **Target SDK**: This is the actual Android SDK version you're currently using to build your Android app. If the user's device is running at a higher version, the user may be warned about possible incompatibility, or your app might even get removed automatically from the user's device after a system update.

Next, we have the **Application** section:

- **Application name**: The name of your app, usually shown under the app icon.
- **Activity name**: The name of the main activity of your app, which can be the same as the application name. In layman's term, activity in the Android app is like individual processes within an app with its own user interface. An Android app can have many different activities that do different things. For example, you can trigger a camera activity that captures a photo from your main activity, and then spawn another activity that uploads the photo to the server and displays the upload progress.
- **Run**: This is the name of the application you want to run. Most projects only have one application so we can just keep the default value.
- **Application icon**: This is where you set the icon for your app. There are several different sizes that you need to set – low DPI, medium DPI, and high DPI icons.

Finally, we will look into the **Permissions** section. Apart from the two options explained in the following, which do what their names imply, the huge space at the bottom is where you add permissions to your Android app. Certain features require permission from the user before it can be used by your app, such as obtaining a device location, accessing file storage, and accessing the camera. For the full list of permissions available on Android, please visit `https://developer.android.com/reference/android/Manifest.permission`. You can add permission to your app by selecting **permission** from the combo box, followed by pressing the **Add** button. To remove a permission, select it on the permission list above the combo box and click on the **Remove** button.

Once you have the `AndroidManifest.xml` ready, you can now build your project and generate the APK file. Do remember to sign your app if you intend to upload it to the app store. To run the app on our mobile phone, we simply click the **Run** button as usual. This time, a window will pop out asking you to select an Android device to run on. Please make sure that you have connected your phone to your PC with the USB cable so that the device will appear on the list here:

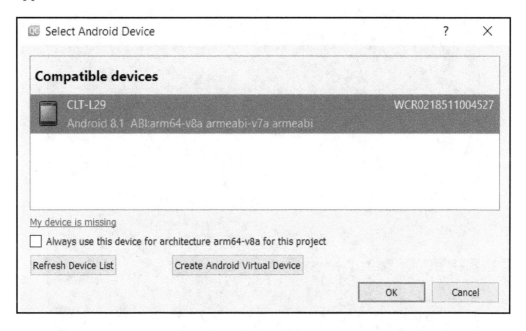

Press the **OK** button and wait for the build process to complete. Once the app has been successfully built, Qt will automatically launch the app on your Android device.

Do note that you can also run your app on an Android emulator instead of running on an actual physical device. Before you are able to deploy your app to an Android emulator, first you need to set up the emulator. You can do so by opening Android Studio, clicking on the **Configure** button at the bottom right of the window, and then selecting **AVD Manager**:

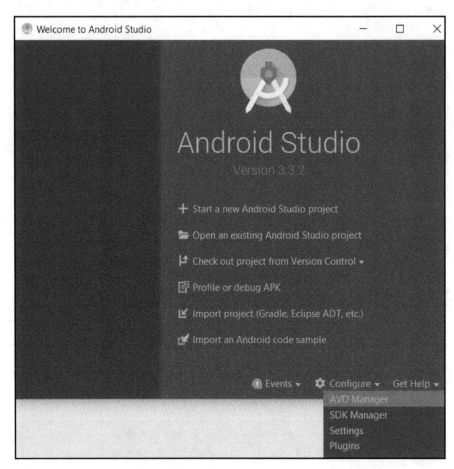

A window will pop out and display the list of the emulators (Android virtual devices) available for deployment. By default, you should see an empty list. You can create a new emulator by pressing the **Create Virtual Device...** button located at the bottom left of the window:

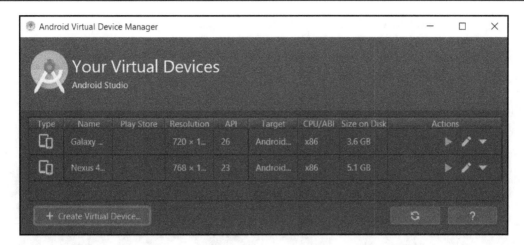

After that, select the device **Category** you want to emulate (that is, phone), select the device model, and then click **Next**:

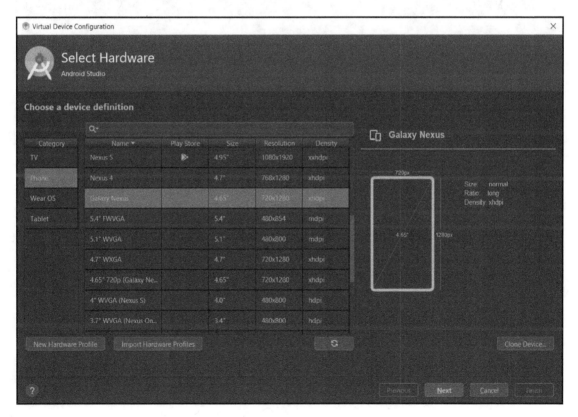

Then, select the Android version for your emulator. If your computer doesn't have the Android image yet, click the **Download** link located next to the Android version name. Once it has been downloaded, you can then select the version and click **Next**:

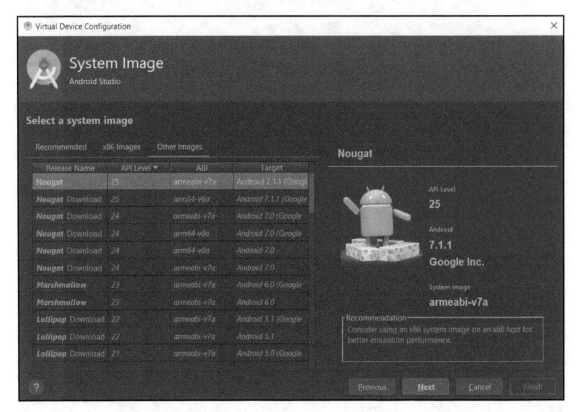

Finally, give your emulator a name, set its start up orientation, and click **Finish**:

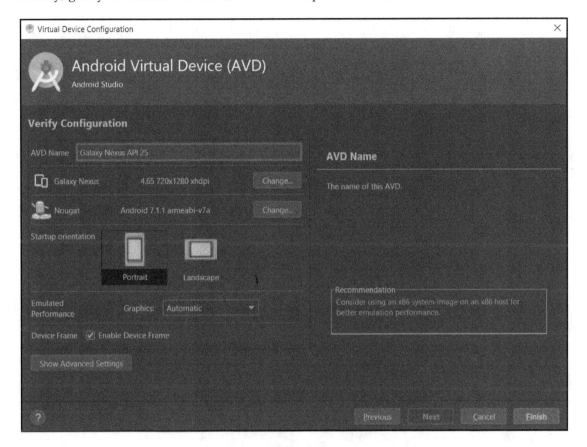

Once you have set up the emulator, you can then test run the emulator and see it in action:

Once you have set up an emulator, it will appear on the device list when you run your Android application from Qt Creator:

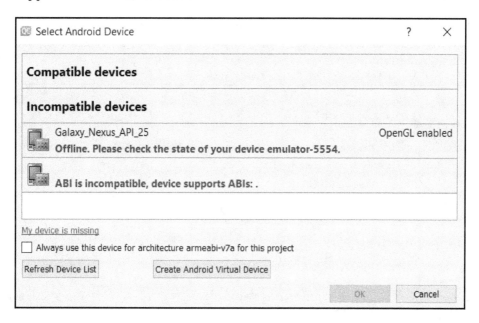

Please be aware that the Android emulator is really slow and not recommended to be used for critical production. Using an actual physical device is still the best way for application development, be it Android or iOS.

In this section, we have learned how to set up and deploy our Qt application to an Android device. Next, we will learn how to implement native functions to iOS and Android applications for better feature support.

Setting up Qt Creator for iOS

One main difference between Android and iOS development with Qt is that you cannot build and run iOS apps on Qt Creator at all, as it is not allowed by Apple. Therefore, Qt Creator can only be used for developing the app and generating the Xcode file. Xcode is the *de facto* programming tool and compiler for all Apple platforms, including iOS. Once the required Xcode files have been generated by Qt Creator, you then have to do the rest on Xcode.

Let's take a look at how we can set up our Qt Creator for iOS development.

First, when you create a new project, you will see quite a variety of different kits available to you. Kits with the word **clang** are for macOS development, which you can also use to test your app's GUI before deploying to an iOS simulator or device. The kit with the keyword **for iOS** is for deploying to a physical iOS device (an iPhone or iPad), while the kit with the keyword **for iOS Simulator** is for deploying to an iOS simulator that comes together with your Xcode installation:

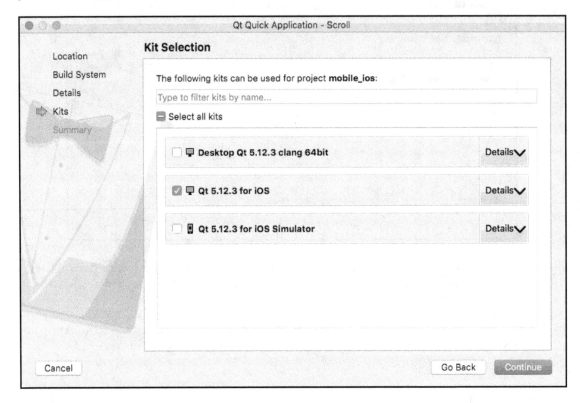

Since you cannot build and run your iOS app for Qt Creator, you can only generate its Xcode files by going to **Build** | **Run qmake**. This will generate the following files in your build folder:

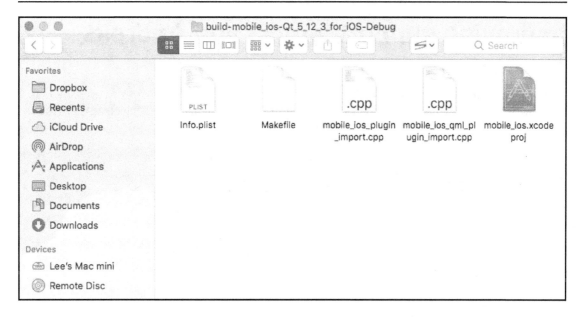

Every time you run qmake, it will generate the make file, Xcode project file, PLIST file for configuration and some CPP files for linking Qt plugins. Do note that every time here, qmake will replace any existing files, so it's better not to edit these files directly as any changes you make will be gone after the next run. You can, however, tell qmake what data to replace when generating these files by writing it in the project file (.pro). Consider the following, for example:

```
ios {
    QMAKE_TARGET_BUNDLE_PREFIX = com.mycompany
    QMAKE_BUNDLE = myapp
    QMAKE_INFO_PLIST = ios/Info.plist
}
```

As you can see, I have added the code in an ios macro so that it will be ignored if we are not building the project for iOS. First, we set our app's bundle prefix as com.mycompany, and then the bundle name as myapp. This will result in com.mycompany.myapp as the full bundle name. Then, we copy over the Info.plist file generated by qmake and place it into the ios folder inside the project directory (or create one if the folder doesn't exist). Then, we tell qmake to copy that particular Info.plist file to the build directory instead of generating a brand-new one. This way, any changes that we made will also get copied over.

That's it. Let's move on to the next topic and learn how we can improve support for iOS and Android applications by supporting native functionalities.

Improving support for iOS and Android applications

Qt not only makes compiling and deploying applications to iOS and Android an easy task, but it also supports native functionalities through Java (Android) and Objective C++ (iOS) coding. In the following sections, we will study both of these.

Calling Android functions from Qt

To call an Android function from Qt, we need to follow a few steps:

1. Create an empty Qt Quick project, which we have done countless times.
2. Open the project file (.pro) and add the following androidextras module to the project:

```
QT += quick
android: QT += androidextras
CONFIG += c++11
```

3. Create AndroidManifest.xml and other important Android files by clicking on the **Create Template** button, which we learned about in the previous *Deploying applications to Android devices* section.
4. Then, create a MyToast.java file in your Qt project directory and open it up using Qt Creator. You must place it in the Android folder where you store your AndroidManifest.xml and make sure the folder structure looks like the following screenshot, otherwise, you won't be able to call it from the code in later steps:

5. After that, reopen our project file (`.pro`) and add the following text to tell Qt to look for Java source code within the directory:

```
contains(ANDROID_TARGET_ARCH,arm64-v8a) {
    ANDROID_PACKAGE_SOURCE_DIR = \
    $$PWD/android
    ANDROID_JAVA_SOURCES.path = $$PWD/android/src/org
        /qtproject/example
        INSTALLS += ANDROID_JAVA_SOURCES
    }
```

The code for `MyToast.java` is very simple. We simply display a line of message on a toast widget when the `notify` function is being called:

```
package org.qtproject.example;

import android.content.Context;
import android.widget.Toast;

public class MyToast extends org.qtproject.qt5.android.bindings.QtActivity
{
    public MyToast() {}
    public static void notify(Context context, String message)
    {
        int duration = Toast.LENGTH_SHORT;
        Toast toast = Toast.makeText(context, message, duration);
        toast.show();
    }
}
```

Once you're done, create a C++ class called `MyToast` and include `QObject` as its parent class. The header file, `mytoast.h`, looks something like this:

```
#ifndef MYTOAST_H
#define MYTOAST_H

#include <QObject>
#ifdef Q_OS_ANDROID
  #include <QtAndroidExtras>
  #include <QAndroidJniObject>
#endif

class MyToast : public QObject
{
    Q_OBJECT
public:
    explicit MyToast(QObject *parent = nullptr);
    Q_INVOKABLE void callToast(QString message);
```

```
};
#endif // MYTOAST_H
```

In the preceding code, we only include QtAndroidExtras and QAndroidJniObject headers if we are compiling the project for Android platform by checking the Q_OS_ANDROID macro. This will prevent a compilation error when you are compiling your project for other platforms, such as Windows or iOS. We then declare a callToast function with the Q_INVOKABLE macro so that we can call it from QML later.

The mytoast.cpp source file also looks very simple, as you can see here:

```
#include "mytoast.h"

MyToast::MyToast(QObject *parent) : QObject(parent) {}

void MyToast::callToast(QString message)
{
    #ifdef Q_OS_ANDROID
    QtAndroid::runOnAndroidThread([=]
    {
        QAndroidJniObject::callStaticMethod<void>
          ("org/qtproject/example/MyToast",
            "notify", "(Landroid/content/Context;Ljava/lang/String;)V",
            QtAndroid::androidActivity().object(),
            QAndroidJniObject::fromString(message).object<jstring>());
    });
    #endif
}
```

In the preceding code, we implemented the callToast function, which triggers the Java notify function through the QAndroidJniObject class. The QAndroidJniObject class provides us with the callStaticMethod function, which can be used to call Java native functions that are static. We declared a static function in the Java code because static functions belong not to an instance of a class, but rather a class itself, which is accessible by all instances of the class and is therefore easier for us to implement in such a cross-language fashion.

This particular callStaticMethod expects no return, and therefore we place <void> behind the function name. As for the function inputs, the first variable is the Java class that we are going to look for, which is org/qtproject/example/MyToast, and the function name that we are going to call is named notify.

Then, we tell the Java function what data type it should expect from the input variables, the first one of which is `android/content/Contact`, followed by `java/lang/String`. The V toward the end is the data type of the returned variable, which in this case is `void`. After that, we submit the variables that are needed by the `notify` function, the first one of which is the context of our application, and the second is the message that we want to display on the toast widget.

Do note that we are running this whole chunk of code within the Android thread, instead of the Qt thread, as the toast widget is part of Android UI. We called `QtAndroid::runOnAndroidThread` and run the `notify` function within the lambda function, which means `notify` will only be called when we are done switching back to the Android thread.

Once you have understood the preceding code, let's move on and open up `main.cpp`. The first thing we want to do here is to include the `mytoast.h` and `QQmlContext` headers:

```
#include <QQmlContext>
#include "mytoast.h"
```

Then, we register our `MyToast` class as a QML type, under a self-declared `MyLib 1.o` library. You will see how this will work out in later steps:

```
QCoreApplication::setAttribute(Qt::AA_EnableHighDpiScaling);
QGuiApplication app(argc, argv);
QQmlApplicationEngine engine;

QQmlContext *context = engine.rootContext();
qmlRegisterType<MyToast>("MyLib", 1, 0, "MyToast");
```

After that, we want to call the `callToast` function when tapping on the screen. So, therefore, let's open up `main.qml` and import the `MyLib 1.0` library that we declared in the previous step:

```
import QtQuick 2.12
import QtQuick.Window 2.12

import MyLib 1.0
```

Once we've imported the library, we can now access the `MyToast` QML type. Let's create one in our QML code and call it `toast`:

```
Window {
    visible: true
    width: 640
    height: 480
```

```
        title: qsTr("Hello World")

        MyToast {
            id: toast
        }
```

After that, create a `MouseArea` object for us to display the toast message. We then call `toast.callToast` when an `onClicked` event is triggered:

```
        MouseArea {
            anchors.fill: parent
            onClicked: toast.callToast("My message here. Hello World!")
        }
    }
```

That's it! Let's build and deploy the app to your Android device. It looks quite empty when launched, but if you tap on the screen, something magical will happen:

Although Qt does not support some of the native Android features, such as the toast widget, we can still implement it ourselves through Java and connect it to our Qt code. That's something really awesome and makes Qt a really powerful development platform.

Calling iOS functions from Qt

Calling iOS functions is quite different from the one we did for Android. The first difference is the programming language for iOS, which is Objective C++ (with the "plus plus" sign) rather than Java. In order for us to integrate iOS functions in our Qt project, we cannot use the usual Objective C language for the class that will be integrated into our Qt project. Instead, we use the Objective C++ language, which is compatible with C++ under macOS and iOS environments. Secondly, there is no **iOS extras** module like you would have with Android. This is because Objective C++ is compatible with C++ and hence we can just create a `trampoline` function in Objective C++ and call it directly, which, in turn, will trigger the native iOS functions that you intend to call.

Let's try it out with a simple example. First, create a new class in your Qt project called `MyClass` and change the `.cpp` file's extension to `.mm`, which tells the Apple compiler, Xcode, that this is an Objective C++ source file (use the `.m` extension for Objective C). Only the `.mm` extension will allow you to mix Objective C code with your C++ code in the same source file, which is why it's called Objective C++.

Then, open up your Qt project file (`.pro`) and make sure these two files only get included in your project if you're compiling for the iOS platform. This is because other platforms don't recognize Objective C++ and will give you a ton of errors during compilation:

```
ios {
    HEADERS += ios/MyClass.h
    SOURCES += ios/MyClass.mm
}
```

After that, open up `MyClass.h` and add the `doSomethingT` function to your file:

```
#ifndef MYCLASS_H
#define MYCLASS_H
#include <QObject>

class MyClass : public QObject
{
    Q_OBJECT

    public:
        MyClass(QObject *parent = NULL);
```

```
            void doSomethingT(QString arg1, QString arg2);

    private:
};

    #endif
```

As you can see from the preceding code, it looks the same as our ordinary C++ Qt code. We called our function doSomethingT, with a capital T at the end of function name, so that we remember this is just a trampoline function. Then, in the MyClass.mm file, we implement our MyClass function, which looks quite a bit different from our ordinary C++ code:

```
#import <Foundation/Foundation.h>
#include "MyClass.h"

@interface MyObject : NSObject
{
    - (void) doSomething:(NSString*)arg1 :(NSString*)arg2
}
@end

@implementation MyObject
- (void) doSomething:(NSString*)arg1 :(NSString*)arg2
{
    NSLog(@"The actual doSomething function being called!");
}
@end

MyClass::MyClass(QObject *parent) : QObject(parent) {}

void MyClass::doSomethingT(QString arg1, QString arg2)
{
    [[MyObject alloc] doSomething:arg1.toNSString()
      :arg2.toNSString()];
    qDebug() << "Doing something:" << arg1 << ", " << arg2;
}
```

It may look a bit strange here at first if you are unfamiliar with Objective C syntax. I intentionally used #import and #include together in the first two lines to show you that you can mix both Objective C and C++ code together in a .mm source file. Then, we create an Objective C class called MyObject that carries the actual doSomething function. We first declare the class and its function between the @interface and @end keywords, and then we implement the class and its function between the @implementation and @end keywords. The doSomething function takes in two NSString variables, namely, arg1 and arg2, which is similar to the doSomethingT function.

After that, we continue to write our code, but this time, in C++. We implemented our `MyClass` class and the `doSomethingT` trampoline function. In the `doSomethingT` function, we initialized our Objective C `MyObject` class and called the actual `doSomething` code here. Luckily, Qt provides us with a `toNSString()` function under the `QString` class, which makes the data type conversion seamless. We also used the `qDebug` function to make sure that we have called this trampoline function successfully. In the `doSomething` function, we used the `NSLog` function to print out a debug message to ensure that it's called successfully.

To wrap everything up, let's look at the following diagram to better understand the whole process discussed here:

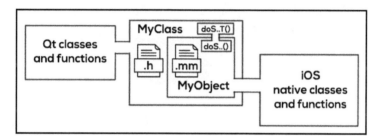

We used the `doSomethingT` trampoline function, which resides in the C++ `MyClass` class, to call the actual Objective C function, `doSomething`, within the `MyObject` class. The `doSomething` function can basically then be used to call any other native iOS functions as you like. In other words, we have jumped between two different realms through a simple trampoline function and are taking full advantage of what Objective C++ allows us to do.

That's it.

In this section, we have learned how we can call iOS functions from our C++ source code. This makes Qt a really powerful development platform because we can now deploy our application to different platforms without creating different sets of projects. Instead, we just use one single Qt project to rule them all.

Summary

Qt for Android gives you an excellent leg up on mobile development, but it's not a panacea. If you're planning to target mobile devices, you should be sure to have a good understanding of the usage patterns for your application's users, as well as the constraints in CPU, GPU, memory, and network that a mobile application must run on.

Once we understand these, however, all of our skills with Qt Creator and Qt carry over to the mobile arena. To develop for Android, begin by installing the JDK, Android Studio, Android NDK, and then develop applications as usual: compiling for the device and running on the device frequently to iron out any unexpected problems along the way.

In our final chapter, we will learn about the bunch of odds and ends in Qt Creator and Qt in general, which will make software development much easier.

13
Embedded and IoT Development with Qt Creator

In the previous chapter, we learned how to create mobile applications using Qt, which makes Qt a really powerful cross-platform development suite. To go even further, Qt has started to add support for embedded devices in recent versions that allow high-performance applications to be run within small hardware with limited computing power. This includes **IoT** (short for **Internet of Things**) devices, medical equipment, automobile displays, manufacturing machines, and more. Unfortunately, Qt for embedded devices is only available if you hold a Qt commercial license.

In this chapter, we will cover the following topics:

- Setting up an embedded Linux image
- Building a cross-compiled Qt application
- Configuring Qt for an embedded project
- Writing your first embedded program
- Deploying a Qt application to an embedded system

In this chapter, you will learn how to set up a Linux image that is used to run on your embedded device, and then configure and build your Qt project so that it supports the device you're running. Finally, you will also learn how to write your first embedded program and deploy it to the hardware.

Technical requirements

The technical requirements for this chapter include Qt (commercial license) 5.13.1 Boot2Qt Emulator, Qt Creator 4.10.1, Windows 10, a GNU Toolchain, Python 2.8, WinFLASHTool, Debian for BeagleBone (or another system), and an SSH server. You also need a physical embedded device, such as the Intel NUC or Raspberry Pi, for deployment.

You can apply for a 30-day trial in order to try out the various features. You will learn how to apply for the trial license in the following section of this chapter. Note that you can still develop your Qt application for embedded devices without using the commercial license, but that will require a ton of manual work and professional know-how. Other than that, you will also need a lot of patience in order to deploy your program to the embedded system without using the automated method provided by the Qt commercial license.

Setting up an embedded Linux image

Embedded devices used to be custom-made individually by hardware manufacturers as the firmware had to be created specifically for the chip soldered to the device. This prevented small companies and hobby developers from designing new products without cooperating with a big manufacturer, which was pretty challenging, especially for hobbyists.

However, our technology has improved significantly in recent years, which means that the chips running our PC and mobile phones have become almost as powerful as the proprietary devices produced by the big manufacturers. This has led to most manufacturers switching sides in order to use the ARM and x86 chips and, by doing so, reduce their cost on research and development. This also allows small companies or hobby developers to easily prototype their software on low-budget embedded hardware, such as the Intel NUC or Raspberry Pi, and still expect it to work on the actual production hardware.

Linux-based systems are currently used by many embedded projects as they are highly customizable due to their open source nature. The embedded Linux system is actually quite different from the Linux systems we usually see running on desktop or server machines. Those Linux operating systems are way too bulky and complex for embedded hardware and will not run well in terms of performance due to limited computing power. Therefore, we need to take away all the unnecessary components from the Linux system and build our very own Linux image, which is small, simple, and optimized for embedded devices.

Before we can set up our embedded Linux system, let's install Qt using a commercial license. Note that you can only build Qt applications for embedded devices using the commercial license. Open source licenses are not allowed and you won't find any of the Qt components required to build the embedded application in the open source packages.

Let's take a look at how to register for the commercial license.

Registering the 30-day trial Qt commercial license

Follow these steps to register for a 30-day trial Qt commercial license:

1. Go to `http://www.qt.i`.
2. Click on the **Download. Try. Buy.** button located in the top-right corner of the web page.
3. Then, click on the **Download Qt Now** button located in the **Try Qt** column. This button will not actually start any download but will trigger a registration form entitled **Request your free trial now**.
4. Fill in the form and click on **Submit my request now** to submit the request form. Note that you must use a business email address to register and not a free email address (such as Gmail, Yahoo! mail, Hotmail, and many others) as this is not permitted. The Qt Company may reject your free trial request if you do so.
5. Wait for a few days before The Qt Company approves your request and sends you an activation link.

Once you have received a 30-day trial license, congratulations! You may start downloading the components for embedded development from the Qt installer.

Installing Qt components for device creation

Once you have logged in to the Qt installer with your commercial account, the installer will display options under the **Qt for Device Creation** section. If you use an open source license, then the following screenshot is something that you might have not seen before:

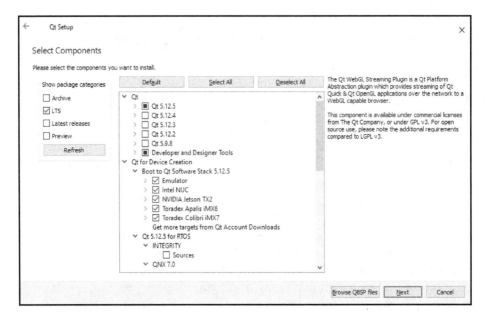

As you can see in the preceding screenshot, by default, Qt provides you with a set of prebuilt Linux images that work well on popular embedded development boards such as **Intel NUC**, **NVIDIA Jetson TX2**, **Raspberry Pi 3**, and **Toradex Colibri iMX7**. If you're using one of these hardware options supported by Qt by default, then you don't have to build your own Linux image from scratch – just download it from the Qt installer.

Qt also provides a Linux image for an emulator, which runs on **VirtualBox**. If you ticked the **Emulator** option and don't have **VirtualBox** installed on your PC, you will get a message box telling you to install this before proceeding:

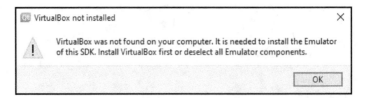

To download VirtualBox, simply go to `https://www.virtualbox.org`. Then, navigate to the **Downloads** page and pick the download option for the operating system you're running (**Windows hosts**, for example). Run the installer and you're good to go. If you don't want to export your application to the device every time there are some minor changes, running on the emulator is the fastest way to test your application.

Writing an embedded Linux image to a storage device

Qt commercial provides us with a handy tool to write a prebuilt embedded Linux image to a thumb drive or SD card. It is a program called **Boot to Qt Flashing Wizard**, or `b2qt-flashing-wizard.exe`, which is located at `Qt/Tools/b2qt`. When you run it, you will be asked to select the device you're running and the Qt version that supports it. The following screenshot shows this:

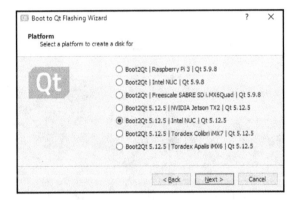

After that, you will be asked to select the storage device to write the Linux image:

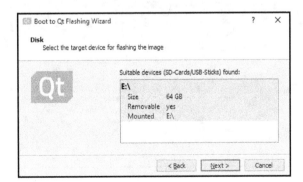

After you have clicked on the **Next** button, the Linux image will be written to the storage device:

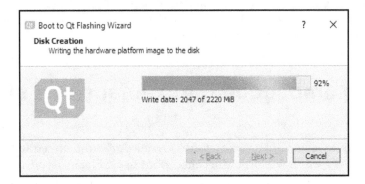

Once it's done, you can then plug your thumb drive or SD card into your embedded device and start booting up your Linux system! You should see the Qt demo being started by default on the Linux system.

The following photograph shows the embedded Qt demo running on my 6-year-old Intel NUC. The performance is really decent even though my machine is pretty old now:

If your device is not officially supported by The Qt Company, then you will need to build your own custom Linux image, which is not exactly an easy task. Qt uses recipes from the Yockto Project (`https://www.yoctoproject.org`) to configure their Linux images, so you should too if you're trying to build your own Linux image.

To learn how to build your own custom Linux image using the tools provided by the Yockto Project, take a look at the documentation at `https://doc.qt.io/QtForDeviceCreation/qtee-custom-embedded-linux-image.html`. Do note that you can only build a Linux image from the source on a Linux system, such as Ubuntu. You can't do it on a Windows or macOS system. Luckily, the Yockto Project also provides us with a build bot that allows us to build on the cloud instead of doing it on our own machine.

In this section, we have learned how to set up an embedded Linux image for device creation on Qt. Next, we will learn how to build a cross-compiled Qt project.

Building a cross-compiled Qt application

Cross-compiling is where you write code on one machine but build it for another machine that runs a different operating system or processor. For instance, you could be developing your application on Windows but build it for a Linux machine; or you could be writing the code on an x86 Linux machine but building the executable for an ARMv8 Linux device.

Cross-compilation is required in the following cases:

- The Qt toolchain or library is not available on the target device you're running
- The target device is really slow and not suitable for compiling the code
- The device doesn't have any display or input method

Qt commercial makes it really easy to cross-compile and deploy your application to different types of embedded devices, so a manual way is not recommended unless the hardware is not officially supported by Qt.

Automated cross-compile using Qt Creator

When you create your project in Qt Creator using a commercial license, you will see more options on the **Kit Selection** page than what you would normally see with an open source license. These kits are the ones that you have selected and installed with the Qt installer. If you don't see these options on the **Kit Selection** page, please open up the Qt installer again and install the missing packages.

If the kits are available, pick the kit that matches your hardware or choose the emulator option if you want to test the application without deploying to the device, as shown here:

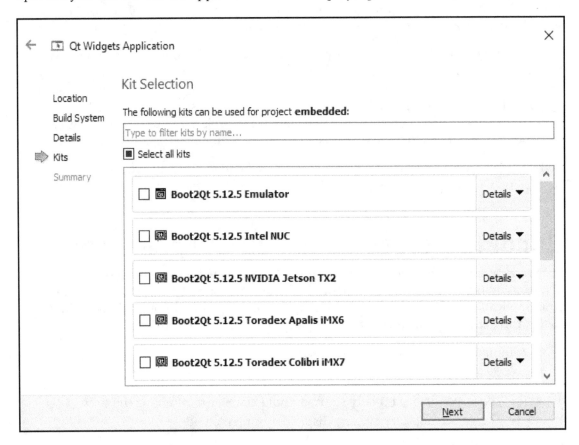

If you are new to device creation on Qt, you probably cannot deploy and run your application on actual hardware yet. We will cover this next in the *Deploying a Qt application to an embedded system* section. For now, let's cross-compile it for the emulator. There are no extra steps required when cross-building in Qt Creator if your hardware is officially supported. Just hitting the **Build** or **Run** button located at the bottom-left corner will do. When you first run the program on Qt Creator, the Qt Launcher will be launched in the emulator instead of your program. This is because the Qt Launcher is the default program to be executed when running the emulator.

The Qt Launcher is essentially the demo gallery that lets you try out different features supported by Qt for device creation:

Once the emulator has been launched, you can try and run your program from the Qt Creator again, and it should now be displayed on the emulator. Do note that the emulator may perform poorly compared to actual hardware due to the need to share resources with your PC.

Manual cross-compile

Manual cross-compile is not recommended unless the hardware is not officially supported by Qt. For instance, the BeagleBone board (`http://beagleboard.org/bone`) is nowhere to be found on the kit selection page when creating a new project. In this case, we have no choice but to manually do it by ourselves. This is because it is a really long and complicated process to set up before you can even begin to cross-compile your project.

If, like me, you're someone who uses the Windows system to develop your application, then you need to download the GNU Toolchain for BeagleBone at `http://gnutoolchains.com/beaglebone`. This package includes the GCC compiler, header files, and libraries that are compatible with the Linux image that runs on the BeagleBone board. You can also download the Linux image from the preceding link instead of the Yockto Project website. Other types of architectures are also supported, such as CubieBoard, Blackfin, and AVR.

Once you have downloaded the installer, run it and install the GNU Toolchain to a local directory:

After you have installed the GNU Toolchain for BeagleBone, install Python 2.8 from `https://www.python.org/downloads` as we will need it for compiling the Qt framework in a moment. Once you have installed it, download WinFLASHTool from `http://sysprogs.com/winflashtool/download` and write the Linux image onto an SD card, as follows:

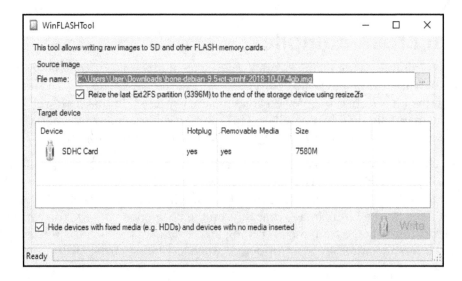

Once you're done writing the Linux image onto your SD card, plug it into your BeagleBone device and boot it up. The Linux system on BeagleBone should have an SSH server installed and enabled by default. If it doesn't, you can do it yourself by using the Terminal commands given here (these might be different if you're not using Debian-based Linux):

1. First, install `openssl-server`:

   ```
   sudo apt-get install openssh-server
   ```

2. Then, enable and start the SSH service:

   ```
   sudo systemctl enable ssh
   sudo systemctl start ssh
   ```

3. Once the SSH server has been started, you can go back to your Windows machine and launch the `UpdateSysroot.bat` batch file, which is located in the `C:\SysGCC\beaglebone\tools` folder. This tool is used to grab all the library files from the target Linux machine and copy them to your Windows machine:

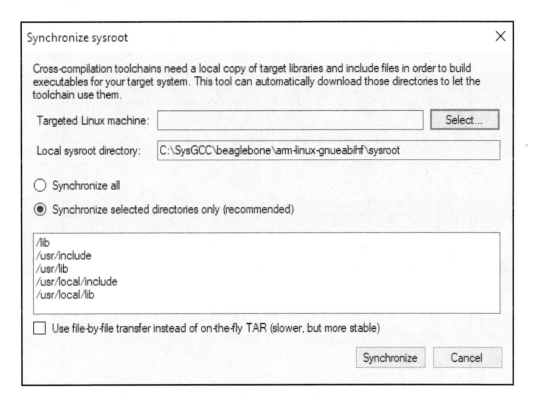

4. Click on the **Select...** button to connect to the Linux machine. If you can't connect using the **username@devicename** format, then use the local IPV4 IP address instead (for example, 192.168.0.140):

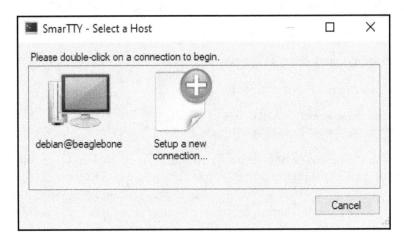

5. Once connected, click on the **Synchronize** button to start grabbing all the library files from the Linux machine. This may take some time to complete:

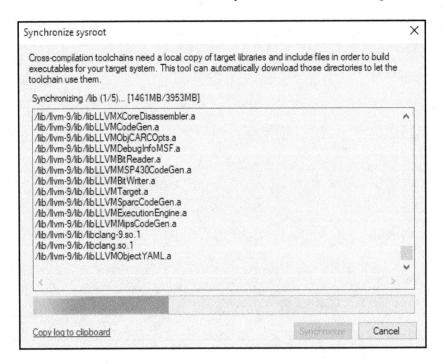

That's it! You can now synchronize the library files between the Linux device and your Windows machine.

After this, we're going to build Qt from the source using the GNU Toolchain and the library files we just grabbed from our BeagleBone. For that, let's take a look at what is required:

1. First, we need to build qmake before using it to build the entire Qt framework.
2. Go to the source folder of your Qt, for example, `C:/Qt/5.12.5/Src`. Then, go to the `/qtbase/mkspecs` directory and duplicate the `linux-arm-gnueabi-g++` folder.
3. Rename the duplicated folder to `linux-arm-gnueabihf-g++` and open up the `qmake.conf` file inside the folder. Change all the `-gnueabi-` prefixes to `-gnueabihf-` so that it matches the folder name, like so:

```
MAKEFILE_GENERATOR = UNIX
CONFIG += incremental
QMAKE_INCREMENTAL_STYLE = sublib

include(../common/linux.conf)
include(../common/gcc-base-unix.conf)
include(../common/g++-unix.conf)

# modifications to g++.conf
QMAKE_CC = arm-linux-gnueabihf-gcc
QMAKE_CXX = arm-linux-gnueabihf-g++
QMAKE_LINK = arm-linux-gnueabihf-g++
QMAKE_LINK_SHLIB = arm-linux-gnueabihf-g++

# modifications to linux.conf
QMAKE_AR = arm-linux-gnueabihf-ar cqs
QMAKE_OBJCOPY = arm-linux-gnueabihf-objcopy
QMAKE_NM = arm-linux-gnueabihf-nm -P
QMAKE_STRIP = arm-linux-gnueabihf-strip
load(qt_config)
```

Since we copied the configuration file, `qmake.conf`, from the `linux-arm-gnueabi-g++` folder and renamed it `linux-arm-gnueabihf-g++`, we must also rename the prefix so that it matches the cross-toolchain package name. The `gnueabi` keyword means that the folder we copied from uses the cross-toolchain package for the `armel` architecture, while the `gnueabihf` keyword we are using for the new folder uses the cross-toolchain package for the `armhf` architecture. The type of cross-toolchain package used will be based on the hardware you're running.

4. Once you're done, open up Command Prompt and create a build folder somewhere outside the source folder and navigate into the build folder:

```
mkdir qt-build
cd qt-build
```

5. Then, we can start the building process by using the following command:

```
C:\Qt\5.12.5\Src\qtbase\configure -platform win32-g++ -xplatform
linux-arm-gnueabihf-g++ -release -opengl es2 -device linux-
beaglebone-g++ -sysroot C:/SysGCC/beaglebone/arm-linux-
gnueabihf/sysroot -prefix /usr/local/qt5
```

The building process will take some time, and, when it's done, you should see that qmake.exe is now located inside qt-build/qtbase/bin. You could encounter some error messages during the building process, but that's OK as long as qmake.exe has been built. To verify this, type the following:

```
..\qtbase\bin\qmake -v
```

You should see the version number of qmake, which means it's a successful build. Next, we're going to build the entire Qt framework. The first thing we need to do is open up the configure file in the qtbase folder in the Qt source directory again, and then add in the highlighted code before displaying the Creating qmake... text:

```
# build qmake
if [ '!' -f "$outpath/bin/qmake.exe" ]; then
    echo "Creating qmake..."
    mkdir -p "$outpath/qmake" || exit
```

Then, run the following command to start configuring the Qt framework. The command is similar to the previous one but with the device-option settings:

```
C:\qt-everywhere-src-5.13.1\configure -platform win32-g++ -xplatform linux-
arm-gnueabihf-g++ -release -opengl es2 -sysroot C:/SysGCC/beaglebone/arm-
linux-gnueabihf/sysroot -prefix /usr/local/qt5 -device-option
CROSS_COMPILE=C:/SysGCC/beaglebone/bin/arm-linux-gnueabihf- -qt-xcb
```

If nothing is going wrong, then you can proceed to build the Qt framework by typing the following:

```
make && make install
```

Do note that every hardware has very different settings and configurations, which may not work the same as the previous example. However, Command Prompt should tell you the problem in case anything happens, so you may need some patience to tweak the configurations until it works for your platform. If your device is officially supported by Qt, then please use the built-in method as described in the previous sub-section, *Automated cross-compile using Qt Creator*.

After the Qt framework has been successfully built, open up `SmarTTY.exe`, which is located at `C:\SysGCC\beaglebone\tools\PortableSmartty`. Then, connect to your device through SSH using SmarTTY, which we have learned about in previous steps. After you have connected, go to **SCP** | **Upload a directory**, as shown here:

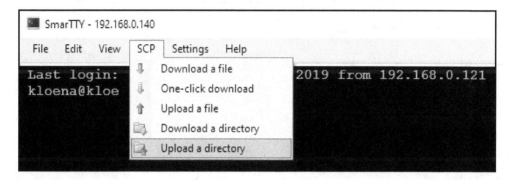

A window will pop out for you to set the directory you want to upload and the target location on the remote device. Set the **Local directory** as `C:\SysGCC\beaglebone\arm-linux-gnueabihf\sysroot\usr\local\qt5` and the **Remote directory** as `/usr/local/qt5`:

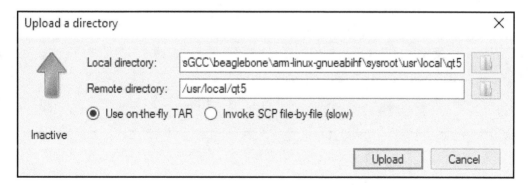

After that, press the **Upload** button to start uploading the files to your embedded device. That's it! You have successfully uploaded the entire Qt library to the embedded device, which you can then run your Qt application on.

Next, we will learn how to manually compile our Qt application for our embedded device. There are some settings we need to look at on our Qt Creator before we can start compiling our application:

1. First, open up Qt Creator, go to **Tools** | **Options...**, and then navigate to **Kits** | **Compilers**.
2. Then, click on the **Add** button located in the right-hand side and select **GCC** | **C++**. Set the compiler settings as shown in the following screenshot:

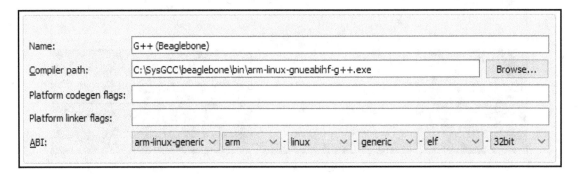

3. Repeat the step for **GCC** | **C** and set the settings as follows:

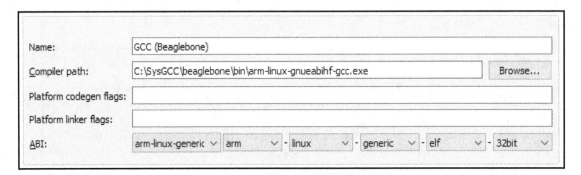

4. After that, navigate over to the **Debuggers** tab and click on the **Add** button. Name the debugger `Beaglebone` and the rest of the settings as follows:

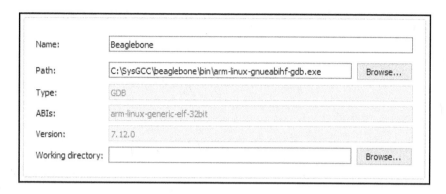

Name:	Beaglebone	
Path:	C:\SysGCC\beaglebone\bin\arm-linux-gnueabihf-gdb.exe	Browse...
Type:	GDB	
ABIs:	arm-linux-generic-elf-32bit	
Version:	7.12.0	
Working directory:		Browse...

5. Then, go to the **Qt Versions** tab and click on the **Add...** button.
6. Select `qmake.exe`, which we built in the previous steps, and name it `Qt Beaglebone %{Qt:Version} (build-qt)`.
7. Finally, go to the **Kits** tab and click on the **Add** button. Name this kit `Beaglebone` and link the compilers, debugger, and Qt version that we have just added in previous steps.

You should now be able to cross-compile your Qt application for your embedded device. You will not be able to launch the resulting executable file to your Windows machine because it is a Linux executable. We will discuss how to manually deploy the application to your device in the *Deploying a Qt application to an embedded system* section of this chapter.

In this section, we have learned how to cross-compile our Qt application on our Windows PC for the Linux device. Let's proceed to the next section and learn how to configure our Qt framework for embedded projects.

Configuring Qt for an embedded project

As you may already know, the Qt framework comes with an enormous set of libraries that may add up to several gigabytes of storage. Even at the minimum, these libraries could take up to 15 megabytes of storage, which is overkill for a small embedded device. To fix this problem, The Qt Company has provided us with a tool for configuring our Qt package before we build the Qt framework from the source for our embedded project. We can pick and choose the features that we want and discard the features that we don't need in order to reduce the Qt library size.

The tool is called the **Qt Configuration Tool** or `qconfig-gui.exe` and is located in the `C:\Qt\Tools\QtConfigGui` folder, as shown here:

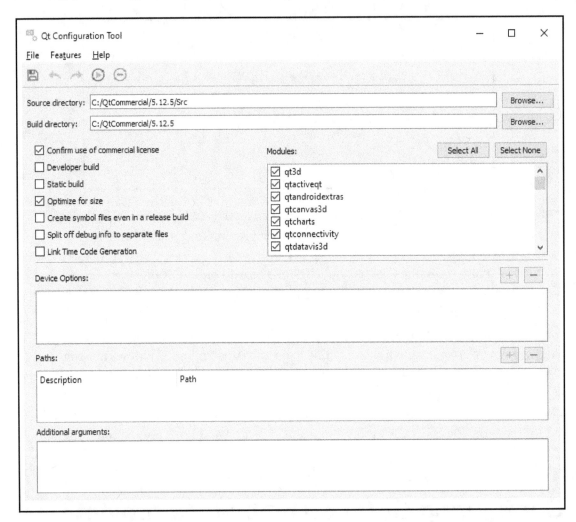

Press the **Run Configure** button to start the configuration process, which will take some time to complete. Once completed, you can open up Command Prompt and build your Qt libraries from the source using the `mingw32-make` command:

```
cd C:\Qt\5.12.5
mingw32-make
```

The building process varies depending on your configuration. The more features you have turned on, the longer it will take to build the Qt libraries. Usually, it will take up to several hours to build because Qt is a really huge library. The building process looks something like this:

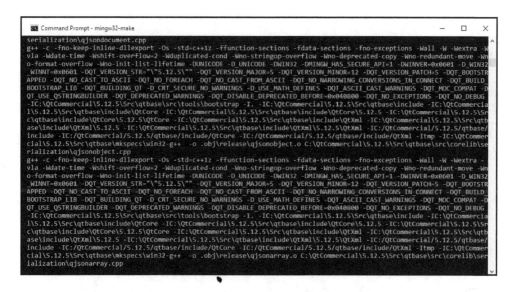

Once it's done, don't forget to run the `install` command:

```
mingw32-make install
```

This will copy all the compiled library files to an appropriate directory, such as `C:\Qt\Qt-5.12.5`. You can reconfigure and recompile again if you find out you need to change the feature list according to your needs.

In this section, we have learned how to configure Qt and make it smaller to fit into our embedded device. In the next section, we will proceed to write our very first embedded program using Qt Quick.

Writing your first embedded program

In Qt, there is no difference between building an application for the desktop, mobile, or an embedded device. You can create your project, as usual, but the only difference will be the building process. Let's create a Qt Quick project by going to **File | New Files or Project** and selecting **Qt Quick Application – Empty**. Make sure that you tick the **Use Virtual Keyboard** option when creating your Qt Quick project.

Open up `main.qml` when you're done. By default, the code contains an `InputPanel` item, which is the virtual keyboard:

```
InputPanel {
    id: inputPanel
    z: 99
    x: 0
    y: window.height
    width: window.width

    states: State {
        name: "visible"
        when: inputPanel.active
        PropertyChanges {
            target: inputPanel
            y: window.height - inputPanel.height
        }
    }
    transitions: Transition {
        from: ""
        to: "visible"
        reversible: true
        ParallelAnimation {
            NumberAnimation {
                properties: "y"
                duration: 250
                easing.type: Easing.InOutQuad
            }
        }
    }
}
```

If you build and run the program on the emulator right now, you will not see anything because the virtual keyboard is hidden from the view. Let's import the `QtQuick.Controls` module and add a `TextField` item to our program:

```
import QtQuick.Controls 2.12

Window {
    id: window
    visible: true
    width: 640
    height: 480
    title: qsTr("Hello World")

    TextField {
        id: textInput
        x: 100
```

```
    y: 100
    placeholderText: qsTr("Enter text here")
}
```

If you run the program on the emulator again, you should see the text field on the screen. Click on the text field to trigger the virtual keyboard:

That's it. Other than the virtual keyboard, all the other items provided by Qt Quick can be used in the same way as desktop and mobile applications. Qt has blurred the line between desktop, mobile, and embedded application development and has streamlined the development pipeline to make the developer's life easier.

In this section, we have learned how to develop our first embedded program using Qt Quick and how to enable the virtual keyboard feature. In the next section, we will learn how to deploy our application to an actual embedded device and make it the default start up program.

Deploying a Qt application to an embedded system

Finally, we will learn how to deploy our application to an actual physical device. We will cover two methods for doing this – the automated way and the manual way. The automated way requires the Qt commercial license and this feature comes together with Qt Creator. The manual way, on the other hand, does not require a commercial license, but it is a much longer process than the former. Let's take a look at each.

Automated deployment from Qt Creator

The Qt commercial license comes with a tool called **Boot to Qt Flashing Wizard**, which we discussed in the *Setting up an embedded Linux image* section. Unlike the manual way of cross-compiling in Qt, which we discussed in the *Building a cross-compiled Qt application* section, the Linux images that come with Qt commercial are optimized for embedded development and support remote deployment from your Qt Creator. That means you don't have to put in any extra effort to make it work.

However, before you can effortlessly deploy your embedded application, you must set up your device in the Qt Creator so that it knows where to export the application. This is actually quite similar to the SSH method discussed in *Building a cross-compiled Qt application* section, but the functionality comes together with Qt Creator itself, so no third-party program is required here.

To set up your device, go to **Tools | Options... | Devices**. Under the **Devices** tab, click on the **Add...** button located on the right-hand side of the window. After that, a window called **Device Configuration Wizard Selection** will pop out:

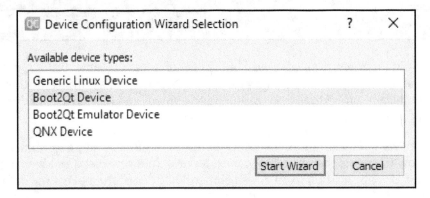

Select the **Boot2Qt Device** option and click on **Start Wizard**. The configuration wizard will take you through several steps to set up your device. The settings should be similar to what you see as follows:

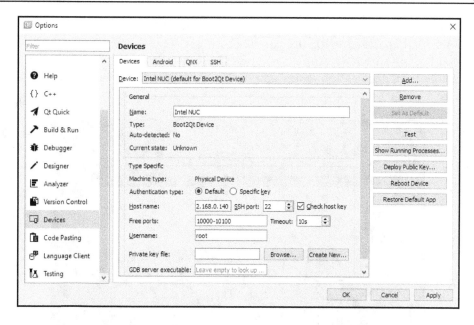

If you can't connect using the `username@devicename` format, then use a local IPV4 IP address instead (that is, 192.168.0.140). The IP address can be found from the Qt Launcher on your embedded device that runs the Linux image provided by the Boot to Qt Flashing Wizard. It is located in the **Network** section under the **Settings** window. Your device must first be connected to a network before obtaining an IP address:

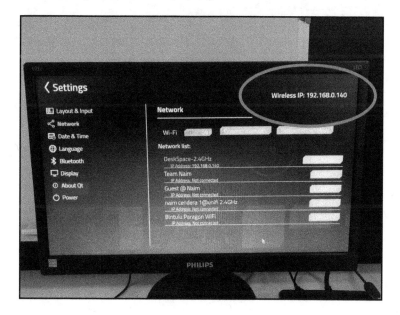

Once you're done, press the **OK** button to close down the **Options...** window in your Qt Creator. After that, make sure you are choosing the correct kit (that is, Boot2Qt 5.12.5 Intel NUC) instead of the emulator. After that, press the **Run** button and wait for a while. You should see that your application is running on the hardware once it has been built and sent to the device:

However, if you restart your embedded device now, the Qt Launcher will be launched at startup instead of your application. To override the default start up application, click on the **Projects** button located on the left panel and open up the **Run** settings interface:

Under the **Deployment** section, click on the **Add Deploy Step** button and select **Change default application**:

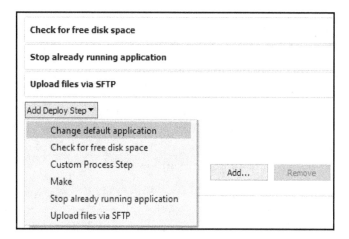

After that, pick the **Set this application to start by default** option and save your project. Run your application from Qt Creator again so that this step will be executed on the embedded device. Then, restart your device and voila! Your program is now the default application to start whenever the device is being turned on.

Manual deployment using SSH

The manual way to deploy your cross-compiled application to the embedded device is through the SSH method, which we have discussed in the *Building a cross-compiled Qt application* section. Before we get started and use SmarTTY to upload our Linux executable, let's take a look at how Qt did it.

If we explore the SD Card or thumb drive that contains the Linux image from Qt, we quickly realize it's not some black magic like we'd imagine. Qt simply stores our Qt application in the `opt` directory, for example, `/opt/myproject/bin/myproject`, and launches it from there.

As for the default start up application, Qt empowers the `systemd` service used by the Debian Linux system. The settings can be found in `/lib/systemd/qtlauncher.service`, which looks something like this:

```
[Unit]
Description=B2Qt Launcher Demo
After=systemd-user-sessions.service
```

```
ConditionPathExists=!/usr/bin/b2qt

[Service]
User=root
ExecStart=-/usr/bin/appcontroller /usr/bin/qtlauncher --applications-root
/data/usr/qt

[Install]
WantedBy=multi-user.target
```

The settings basically tell `systemd` to launch this service after `systemd-user-sessions.service` has been launched. Then, it will look for the shortcut link called `b2qt`, which is located at `/usr/bin/`. The `b2qt` shortcut essentially links to our Qt application (that is, `/opt/myproject/bin/myproject`) and launches it.

If the shortcut link doesn't exist, then it will launch the Qt Launcher instead. It is that simple. Therefore, if we want to imitate that method, we can first upload our application to the `opt` directory of the device using SmarTTY by going to **SCP | Upload a file**:

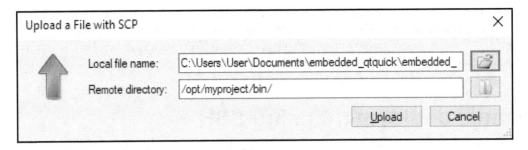

Once you have uploaded the executable, open up `/lib/systemd` and create a new file with the `.service` extension. You can copy the preceding script and change it to your liking, such as adding a custom description name, a custom directory path, and more. Then, run this command to enable your customized service:

```
sudo systemctl enable yourservice.service
```

Note that this only applies to a Linux system that uses `systemd`, such as Debian. If you are using a Linux system that runs some other start up managers/init daemons, such as `initd`, `Runit`, `Upstart`, or many others, then you cannot use the preceding method. There are plenty of resources on the internet that can teach you how to do it with those alternative start up managers.

In this section, we have learned how to deploy our Qt application to an embedded device, using both automated and manual methods.

Summary

In this chapter, we went through a long journey of learning how to empower Qt's cross-platform capability and created our first application for embedded devices. We learned how to set up an embedded Linux image and write it onto an SD card or thumb drive to run it on the device.

Then, we learned how to cross-compile a Qt project from a Windows machine and export it to the Linux device. This really is a time-saving approach as embedded devices are often not powerful enough for compiling source code, and therefore it is really handy for us to be able to compile it using a different, more powerful setup and deliver it to our production device remotely without even connecting it with a USB cable.

Other than that, we also learned how to configure the Qt framework and reduce its size so that it can fit into the embedded device. This is really important because embedded devices (that is, wearable devices, smart robots, medical devices, and so on) are often very small in size and have very limited storage.

After that, we also learned how to trigger the virtual keyboard in our first embedded program. This is also extremely important as most embedded devices have no keyboard or mouse for user input; therefore, the virtual keyboard plays an important role to ensure users are able to key in information without the need for a keyboard.

Finally, the coolest part of this chapter is when we learned how to deploy our application on an actual embedded device and see our hard work come to fruition. I really hope that more and more people can become empowered by using this information and produce a really awesome product that can perhaps change the world for the better.

In the next chapter, you will learn some tips and tricks to help you to improve your project's development workflow and productivity.

14
Qt Tips and Tricks

In the previous chapters, we discussed what makes Qt great for software development: how to edit, compile, and debug applications; how to profile their execution and memory performance; how to localize them for different regions of the world; as well as how to make mobile applications that run on Android phones and tablets.

In this chapter, we will discuss a collection of tips and tricks that you should know about when using Qt Creator and Qt, which will have you writing software like a pro.

We will cover the following topics in this chapter:

- Writing console applications with Qt Creator
- Integration with version control systems
- Configuring the coding style and coding format options
- Applying a new theme to Qt Creator
- Setting the Qt Quick window display options
- Building projects from CMake and the command line
- Running multiple debuggers simultaneously
- Learning more about Qt

Technical requirements

The technical requirements for this chapter include Qt 5.12.3, MinGW 64-bit, Qt Creator 4.9.0, and Windows 10.

Writing console applications with Qt Creator

Remember `Hello World` in `Chapter 1`, *Getting Started with Qt Creator*? That was a console application – about as simple a console application as you can write. Let's recap the code: We created a new Qt console application and, in `main.cpp`, we wrote the following lines of code:

```cpp
#include <QCoreApplication>
#include <iostream>

using namespace std;

int main(int argc, char *argv[])
{
    QCoreApplication a(argc, argv);
    cout << "Hello world!";

    return a.exec();
}
```

Any valid C++ file is valid in a Qt application, including **Standard Template Library** (STL) code. This is especially handy if you need to write a small tool in C++ and haven't learned a lot about Qt yet – everything you know about C++ (and even C, if you prefer) is accessible to you in Qt Creator.

Although Qt is most widely known as a GUI toolkit, it's worth mentioning that the Qt Core library, a part of every Qt application, including Qt console applications, includes a bevy of utility and template classes, including the following:

- Collection classes, including `QList`, `QVector`, `QStack`, and `QQueue` to keep lists and vectors and for the last-in-first-out and first-in-first-out data storages
- Dictionary classes (otherwise known as **hash tables**), including `QMap` and `QHash`

- I/O for a cross-platform file with `QFile` and `QDir`
- Unicode string support with `QString`

Why would you choose Qt's classes over what vanilla C++ provides you? There are a few reasons:

- **Memory performance**: Unlike STL collections, Qt collections are reference-based and use copy-on-write to save memory. Qt collections typically consume less memory than their STL counterparts.
- **Iteration**: Iterating over Qt collections is safe, with guarded access to prevent you from walking off the end of a collection.
- **Readability**: Using Qt code and libraries throughout an application provides a uniform look and feel that can make the code easier to maintain.
- **Portability**: On some embedded platforms where Qt is available, STL might not be present. However, this isn't nearly the problem that it was when Qt was first being written.

It's worth noting that Qt's collections are often slightly slower than their STL counterparts. When using a Qt class for data, you're often trading memory performance for speed. In practice, however, this is rarely a problem.

The `QFile` and `QDir` classes deserve a special mention because of one thing—portability. Even directory separators are handled in a portable way; directories are always demarcated by a single /, regardless of whether you're running on macOS, Linux, or Windows, which makes it easy to write the code in a platform-agnostic way and to ensure that it runs on all the platforms. Under the hood, Qt translates directory strings to use the platform-specific directory separator when accessing files.

Next, we will learn how to integrate our Qt Creator with a version control system.

Integrating Qt Creator with version control systems

Nearly all large projects require some sort of version control to coordinate the changes made to the same files by different users and to ensure that changes to a source base occur harmoniously. Even a single developer can benefit from using version control because version control provides a record of what has changed in each file that the developer has edited and provides a valuable history of the project over time. Qt Creator supports the following version control systems:

- Bazaar (supported in Qt Creator version 2.2 and beyond)
- CVS
- Git
- Mercurial (supported in Qt Creator version 2.0 and beyond)
- Perforce (supporting Perforce server version 2006.1 and later)
- Subversion

Aside from these Qt Creator also supports some commercial version control hosting services, including the following:

- GitHub
- GitLab

The first thing you need to do is set up some version control software for your project. How you do this depends on the version control system you choose (it might be dictated by your organization, for example, or you might have a personal preference from working on past projects), and will differ from system to system. So, we won't go into it here. However, you need to have a repository to store the versions of your source code and have the appropriate version control software installed on your workstation with the appropriate directories containing the version control binaries in your system's PATH variable so that Qt Creator can find them. It's important that you are able to access the version control commands from your system's shell (such as PowerShell or your local Terminal prompt) because Qt Creator accesses them in the same way.

Once you've done this, you can configure how Qt Creator interacts with version control by navigating to **Tools** | **Options...** | **Version Control**. The following screenshot shows this window:

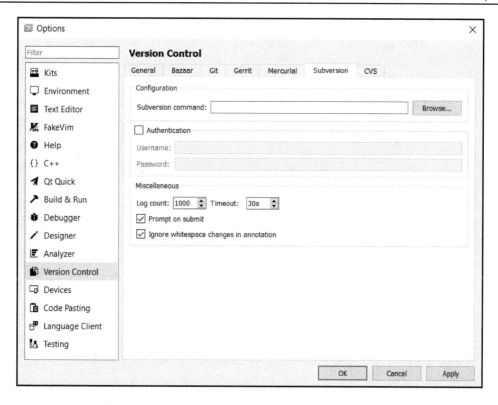

There are general configuration options, which apply to any version control system you're using, and then there are specific options for each flavor of version control that Qt supports. The following are the general options:

- A script that can be run on any submission message to ensure that your message is formatted correctly or contains the right information
- A list of names and aliases for your source code control system
- A list of fields to include in each submission message
- The SSH prompt command used to prompt you for your SSH password when using SSH in order to access your version control system

Some version control systems, such as Git and Mercurial, support local version control repositories. This comes in handy if you're flying solo on a development project and just need a place to back up your changes (of course, remember to back up the source code repository directory as well). If you're using one of these systems, you can use Qt to create the local repository directory directly by selecting **Create Repository** under **Tools**, or by going to **File | New File or Project** and then going to the last project management page. Of course, to do this, you'll need to have your version control software installed first.

You can find out more about how Qt Creator integrates with version control systems by taking a look at the Qt documentation at `https://doc.qt.io/qtcreator/creator-version-control.html`.

If you install and configure a version control system, the various commands available from this system are added in a submenu to the **Tools** menu of Qt Creator. From there, you can perform the following steps:

- View the version control command output by navigating to **Window** | **Output Panes** | **Version Control**.
- View different output (a comparison between two files with the same name of different versions) from your version control system, letting you see what's changed in a file you are editing from what's in the repository.
- View the changelog for a file under version control by selecting **Log** or **Filelog**.
- Commit a file's changes to the system by selecting **Commit** or **Submit**.
- Revert the changes to a file by selecting **Revert**.
- Update your working directory with the current contents of the version control system by clicking on **Update**.
- Use additional per-version control commands to support branches, stashes, and remote repositories.

If you're just starting out and need to choose a version control system, perhaps the best thing to do is to look at the comparison of various systems on Wikipedia,

at `http://en.wikipedia.org/wiki/Comparison_of_revision_control_software`, and get familiar with one. Personally, I prefer Git for my work, using both local repositories and hosted repositories such as GitHub. It's free, fast, has good support for branching, and is well supported by Qt Creator.

Next, we will look at setting up third-party hosting services for your version control system, such as GitHub and GitLab. It is actually pretty straightforward for these services. You can log in to these services through Git pretty much the same as your self-hosted repository.

Setting up your GitHub repository

First, register a GitHub account if you haven't got one. The registration page is located right at the front page of the website at `https://github.com`. Then, once you have completed the registration process, click on your profile picture located at the top right corner, followed by clicking on the **Your repositories** option on the drop-down menu:

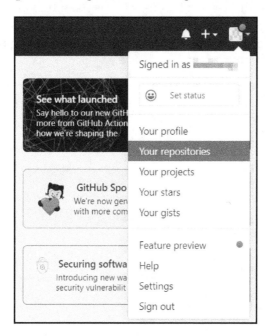

There, you will see a **New** button in green. Press the **New** button to create a new GitHub repository for your project. You will then be directed to **Create a new repository** page, where you can create a new repository by inserting the repository name next to the owner drop-down box:

After that, you can set whether the project is a **Public** or **Private** project by checking one of the options. Then, check on the **Initialize this repository with a README** option since you are creating a fresh new repository. The README file created by GitHub will be the front page of your repository.

You can also set the .gitignore option, which tells GitHub to ignore some of the files that are meant as temporary or user-specific files, such as make files and the user's project settings file (.pro.user). Select the **Qt** option in this case, as we are developing Qt projects in this book. You can also add a license to your project by selecting one of the options in the **Add a license** drop-down box:

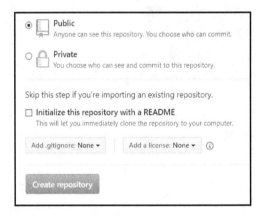

Once you've clicked the **Create repository** button, you will be brought to the following page:

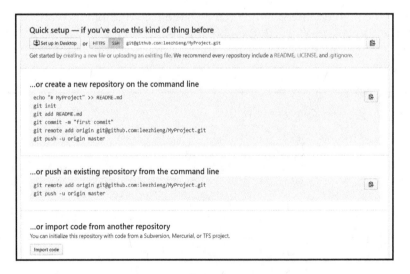

These are the commands you can use for linking your project to GitHub. However, you can also do this in Qt Creator. Go to **Tools | Git | Create Repository...** and then, select your project folder and click on **Select Folder**. This will create a local repository that works on your PC. The Git system is able to link to two repositories – a local one and a remote repository. You must commit your code to the local repository first before you can push it to the remote server.

Now that you have created your local repository, let's proceed with the remote repository:

1. Go to **Tools | Git | Remote Repository | Manage Remotes...**. A window will open that shows you the current remote server that you have connected to, which is empty for now.
2. Click on the **Add...** button and add your GitHub URL to the remotes list. The URL can be found on the **Quick setup** web page, as shown in the previous screenshot.
3. Once you have linked the GitHub account, you can then try and click the **Fetch** or **Push** button to verify the connection:

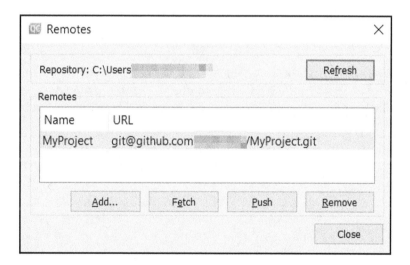

If the SSH link failed to work, you can also switch over to the HTTPS link by clicking on the **HTTPS** button on the **Quick setup** web page.

To commit your code to your local repository, simply go to **Tools | Git | Local Repository | Commit....** A window will appear on your Qt Creator that looks like this:

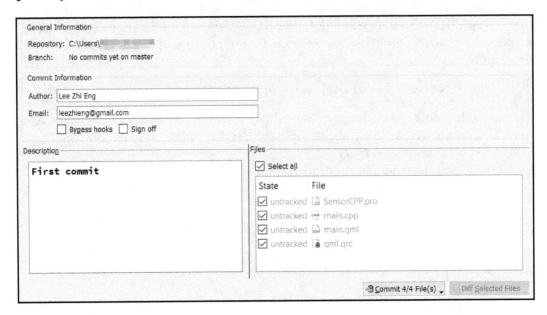

Select the files you want to commit, type in the description and click the **Commit** button. After that, you can proceed to **Push** the code to your GitHub repository. You may see an error like the following if you go to **Tools | Git | Remote Repository | Push**:

```
fatal: No configured push destination.
Either specify the URL from the command-line or configure a remote
repository using

    git remote add <name> <url>

and then push using the remote name

    git push <name>

The command "C:\Program Files\Git\cmd\git.exe" terminated with exit code
128.
```

This is because Git doesn't know which remote server is the default one to push to, and there is no solution in Qt Creator, so you have to use the `git` command to achieve this:

```
git push -u "resp" master
```

Here, `resp` is your repository name and `master` is the master branch of the repository.

Alternatively, you can use the **Git Gui** tool every time you want to push your project. Go to **Tools** | **Git** | **Git Tools** | **Git Gui**. A window like the following will appear:

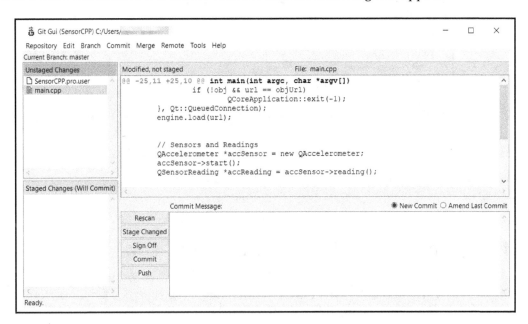

You can make your commit and push over here as well. If you go to **Remote** | **Push**, a window will pop up, which allows you to select the remote server you want to push to:

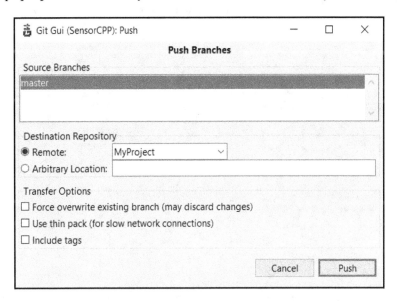

Once you click the **Push** button, you will see the success status as follows:

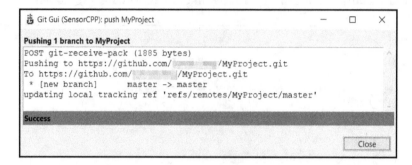

In this section, we have learned how we can link our Qt Creator to our GitHub account. Next, we will look at how we can do the same for GitLab.

Setting up your GitLab repository

GitLab is actually pretty much the same as GitHub. To create an account, go to `http://gitlab.com` and click on the **Register** button located in the top right corner. Once you have created an account and have logged in to GitLab, you will see the following screen:

Click on the **Create a project** button and it will bring you to the new project page. Similar to GitHub, you are required to fill in the project name and other information about your project:

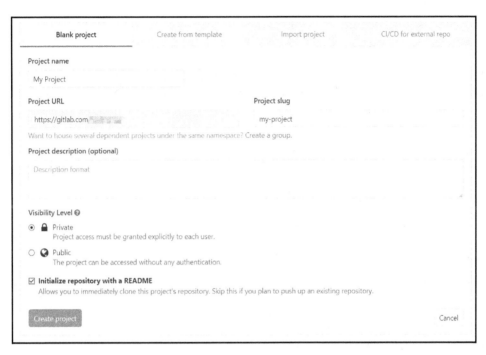

Once you are done, click on the **Create project** button to complete the process. To get the URL, go to the **Project** page from the top panel and click on your repository. After that, click on the **Clone** button and the URL will appear on the pop-up panel:

After that, you can follow the steps in the GitHub example and apply the URL to your Qt Creator.

Next, we will look at how we can configure the coding style and coding format from Qt Creator.

Configuring the coding style and coding format options

Readable code is crucial, and Qt Creator's default coding style is one that most people find very readable. However, you might be on a project with different coding guidelines, or you might just find that you can't bear a particular facet of how the Qt Creator editor deals with code formatting; maybe it's the positioning of the brackets or how a switch statement gets formatted. Fortunately, Qt Creator is extremely configurable. Go to **Tools** | **Options...** | **C++** and configure how Qt Creator will format your code, as shown in the following screenshot:

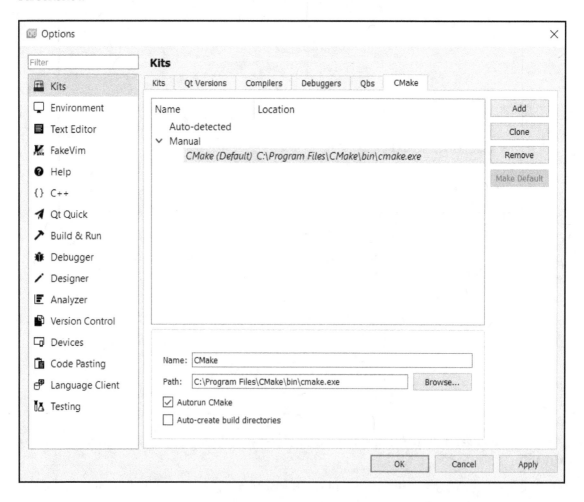

The basic dialog lets you pick popular formatting styles, such as Qt's default format or the format used by most GNU code. You can also click on **Edit...**, which brings up the code style editor, which you can see in the next screenshot:

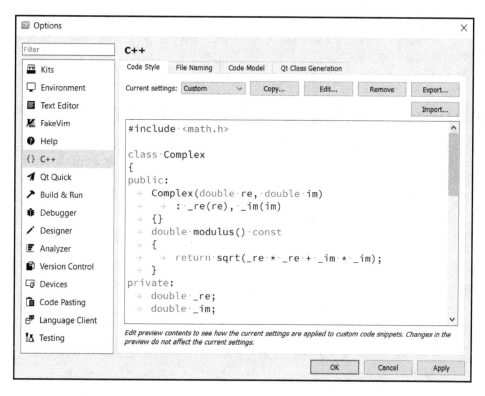

You'll want to begin by copying a built-in style and editing it to suit your tastes; from the edit **Code Style** dialog, you can select whether tabs are spaces or tabs, the number of spaces per tab stop, as well as how line continuations are handled. Each pane lets you adjust specific aspects of code formatting, as follows:

- The **Content** pane lets you adjust how class bodies are formatted, including spacing for public, protected, and private declarations.
- The **Braces** pane lets you control formatting that pertains to braces.
- The "**switch**" pane lets you control the `switch` and `case` statement formatting.
- The **Alignment** pane lets you control how code is aligned between consecutive lines.
- The **Pointer** pane lets you control spacing around pointer declarations.

It's easy to go crazy with all these options, but I urge you not to; what looks good at first glance is often an unreadable mess when you see it day after day. If you're just getting started with Qt, stick to the default formatting and remember the old adage to "do no harm" when it comes to editing the existing code – match the formatting that's already there.

Continuing with appearance, let's move on to learn how we can change the look and feel of our Qt Creator instance.

Applying new themes to Qt Creator

Other than configuring the code style, Qt Creator also allows us to change the color scheme and style of the entire program. This helps us change the user interface appearance! You can do so by going to **Tools | Options... | Environment** and you will see the **Theme** option under **User Interface** settings:

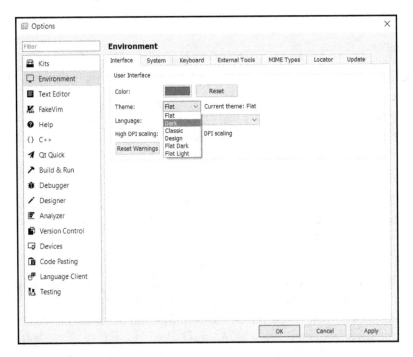

By default, Qt Creator is using the **Flat** theme, which is what we are familiar with all this time. Qt also provides us with some of the newer options, such as **Dark**, **Design**, **Flat Dark**, and **Flat Light**. Do try them out and see whether any of them fit your taste! Do note that you may need to restart Qt Creator in order for the change to happen.

There are some other third-party themes for Qt Creator that are worth mentioning here:

- Dracula theme: `https://draculatheme.com/qtcreator`
- Blue Sky theme: `https://github.com/foxoman/bluesky`
- Dark and Light themes by Ildar Gilmanov: `https://github.com/gilmanov-ildar/qtcreator-themes`
- Arc theme: `https://github.com/elmodos/qt-creator-arc-theme`

You can download these themes and copy the `.xml` file to the following directory:

- **Windows**: `%APPDATA%\QtProject\qtcreator\themes`
- **macOS**: `~/.config/QtProject/qtcreator/themes/`
- **Linux**: `~/.config/QtProject/qtcreator/themes/`

Then, restart Qt Creator and you should be able to find the theme name on the `Theme` selection box.

If you are not happy with the theme's color scheme, you can still tweak it a little by going to **Tools | Options... | Text Editor | Font & Colors**. Here, you will see a selection box that allows you to change the color scheme of the code editor:

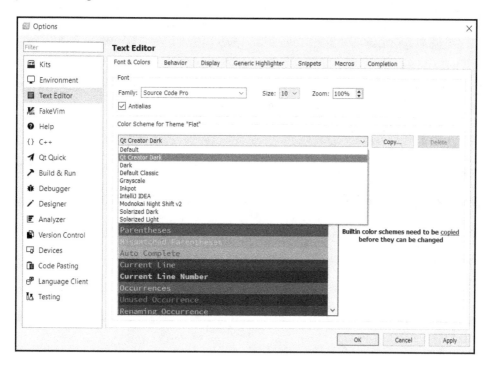

You can go even a bit further by changing each of the options available for the color scheme. However, you can't change the original setting, but instead, you need to first duplicate the selected color scheme by pressing the **Copy...** button. Then, a small window will pop up and ask you to insert a name for the newly copied color scheme. Once you have created the new color scheme with the copied attributes from the previous color scheme, you can then start to mess around and change any settings you like. That's what I'm talking about!

Qt Creator really gives us the flexibility to customize the look and feel of the tools so that we feel at home when using it.

Let's move on to something different. Besides adjusting the theme of the Qt Creator, we can also make our Qt Quick window stand out from the ordinary. Let's take a look at how we can change the setting of the Qt Quick window display options.

Setting the Qt Quick window display options

Qt Quick is great for building applications for non-traditional computing environments, such as set-top boxes or automotive computers. Often, when working with Qt Quick, you'll want an application that doesn't have all the usual windows (such as the close box) around the contents of the window in these settings, because you're trying to present a unified user interface based on your Qt Quick application, rather than the windowing toolkit on the host platform.

You can easily set windows options by editing the `main.cpp` file in your Qt Quick project. By default, it looks similar to the following code snippet:

```cpp
#include <QGuiApplication>
#include <QtQuick/QQuickView>

int main(int argc, char *argv[])
{
  QGuiApplication a(argc, argv);

  QQuickView view;
  view.setSource(QUrl("qrc:/qml/main.qml"));
  view.show();

  return a.exec();
}
```

This code creates a Qt Quick Application Viewer, sets its main QML file (the first file to be loaded) to the indicated file, and then shows it before starting the application's event loop. Fortunately, QQuickView has a setFlags method that lets you pass the Qt::Window flags to the window it initializes in order to display your Qt Quick application. These flags include the following:

- Qt::FramelessWindowHint: This indicates that the window should be borderless (this works on Linux systems but not on Windows).
- Qt::Popup: This indicates a pop-up window. You can use this on Windows to get a nearly borderless window with a slight drop shadow.
- Qt::WindowStaysOnTopHint: This indicates that the window should stay on top of all other windows.
- Qt::WindowStaysOnBottomHint: This indicates that the window should stay under all other windows.
- Qt::Desktop: This indicates that the window should run on the desktop.

We will show you how you can use these flags in the upcoming example C++ code.

 A complete list of the flags can be found in the Qt documentation at https://doc.qt.io/qt-5.9/qt.html#WindowType-enum.

You can also adjust a window's opacity using the setOpacity method of QQuickView.

Say, for example, that we want a blue window with no border, but a slight drop shadow of 75 percent opacity to hover over all other windows of our Qt Quick application. We'd change the QML to read as follows:

```
import QtQuick 2.12

Rectangle {
    width: 360
    height: 360
    color: "blue"
    Text {
        text: qsTr("Hello World")
        anchors.centerIn: parent
        font.pointSize: 18
    }
    MouseArea {
        anchors.fill: parent
        onClicked: {
            Qt.quit();
```

```
            }
        }
    }
```

Note the `color: blue` declaration for our top-level rectangle. Next, we will modify `main.cpp` to read as follows:

```cpp
#include <QGuiApplication>
#include <QtQuick/QQuickView>

int main(int argc, char *argv[])
{
  QGuiApplication a(argc, argv);

  QQuickView view;
  view.setOpacity(0.75);
  view.setFlags(Qt::Popup | Qt::WindowStaysOnTopHint);
  view.setSource(QUrl("qrc:/qml/main.qml"));
  view.show();

  return a.exec();
}
```

The key lines here come just before `view.setSource`: the `setOpacity` method sets the main window's opacity, and the `setFlags` method sets the flags for the main window to be a popup that will be on top of all other windows. Upon running the application, we will see something similar to the following screenshot:

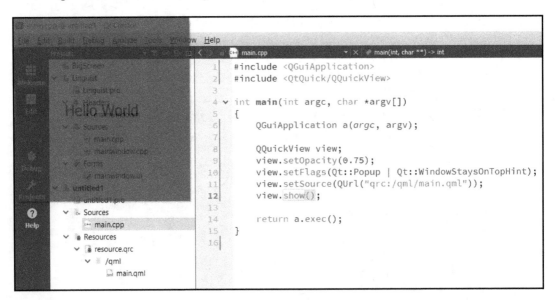

You can use this trick to come up with a variety of effects for how your Qt Quick application is displayed.

We have learned how we can set the window display option for our Qt Quick application. So next, we will learn how we can build our project directly from the command line.

Building projects from CMake and the command line

Sometimes, you need to build a project from the command line. Maybe you're working on Linux and you're just more comfortable there, or you've got a remote session running on your desktop while you're in a meeting. Or, maybe you want to automate builds on a build server and need to know how Qt performs its compilation magic for your builds.

Building using qmake

The trick lies in qmake: Qt's meta-make system that manages the generation of make files for the compiler toolchain you have already installed. The qmake command takes the `.pro` files, which you first saw in Chapter 2, *Building Applications with Qt Creator*, and generates the `make` or `nmake` file necessary for your toolchain to build your application. Let's see how this works:

1. First, ensure that you have your compiler and set utility in your system path; how you do this varies from one development environment to another. Next, be sure to have commands for Qt's build system in your path – this happens by default if you've installed Qt on Linux using the package manager, and is easily done on macOS or Windows by editing your path to include the appropriate `bin` directory from the Qt tools you installed earlier.
2. Next, open up a command window and change to the directory containing your project: your `.pro` file should be at the root of this directory. Type `qmake` and then enter either `make` (if your build system uses make) or `nmake` (if you're using a Microsoft Windows toolchain). That's all there is to this!
3. If you have a C++ project, Qt or not, and you miss the `.pro` file, qmake can create this for you with the following command:

```
qmake -project
```

With this command, qmake explores all the C++ files in the folder and subfolders and writes a generic PRO file. Then, you can edit this file to change the target name or to add some `qt` modules as shown in the following statement, but in general, you will obtain a good result:

```
qt += qt network xml
```

We have learned how we can build our Qt project using qmake. Next, we will learn how to use CMake to build our project.

Building using CMake

CMake is a set of cross-platform tools used for generating make files for different types of projects, such as Visual Studio and Qt. CMake uses a simple configuration file called `CMakeLists.txt` and can be easily modified to suit your needs. Since CMake is a third-party tool, you don't get much information from Qt's official documentation. Instead, you can read the documentation provided by CMake at `https://cmake.org/documentation`.

Therefore, if you decided that you prefer to use CMake instead of the default qmake provided by Qt, you then no longer create a `.pro` project file for your Qt projects. Instead, you create `CMakeLists.txt` as your project file and manually add the paths to your source files, libraries, and compiler settings into the `CMakeLists.txt` file by hand. You also can't create a new Qt project from Qt Creator as it comes with the qmake project file (`.pro`) by default.

Qt Creator supports CMake 3.0 and above, which means the latest version will work out of the box on your Qt Creator. If you have installed CMake on your computer, Qt Creator will automatically look for CMake through the `PATH` setting. If you have not, please go to `https://cmake.org` and download the latest version of CMake.

You can set up CMake in Qt Creator by going to **Tools |Options...** and select **Kits | CMake:**

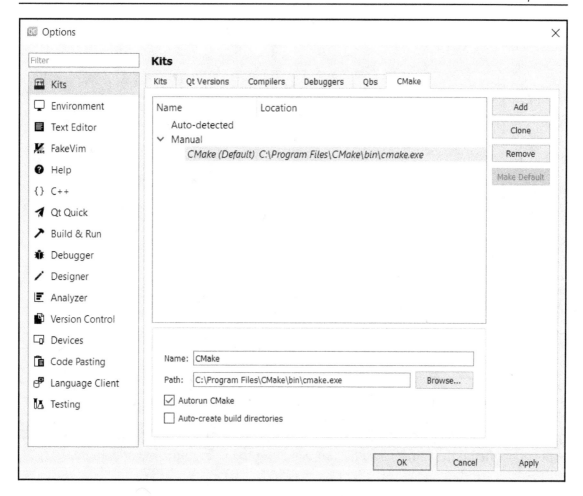

If Qt Creator doesn't detect your CMake directory, you may click the **Add** button to
manually set the directory path. When you checked the **Autorun CMake** checkbox, Qt
Creator will automatically run CMake whenever you made any changes to any of
the CMakeLists.txt files.

After that, go to the **Kits** tab and make sure that the kit you are running on your project has the CMake tool selected:

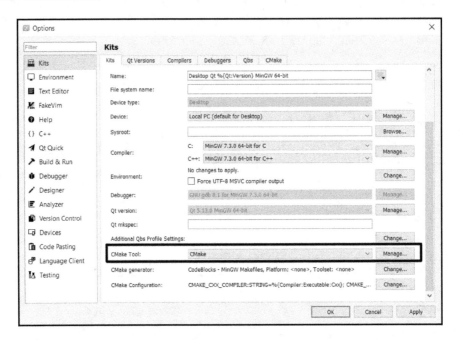

Once done, we can now start creating our first Qt project that runs CMake by creating a `CMakeLists.txt` file in the desired directory. After that, open the file using Qt Creator. The first thing you need to add to the file is the minimum CMake requirement so that we will get notified if the CMake installed on our computer is anything lower than that version:

```
cmake_minimum_required(VERSION 3.0.0)
```

Then, set your project name and ask CMake to look for the header files in the build directories:

```
project(MyProject)
set(CMAKE_INCLUDE_CURRENT_DIR ON)
```

After that, enable the following three options so that CMake will handle the `moc`, `uic`, and `rcc` build targets for you automatically by scanning the headers and source files at build time, which makes your life easier:

```
set(CMAKE_AUTOMOC ON)
set(CMAKE_AUTOUIC ON)
set(CMAKE_AUTORCC ON)
```

Then, we need to include Qt 5 components in our project so that it can be compiled and run properly. There are two ways we can add these components – the first is by adding them one by one:

```
find_package(Qt5Core REQUIRED)
find_package(Qt5Widgets REQUIRED)
```

However, I prefer the second way, which is to add all the required components all at once:

```
find_package(Qt5 COMPONENTS Core Widgets REQUIRED)
```

If you have any C++ source files, Qt Quick files (.qml), Qt form files (.ui), Qt resource files (.qrc), and so on that you want to add to your project, you can do so by using the add_executable command. Consider the following, for example:

```
add_executable(MyProject main.cpp mainwindow.cpp mainwindow.ui
resource.qrc)
```

After you've saved the CMakeLists.txt file, Qt Creator will now refresh the project and display the source files on the **Projects** panel on the left. You may notice that the project tree looks a bit different from the ordinary Qt structure used by qmake:

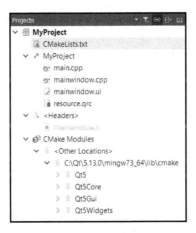

Finally, we must link Qt libraries to our project so that it can be compiled and run properly:

```
target_link_libraries(MyProject Qt5::Widgets)
```

Now, our CMakeLists.txt file looks something like this, which is very short and simple:

```
cmake_minimum_required(VERSION 3.0.0)
project(MyProject)
set(CMAKE_INCLUDE_CURRENT_DIR ON)
```

```
set(CMAKE_AUTOMOC ON)
set(CMAKE_AUTOUIC ON)
set(CMAKE_AUTORCC ON)

find_package(Qt5 COMPONENTS Core Widgets REQUIRED)
add_executable(MyProject main.cpp mainwindow.cpp mainwindow.ui
resource.qrc)
target_link_libraries(MyProject Qt5::Widgets)
```

You can now hit the **Run** button on the Qt Creator to kickstart the build process. Your program should be running automatically in a few seconds provided there is no error during the build process. But of course, the preceding example is only the most basic configuration to kickstart your project in CMake. If you need to learn the more advanced settings, please visit https://doc.qt.io/qt-5/cmake-manual.html and https://cmake. org/documentation.

That's it. We have gone through how we can make use of CMake in our Qt project and got ourselves familiar with the basic configurations for our CMakeLists.txt file. Next, we will learn how we can run multiple debuggers simultaneously.

Running multiple debuggers simultaneously

Oftentimes, our project is not merely a simple hello world application that runs only a single executable, but can be a collection of executables of different types that run on servers, client computers, or even mobile devices simultaneously. For example, your end user could be running the app you built from Qt, which runs on their mobile device. Then, you have a server application that is also built from Qt that processes information sent from the user's app. Finally, you provide your server admin with management software that you built with Qt that runs on their PC.

To build and maintain such a huge application, we need to make sure it is always easy and keeps things together. To ensure that we can easily edit, build, and debug all the different applications, we use something called subdir to group these projects together into one in Qt. To do that, we put all the three example programs we described into a folder and create an empty .pro file in it. The directory looks something like this:

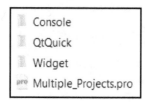

Each of the project subfolders is just like an ordinary Qt project folder and has its own project file (`.pro`), but we will use the main project file outside of these folders to group them together into a single master project. Then, open up the main project file and add the following code:

```
TARGET = Multiple_Projects
TEMPLATE = subdirs
CONFIG += ordered

SUBDIRS += \
    Console \
    Widget \
    QtQuick \
```

As we can see, it's very short and simple. The `TARGET` setting simply gives this project a name, which in this case I simply called `Multiple_Projects`. The `TEMPLATE` setting, which we usually set as `app`, is now `subdirs` instead, because we only use this project file to group the other projects together, and not to build an actual program. We add the `ordered` keyword to the `CONFIG` setting so that the directories listed later will be processed in the order in which they are given. Finally, we add the individual project folder into our master project file by adding it to the `SUBDIRS` settings variable. Once you save the project file, you will see the project structure has now been updated. You will now be able to see all the sub-projects in the project tree:

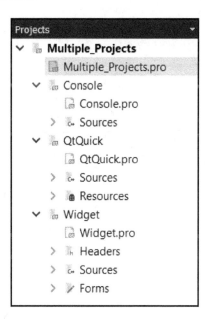

This way, it is easier for you to edit, build, and debug all the sub-projects easily without the need to open each project separately. You can now even put them into the same version control repository and commit/update the entire project on the fly. This is especially handy when collaborating with a team of programmers.

You may notice that when you try to run all these programs, Qt Creator may close the first program before running your second program, and so on. This default behavior can be altered by going to **Tools** | **Options...** | **Build & Run** | **General** and changing the option for **Stop applications before building** to **None**:

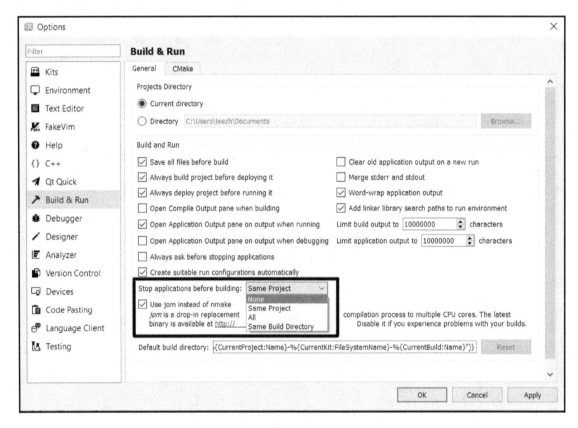

This way, you can run and debug the programs simultaneously and look at the debug messages of all programs on your Qt Creator at the same time, making your debugging process simpler and swifter:

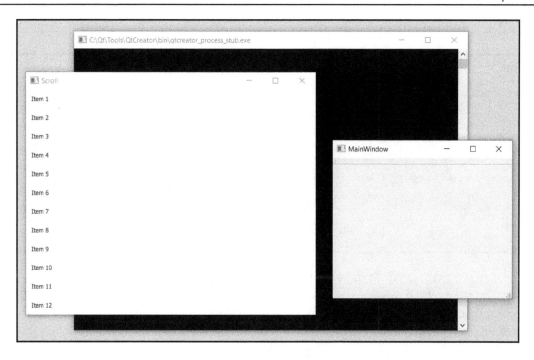

One last tip is that if you want Qt Creator to launch all three programs at the same time instead of running them one by one, you can go to the **Projects** interface, and then open up the **Run Settings** page by clicking on the **Run** icon under your preferred kit:

After that, add a new **Run configuration** by choosing the **Custom Executable** option:

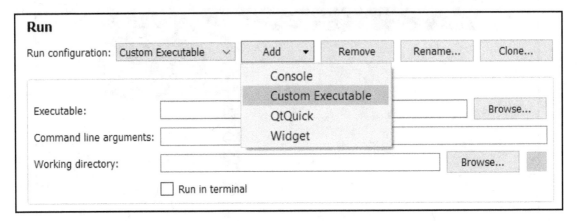

Then, click the **Browse...** button at the **Executable** setting and link it to a batch script that helps you to launch all three programs simultaneously. You also need to select the working directory by clicking on the **Browse...** button at the **Working directory** setting. It's not recommended to use the batch script but if you really want to do so, you may.

We have learned how we can group different Qt projects together and run debuggers on these projects simultaneously. Next, we will learn about what Qt Assistant is and how to access it from our Qt Creator.

Learning more about Qt

In the first few chapters, I pointed you to the **Help** panel of Qt Creator as well as the editor's facility for the autocompletion of class members when editing code. Qt Creator's help view is really a subview of **Qt Assistant**, the full documentation for Qt. This should be installed by default if you install all of the Qt installations; the documentation is packaged as HTML files locally. Much of this documentation is also available on the web, but it's much faster to access it this way.

When we start Qt Assistant from the Qt SDK (either from the command line with `assistant`, or by finding it in the installed list of applications), we should see something similar to the following screenshot:

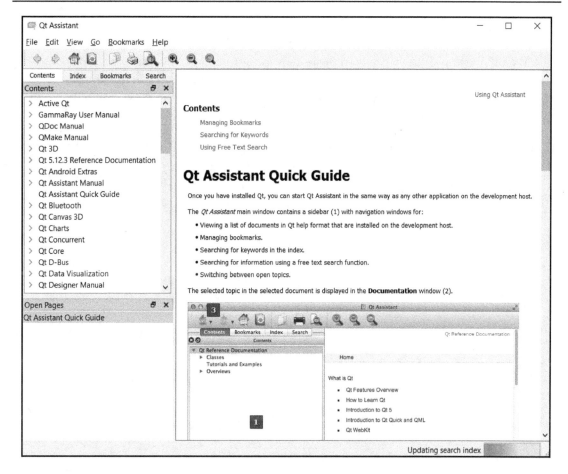

Qt Assistant is the definitive place to learn about Qt. In the column on the left-hand side, you can see a table of contents; the best place to start is with Qt Core, and then either Qt GUI or Qt Quick, depending on whether you want to write GUI or Qt Quick applications. The main view on the right-hand side is just like a browser window, complete with hyperlinks to the related sections.

Also, inside Qt Assistant, you can add bookmarks to frequently accessed pages, see an index of all the terms in the documentation, and quickly search for terms using the search tab in the column on the left-hand side. It's an invaluable resource and as easy to use as an e-book.

Finally, if you prefer to use the web to learn about things, don't forget Qt's extensive online documentation, available at `https://doc.qt.io`. There's also the Qt Project forums at `https://forum.qt.io`.

Summary

Qt and Qt Creator provide a great environment for application development, irrespective of whether you're writing console, GUI, or Qt Quick applications. You can mix and match standard C++ code with Qt, making the most of your existing skills. When doing this, you can add in things such as version control and command-line builds to your tools, giving you the ability to work in large teams and perform unattended builds of large projects using Qt. Qt has great documentation too, both bundled with Qt Creator and on the web.

With what you've learned in this book and what's available, the sky's the limit for your application development goals!

Other Books You May Enjoy

If you enjoyed this book, you may be interested in these other books by Packt:

Hands-On Embedded Programming with Qt

John Werner

ISBN: 978-1-78995-206-3

- Understand how to develop Qt applications using Qt Creator on Linux
- Explore various Qt GUI technologies to build resourceful and interactive applications
- Understand Qt's threading model to maintain a responsive UI
- Get to grips with remote target load and debug using Qt Creator
- Become adept at writing IoT code using Qt
- Learn a variety of software best practices to ensure that your code is efficient

Qt5 C++ GUI Programming Cookbook - Second Edition
Lee Zhi Eng

ISBN: 978-1-78980-382-2

- Animate GUI elements using Qt5's built-in animation system
- Draw shapes and 2D images using Qt5's powerful rendering system
- Implement an industry-standard OpenGL library in your project
- Build a mobile app that supports touch events and exports it onto devices
- Parse and extract data from an XML file and present it on your GUI
- Interact with web content by calling JavaScript functions from C++
- Access MySQL and SQLite databases to retrieve data and display it on your GUI

Leave a review - let other readers know what you think

Please share your thoughts on this book with others by leaving a review on the site that you bought it from. If you purchased the book from Amazon, please leave us an honest review on this book's Amazon page. This is vital so that other potential readers can see and use your unbiased opinion to make purchasing decisions, we can understand what our customers think about our products, and our authors can see your feedback on the title that they have worked with Packt to create. It will only take a few minutes of your time, but is valuable to other potential customers, our authors, and Packt. Thank you!

Index